KYRENIA'S LEGEND

THE LIFE AND TIMES OF
COSTAS CATSELLIS

Armida Publications is a member of the Independent Publishers Guild (UK),
and a member of the Independent Book Publishers Association (USA)

www.armidabooks.com | Great Literature. One Book At A Time.

Summary:
This deeply engaging biography recounts the story of Costas Catsellis, a man whose achievements
will forever be ingrained within the history of Kyrenia, Cyprus. From his humble upbringing in this
forgotten corner of the vast British Empire during the height of the colonial era, to his ambitious
journeys across the Atlantic Ocean to the land that promises everything; America. There he learns
the subtle art of cooking, and gambles away a fortune in the stock market before volunteering with
the US Army during WWI. His journey continues until his final return to Cyprus with dreams
of having a family and leaving his mark on his beloved Mediterranean coastal town of Kyrenia.

[1. Biography - Business. 2. Biography - Personal Memoirs.
3. Biography - Cultural, Ethnic & Regional / General. 4. Biography - Historical
5. History - United States / 20th Century.
6. History - Middle East / General. 7. Travel - Europe / Cyprus.]

———

English translation by: Irena Joannides

Cover design by: Armida
Front cover image: On the left, the first and second Sea View hotels just behind the Kyrenia
Municipal Seawater Baths. On the right, the Dome Hotel with its first two Byzantine domes.
Back cover image: Postcard of the port of Kyrenia during the 1920s. *(Additional information on pg 319)*

———

Many thanks to the
Ministry of Education and Culture of the Republic of Cyprus
for financially supporting the translation of this work.

———

First published in Greek by Chrysopolitissa Publications in 1994 as: *Κερύνεια. Ο άνθρωπος/τόπος.*

First edition: December 2017

ISBN-13 (paperback): 978-9963-255-56-6

KYRENIA'S LEGEND

THE LIFE AND TIMES OF COSTAS CATSELLIS

A biography by

RINA KATSELLI

English translation by

IRENA JOANNIDES

ARMIDA

This book is dedicated to
Costas Zambarloukos
Despina-Maria
and Stavrini-Christina

TABLE OF CONTENTS

Author's Note

I have left the names of the various locations where C. Catsellis had worked in America as he had told them to me. It should be noted that as these events took place a long time ago, some of the locations could not be verified.

Translator's Note

The original Greek text was recorded as it was narrated by Costas Catsellis in the local dialect of Kyrenia. Vocabulary, syntax and pace were highly idiosyncratic. The challenge in the translation was to render his narrations into easy to read English, while maintaining something of the original delivery.

Chapter 1

Afternoon Tea with my Daughter-in-Law

Kyrenia, 1964

Early afternoon, north veranda; the sea across, I am watching the waves. They are born, they flow, they grow, they rise, they fall, they vanish – each in its own way, never two alike. Millions, billions of waves, century after century, each with its own shape; the sea never repeats herself.

But I... every day at this time, with a strong tea served on the table next to me, one of a kind in Cyprus, a special order for my hotel from Ceylon via England, delivered in large tin boxes. The metallic teapot is not like the old ones yet, heavy and silver-plated, it still bears the emblem of a lion holding the flag with a large calligraphic "C." I am C: seventy-six years old, over the hill, nearly out to pasture...

What hill? What pasture? Everything's upside down: the hill, the pasture, the country, my children, my grandchildren, my employees... I have given most of my employees a leave of absence; the few that are still here, at the hotel, have nothing to do. They talk amongst themselves in low voices, with their arms folded and with fear coiled inside their eyes. Many Kerynians pass by the hotel to hear and discuss the latest news; all with the same gaze, all of Kyrenia is afraid. I am afraid! Who am *I* to say that I have lived?

"What you're asking for is so boastful. And it's not like I have lived such a grand life!" I tell her.

"You're not the one to judge that!" she says sharply and sits down across from me.

The waiter arrives with a large teapot for four people, milk, a clean cup, cake — everything ordered by her before she came to sit here with me. And she is determined! Milk pitcher in hand, she begins preparing her first cup; she can drink tea, one cup after the other, until dawn. She is in mourning and the black clothing only emphasizes the intense rosiness of her cheeks. I am looking for a way out, but how do I evade her?

I avoid looking at her; I worry. Worry has always been my bread and butter. But to worry about a thing like this…? World War II: Anxiety, insecurity, fear, but the whole world was in the same boat then. Countries destroyed, cities turned to ashes. Our small corner of the world saw the least destruction. What destruction? Nothing happened here! Only the volunteers saw action, some 37,000, and not all of them on the front lines. During the last world war, even if the volunteers represented one tenth of the population of Cyprus, we did not feel like this; there was a tenacious collective resistance in the air from so many nations, which believed that their citizens were sacrificing themselves for freedom and high ideals. Now everything is upside down and those same countries are not supporting us; they will not even speak up for our independence to help restrain Turkey that is hell-bent on grabbing our land. What is their position? Do they support us? No one knows what's going to happen, no one speaks openly. Suspicious things! I tell her that the Americans surely want Turkey to invade our country because they expect to get a foothold here as well, because of NATO. The British, on the other hand, also support the Turks because they resent us for ousting them, even though they maintain two army bases on the island and hold Troodos for themselves, having set up their enormous spy radars there. I ask for her opinion but she keeps at it, notebook and pencil in hand.

"So are you going to start at the beginning?" she asks.

Something firms up inside me but then retracts again.

"What on earth do you want me to tell you?"

"Your life story from the beginning!" she says sharply.

I sigh! Before all this trouble began, I was sure of everything. I liked the idea but now with everything upside down and with her sitting there insisting teacup in hand... Her determination raises some certainty inside me that melds with fear, confusing me, making me flush, leaving me tongue-tied.

"Can we start, Father?" she asks and sets down her teacup.

She calls me "Father"! Her father Stavris, the son of Kyriakos Lordos, a big tall man, has been dead for over a year —assimilated at the cemetery's entrance (first grave to the left) in the company of his father. His shouting is no longer heard all the way to the port. His bicycle, which tilled the roads and outskirts of Kyrenia for years, lies rusting and abandoned God knows where, and the white dog, which always chased after him, dead on his grave from sorrow.

"But you have already agreed... Come on, Father!" she pleads with me and smiles, while preparing her second cup of tea.

I did agree before the unrest but now my mouth refuses to open; it won't be pried open even with a knife. I don't want to do this! What I do want is to have my hotel full again, to barely keep up in the kitchen, not to have a moment's rest. I don't want to sit around recounting my life story! What life? The life that, because of this situation, is about to be dragged down the river along with the entire country? All my guests are gone and I, with my hands tied, find no peace, like the waves of a stormy sea during a fierce tramontane. And at night, the threatening lights of the Turkish warships a living nightmare... I watch them for hours; without work, I feel rested. I do not even need the three hours of sleep that would normally be enough for me in twenty-four. Wide-awake with no way of burning up anxiety even for a little while, during those twenty-two hours that I am awake of the twenty-four. And now, after tea, I am idle and restless like the waves of the sea... No, no, the waves are working; they are enriching the sea with oxygen, giving life to marine plants and creatures. The waves are at work as always; I am the one sitting around with nothing to do. This is hell! Having already finished her second cup, she smiles at me while pouring her third.

"When were you born? Do you know?"

CHAPTER 2

THE FIRST YEARS

Kyrenia, 1888-1902

No. 183[1]
Name: Costas Charalambou
Place of Birth: Karakoumi Village
Date of birth: 13.11.1888
Godmother's Name: Polyxeni Gr. Demetriadou
Note: On 24.1.1888 Constantinos Gregoriou Demetria-
des succumbed to revolver wounds at age 19.

Karakoumi – Karmi

My date of birth is November 26, 1888, according to the new calendar. On the eighth day I am given the name Socrates in church. Hadjiglioris, the first notable of Kyrenia, agrees to have his eldest daughter Polyxeni baptize me but wants to name me Costantinos, after his son who died of revolver wounds earlier that year. So I am baptized Costas in memory of that young man. My father agrees, never opposing Hadjiglioris, who also baptized my brother Glioris; the first notable and my father are related by the Sacrament of Baptism. My father, Charalambos Kyriakou, hails from Karakoumi, a small village. Our one-room home is located approximately fifty fathoms from the sea. My mother hails from the village of Karmi, which is up on the mountain, almost directly

---

1 Father Yiannis Paphitis, "Record of Births in Kyrenia from the Year 1880 until the Year 1905," pg. 12.

beneath Ais Larkos. In Karmi they name their children after ancient Greek gods and men. My mother's name was Athena. I remember her holding my hand; we were walking along a footpath.
It was Easter, at dawn, and we were returning to the village from
Kyrenia. I remember feeling sad because we had left Archangelos
Church – the huge bonfire in its courtyard, the people holding lit
candles, the young men ringing both the bell and the semantron
and setting off firecrackers. Men firing shots into the air and the
priests, in their glittery bedecked vestments, chanting "Christ has
Risen!" It's like I am there now – holding her hand and trying
to keep up with her pace until, from one side of the village, my
eldest sister appears, head uncovered, hair tousled... She is waving her hands and shouting things that I do not understand. In the
commotion my hand slips out of my mother's so I grab onto her
skirt but it, too, slides out of my grip. She tumbles down into the
stream next to the footpath... I am very frightened.

"Ma! Ma..."

Nothing! This is the only memory I have of my mother; I do not
even remember her face.[2]

I remember the second one more vividly although her face has
completely faded from my memory, too. I am in a nice konak[3]
in the middle of a chiflik,[4] which has everything: flowers, trees,

2   The childhood story of Costas Catsellis, until his graduation from
elementary school, is given in the novel by Rina Katselli, *Kyrenia: From the
Mouths of Elders III*.

3   Konak (Greek: κονάκι): A Turkish word for "house" at the time of the
Ottoman Empire, especially one used as an official residence.
[Translator's note: Commonly used words of a non-Greek origin such a
"konak" have been preserved in the translation in the interest of rendering the
local colour and the era. Most are remnants of the period of the Ottoman rule of
Cyprus, which ended in 1878, only ten years before the birth of Costas Catsellis
in 1888.]

4   Chiflik (Greek: τσιφλίκι): A Turkish term for a system of land management
in the Ottoman Empire.

running waters… My second mother spoils me with affection and dresses me in a sailor's uniform. Her name is Marianna. She is the mistress of the attorney Pericles, who keeps her in a house on his chiflik. And this is why I lose her, too. Elengou and Maria, my mother's sisters in Karmi, are incensed that an unwed woman is raising me. They say it's a sin that brings shame on their family.

Aunt Elengou has no children of her own, so she arranges with my father to have me brought to her. In Karmi her one-room house is smaller than my paternal home in Karakoumi. Her husband Tzambris works as a labourer anywhere he can get employment, if and when he can get it. The man certainly likes to drink! The wine gourd is always in front of him; he raises it up and drinks straight from its mouth.

Karmi is a lovely village,
but all of it is rocky;
it has pretty girls
like pomegranates rosy.

Karmi is a nice village,
but it's full of kartamilles;[5]
some are lame, some are hunched
and some have eye gunk.

Life is primitive in Karmi but at least I go to school, which is among oldest and best in the area. The villagers are poor but hold onto it by the skin of their teeth, paying the teacher's salary with money they can't spare. Georgios Stavrides is our teacher this year. My education begins with him. We are afraid of him but we study. He writes poetry, loves nature and beautiful things, so we find

---

5 Kartamilles (Greek: καρταμίλλα/καρταμίλλες): A small bittersweet plant that grows on riverbanks. When villagers were out in the fields, they would collect these greens to eat with bread and olives, thereby adding more flavour to their meals.

ways to get out of the classroom. Eleni, one of our classmates, is quite pretty; her hair is styled into two long, well-groomed braids with a huge silk bow at each end. She is the teacher's pet, so we coax her into asking him for favours.

"Ask him to take us on an excursion, Eleni!" we convince her and she cajoles the teacher.

"Sir, please take us on a field trip! Please, Sir..."

The teacher appears to be undecided but there's no escaping her – her smile forces him to oblige. He takes us on a trip to Ais Larkos!

It's spring. Flowers everywhere, verdant green, aromatic bushes: myrtle, savoury, chamomile, marjoram, mint. And trees: cypresses, pines, planes, olives, carobs... The teacher talks to us about the castle, about Hilarion, the sainted ascetic who lived on this peak, about the houses of Rigaina, about the conquerors... I have heard it all many times before both in class and from my aunts. I'm bored so I wander off with three or four other boys. We chance upon a group of English visitors, who have arrived on mules at the entrance of the castle. They are dressed in white and wear wide-brim hats. The women are plump, fair-haired and blue-eyed; their dresses, full of ruching and falbalas, look brand-new. We are scrawny and barefoot. We observe the English visitors with unbridled curiosity; they smile and give us ham sandwiches. None of us has seen anything like this before... Not trusting the strange ingredient, we toss the ham and eat only the bread. When the teacher catches up to us, he notices the ham on the ground.

"You tossed the cured ham and ate the bread by itself?"

By itself, yes, but what a lovely and soft white bread it was, smothered in butter! Could it be that what we tossed was just as scrumptious? Carefully, so as not to be seen by the teacher, we pick up the ham and clean it as best we can. The slices that fell on grass have no dirt on them. Our teacher was right – thin, pink slices of cured ham are indescribably delicious! Late afternoon I slip away again along with a few other students. We wander off and darkness begins to fall; the landscape loses its beauty and turns wild. The sea below is not a dazzling blue anymore; now it is dark, like the sky above the trees. Everything goes dark, almost pitch black... We want to join the others but cannot find our way back. We are lost! Unable to see where we are going, we run around here and there, gripped by fear. Finally we hear the teacher calling our names. We run toward his voice, guided by the sound; it would not matter if he beat us until we bled, as long as we can reach him. We join the others at last! Yet the teacher does nothing to us, no punishment whatsoever; he only sighs with relief.

"Let's head back to the village," he says. "It's getting dark."

Always cooped up indoors, we are often bored in class. We yearn for another excursion but young Eleni is not at school. She is at home sick. Who is going to ask the teacher?

"Come on, Costis, ask him to take us on a field trip. So we can get some sunshine, if nothing else..." my classmates urge.

Truth be told, we are hungry for the sun. Karmi is wedged on the north side of the tall mountain; it has a lovely view of the sea but the hours of direct sunlight are few, only around noon. That's why many locals die of consumption; their lives are very hard and filled with dearth.

"Come on, Costis, ask him!"

After a great deal of coaxing I muster enough courage. I dare!

"Sir, please take us on a field trip," I plead with the teacher but he, hunched over a book, does not respond.

So I ask again:

"Even if it's only for a walk. Please, Sir..."

The teacher looks up from his book and smiles, but not in the way that he smiles at young Eleni.

"Costantis Kolofantis with the short breeches, run up, run down; there's the turd, swallow it down!" he recites.

Everyone bursts out laughing but "Costantis Kalofantis" sticks. My fellow students tease me and I get into fights – the nickname really bothers me.

But there are also other things in Karmi that make my life difficult, like the chores that I have to do for my uncle and aunt. It's
not easy taking the donkey out to the fields because he is huge and
I am afraid of him. His stall, in the awkward small stable, does not
fill up easily with hay and the saddlebag with the barley is hung
too high. I climb up to the saddlebag with difficulty, put feed in a
basket, come down and spread it in front of the animal, which is
anxious to eat. The donkey drools all over me; worse still, since
there isn't much space, I have to pass behind him. I am terrified of
his hind legs because they kick! In Karmi I am always gripped by
fear, by a premonition that something terrible will happen. And
disaster strikes in a way that I never expected, when my uncle
sends me to the coffee shop to fetch wine. On the way back, a
feral dog bites my leg. The wine gourd lies broken on the cobble-
stone and the dog won't let go. I scream, the neighbours save me,
but my left leg is shred to pieces. It becomes infected, fills up with
pus, and I burn up with fever. My aunts do their best to take care
of me but their home remedies are primitive: balsam leaves, reed
shavings, onion skins. To make matters worse, they are out all day
doing chores! Home alone in bed, on a mattress stuffed with seaweed, I writhe in pain, hoping that my leg will be amputated so I
can finally be free from the constant aching and from what is even
worse, the hallucinations.

All the monsters in the universe descend from the ceiling
beams: dog-shaped dragons, evil goblins, serpents… I sweat pro-
fusely, screaming day and night from pain and from fright. My
aunt Elengou loves me. Fearing that the dog was rabid, she makes
a big decision: On the fortieth day since the bite, she holds a "dog
wedding"[6] for me. She invites everyone in the village, including
the priest; she brings fiddles, lutes, dumbeks, tin cans, whatever
can be used to make a lot of noise… She goes to great expense and
slaughters all her chickens to feed so many people. All night long I

---

6 The "dog wedding" (Greek: σκυλόγαμος) was a Cypriot custom carried
out as a remedy for those who had been bitten by rapid dogs.

want to sleep but they won't let me doze off even for one minute.
The guests eat and drink, making as much noise as possible. They
take turns watching over me, shaking me violently the moment
they see my eyes closing. At dawn they put me on the large donkey and, forming a procession, parade me around the village. I am
on the animal at the front and behind me a crowd bangs tin cans,
anything you can imagine. Complete pandemonium... The night
of the dog wedding is an indescribable torment. Am I saved by it
though? I don't know, but I do not die.

My father rushes to Karmi to bring me home. In Karakoumi
my leg still aches but everything else is tolerable and there's always someone with me at the house. I have six siblings: Polyxeni,
Styliani, Milia, Antonis, Glioris, and Eleni,[7] who is younger than I
am. My eldest sister cleans the wound twice a day with salt water,
applies ointment and wraps it with clean white pieces of cloth,
which quickly fill up with pus again. Styliani takes the pieces of
cloth, pours hot lye on them, and beats them with the washing bat
until they are clean. Milia brings me fresh water from the jug, and
Eleni always plays next to me. At night my father and brothers return home. Since I am never alone, no dragons, beasts or monsters
descend from the ceiling. The wound slowly builds up a brown
scab, like a burnt bread crust. I get out of bed, start walking again,
and eat with the others from the large earthen bowl in the middle
of the woven flat basket, on the stool. It's summer and we always
eat what we grow in our fields: fried red gourds, eggplants, green
black-eyed peas, dry legumes (fava and white beans), bulgur pilaf
with lots of fried onions. I have a good appetite and I am happy
when my eldest sister's fiancé Argyros, a builder from Pano Kyrenia, visits because then we have chicken. I start to leave the house.

---

7 No 26: Antonios Charalambou, born 20.2.1882.
   No 92: Gregorios Charalambou, born 5.11.1884.
   No 291: Eleni Charalambou, born 14.11.1893.
   (Father Yiannis Paphitis, "Record of Births in Kyrenia from the Year
1880 until the Year 1905," pgs. 2, 6 and 16.)

The sea is a magnet for me; I dip into its waters and collect tasty limpets from the rocks. My leg stings but the pain is tolerable and Polyxeni no longer has to do salt washes at home because, at the sea, there's no shortage of salt water. My father gets very angry; he keeps shouting, afraid that I may drown but, since he is gone for work all day, I go to the sea anyway. I learn to swim and dive. Only my sisters are at home and they keep yelling at me:

"That's enough, Costis! Enough!"

I am not afraid of them, so I do not listen.

"Enough, Costis!"

But I cannot get enough of the sea!

Kyrenia's Primary School

When I turn seven, my father tells me:

"Costis, I want to you go to school, to get ahead in life, not like your brother Antonis, who ended up a carpenter because he doesn't like school, or like Glioris, who left school halfway to wander 'round here and there!"

Every morning I have to walk two miles from the village to the school in Kyrenia. There is no proper road – just a path along the coast where, in two or three places, I have to cross dry rivers since there are no bridges. It's not that I have to walk two miles at dawn but that I am always scared: I am certain that every tree conceals a ghoul, that dragons hide behind bushes, that dogs and evil men lie in wait. With every step my heart pounds in anticipation of some horrific encounter. But the real hazard is elsewhere: the fast-moving waters that fill the dry rivers when it rains. My father comes with me on those days. He dives into the raging waters while I, high up on his shoulders, do not even get wet. I discount the rapids that could easily carry us both away; I am not afraid because, when my father is with me, I am certain that no ghoul would ever show up and that he could protect me from any evil man. When we arrive at the cemetery where he works as a rock carrier – they are building a tall, thick wall around the grounds – I make my own way from there. The first houses of Kyrenia are a stone's throw away and I can walk to school on my own. Worst of all are the days when I do not go to school, when they are not holidays: I stay at the village, having been expelled, because my father did not pay my tuition. I feel bad because I love school and hate to miss out on classes. Above all, I hate being away from my friends, especially Yiannis Vrahas. He is a good-natured boy that loves to joke around. One day he notices that our friend, Spyros Charalambou, is pensive.

"Spyros's ewe must've croaked!" he says and we burst out laughing.

Spyros gives us a dirty look. No, his ewe did not die; this is how he gets every time his mother is in labour. Being the family's only son, he is afraid of losing the distinction. His mother gives birth to another daughter and, on the following day, our friend's face – plump, like a small loaf of bread – beams with joy. But I have a problem with his father because he chases me away when I bring my oxen to the edge of his field. He won't allow it! Not that I deliberately take my father's animals to graze on other people's pastures but we have only a few strips of land in Karakoumi and my father says that the animals need to graze, otherwise they will die of hunger. I have no choice; feeling pressured and frustrated by the situation, I take it out on my friend Spyros.

"Spyros, come here. Someone's looking for you!"

He runs out of the classroom and I point to the balcony across the street where one of the two daughters of the shoemaker Hadjilambros is standing.

"Your fiancée, Mirou, is looking for you. She's up on the balcony, over there..."

Enraged, Spyros picks up a stone to throw at me. I run; he chases me; we tumble down the steps of Archangelos Church; he catches up to me outside the caves. He grabs me by the ears and pushes me against the rock, while I dig my nails mercilessly into his cheeks. We both squeal and the teacher comes out of the classroom.

"What's going on, boys?" he asks.

We pretend not to know what he is talking about; we fight but we are friends, inseparable. We do not involve teachers in our squabbles.

Our first teacher, Kyrillos Pavlides, is good; the only problem that we face is that the school moves every year. First it is housed in one or two small rooms next to the church. But when the students multiply, it moves from Archangelos's rock to the two front rooms of Father Yiannis Paphitis's house, next to the sea. The priest's family lives in the two rooms at the back of the house. The devout priest spends his days in a cave in his back yard. The cave was carved out of the foot of Archangelos's rock a long time ago; it's an ancestral tomb! Father Yiannis sits there and reads his religious books but his wife's chickens annoy him; he tosses pebbles at them so they'll stay away from him. The classrooms are comfortable enough but the toilet is a source of distress. Built across the house, at the edge of the rocks that extend out into the sea, it is always clean. It never smells badly because its cesspit is constantly washed out; it empties directly into the salt water. The problem is that we slip trying to reach the toilet, since most of us go barefoot both in summer and winter. On the way there the waves do not frighten us because we are compelled by the need to go but, once we have relieved ourselves, we cannot muster enough courage to return. Every so often, three or four of us get stuck there. Holding on to the wooden structure's dilapidated walls, we call out for help while the raging sea froths at our feet. The teacher has to call on the hamals[8] from the nearby port to carry us to safe ground on their strong shoulders.

---

8 Hamal (Greek: χαμάλης): A porter in the Middle East and Orient; a word of Arabic origin.

WEDDING[9]
Date: 19.1.1897
Newlyweds: Argyros Hadjinicola and Polyxeni Charalambou from Karakoumi.

My sister, a bride in Pano Kerynia, dressed in white lace; I remember it like it were yesterday! Argyros, the groom, throws the large pomegranate in his hand onto the closed front door of his house with all his might. The fruit breaks apart and the red seeds fly everywhere, staining my sister's dress. Everyone is delighted the more stains on her wedding dress, the more children she will have. There are many people at the wedding feast. The fiddle and lute players play nonstop, and Polyxeni, now married to the builder Argyros, moves into his house in Pano Kyrenia.

In the following year the school moves to the old warehouses at the port. I like the ships and the people of the sea – the captains, the sailors, the hamals. For the school year prior to my last, the school returns to the heights of Archangelos's rock, north of the church, in newly built rooms commissioned by the church committee. There are more students this year so the Kyrenia School for Boys has two teachers. One is Georgios Stavrides, who was my first teacher in Karmi. Fortunately, he teaches the lower grades, so the story of "Costantis Kolofantis" and the nickname have been forgotten. We, the older students, are taught by Yiannis Hadjitzypris, who is the best teacher I have ever had. He teaches Greek history in his own special way. He also educates us on the contemporary trials and tribulations of Greece, often moving us to tears. The tears that we shed are real, but there's another reason for them as well: Voluntary enlistment is not allowed at our age, so we cannot fight for the motherland. When Kyrenia's older youth catch wind of this, they make fun of us.

---

9 Father Yiannis Paphitis, "Record of Births in Kyrenia from the Year 1880 until the Year 1905," pg. 39.

"Eat your hearts out! We're volunteering to fight but you're too young. They won't accept you as volunteers in the Hellenic Army."

We work very hard as volunteers all the same, cleaning the area under the rock where the school is located, all the way to the dark mouths of the ancient caves where the neighbours keep their animals. The task is initiated and directed by our teacher, Yiannis Hadjitzypris, whose lessons extend beyond history to the entire breadth of our culture. The clean yard now functions as a gymnasium. Our teacher orders some wooden weights that look like bottles[10] and shows us how to exercise with them. The body needs exercise, he says, and teaches us the history of the Olympic Games. He also tells us that the Olympic Games are being re-vived internationally in our times. Yiannis Hadjitzypris is the only teacher who never asks for explanations when I raise my hand in class; he immediately gives me permission to go outside to vomit. I vomit frequently because of malaria. When the nausea starts, I feel dreadful; I must rush out of the classroom to expel bile. My mouth becomes as bitter as venom but mercifully, immediately after I vomit, my guts settle down and the torment stops.

A poor, small grower and rock carrier-labourer with many children and daughters that need dowries, my father can never spare any allowance for me; this is the source of my greatest dis-tress. And the taxes make a bad situation worse; based on Otto-man legislation and collected pitilessly by the British, the tax de-prives us of 10% of our meagre harvest. It's not that I am barefoot and dressed in threadbare clothes or that, being always penniless, I do without the sweets and other goods from Kyrenia's shops; school excursions are my greatest torment because I cannot join in the roasting feast. All my schoolmates contribute their share and collect money to buy meat for souvla.[11] Meanwhile, I cannot

---

10 This is most likely a reference to "Indian Clubs," exercise equipment used for developing strength.

11 Souvla (Greek: σούβλα): A popular dish from Cyprus, which consists of

chip in even with half a piastre. Far worse than going hungry with the smell of roasting meat in my nostrils is that I am excluded from the enjoyment of the group. One time, during an excursion to Hadjiyiorkos's paddock at the river of the Thermia Chiflik, I get lucky: Panayis, the son of Hadjiyiorkatzis, offers to pay my contribution for a live common swift. I agree. I eat the meat with fresh bread and have a good time with my friends! Before long I manage to catch another live common swift, with which I re-pay my debt. This is when I realize that the black and white birds can fetch a few pennies. One piastre=ten para, forty para=one grosi,[12] nine grosia=one shilling, twenty shillings=one lira![13] I sell the birds for one or two piasters each. They are in demand, so they sell quite easily. I chase them feverishly. I find out where their nests are located, when they lay their eggs, when they hatch and have young. One day, while my hand is fumbling about in a nest on the roof of an old house, it comes across the cold body of an-other hunter – a snake that is also looking for eggs or hatchlings. Startled, I jump away and nearly fall. The incident frightens me so much that I stop hunting the birds. As a result, I lose those few piastres that I used to earn.

Worst of all, I am expelled from school again because my father cannot pay my tuition. Beyond feeling dreadful about not being able to go to class or about missing, in total, two years of school due to non-payment, now that I am older, I am also ashamed. I am ashamed of being so poor. I do not want to stay in Karakoumi to take our few animals out to pasture or work in the fields. I want to be in school; I want to be in class, to learn from the teacher

---

large pieces of meat cooked on a long skewer over charcoal.

12 Grosi/grosia (Greek: γρόσι/γρόσια): A denomination of the lira derived from the Turkish word "kuruş."

13 The Cypriot pound, also known as the lira, was the currency of Cyprus until the Republic of Cyprus adopted the euro.
[Translator's note: Since Cypriots always referred to their currency as "the lira," this term is used instead of "the pound."]

that I love and admire so much. I go down to Kyrenia, pass the gymnasium, come to the caves, and hide in their darkest corner. The caves are ancient tombs and I feel so awful that I want to die. After being there for a while, I feel the need to relieve myself. As my hot urine washes away the soil, it reveals a shiny object on the ground. I pick it up, examine it, and realize that it's a gold coin. But what exactly? I have never seen anything like this before. At recess, when my classmates come out to the yard, I show the coin to my friend Yiannis. Achilleas approaches to have a look as well.

"I'll trade you for a shilling. What do you say? Do we have a deal?" Achilleas proposes.

Standing behind him where he cannot be seen, Yiannis motions "no" to me, but I have other things to consider as well.

"The coin doesn't belong to me; I have to bring it to the teacher," I decide and Achilleas starts cussing under his breath.

The teacher says that it's a half golden lira! He calls the crier Hadjiportolos from across the street:

"The person who has lost a half golden lira should claim it from the teacher, Yiannis Hadjitzypris…"

Michalis the barber turns up, but the teacher does not simply hand over the coin. He stops the lesson and questions him: "When and where did he lose the coin? Has he told anyone about it? Who has he spoken to about this?" When Michalis trips over his words, it becomes clear that the coin does not belong to him. Then the teacher says that the rightful owner of the coin is the one who has found it, meaning me! A half golden lira that belongs to me… I could never have imagined such a thing in my wildest dreams!

"What are you going to do with it, Costas Charalambou?" the teacher asks.

I do not have to give the matter much thought.

"Four shillings will go toward the tuition that I owe, Sir, and I will give the other six to my father."

The teacher makes me stand on the chair at his desk.

"Costas Charalambou has made a very prudent decision and should serve as an example to all of you!" he tells the class, looking quite pleased with me.

I am also quite pleased because I can go back to school; I do not have to miss the lessons of the teacher that I love and admire. Yiannis Hadjitzypris is pure gold himself! But he has problems with the other teacher, Georgios Stavrides. One day, when my teacher punishes the son of Master Panayis, Stavrides glares at him and says antagonistically:

"The young students are my responsibility. I will not allow anyone to intervene, let alone punish one of them!"

My teacher, a good natured man, does not tell him that the kid, who is a monster, was making a racket, refusing to get in line, thereby delaying the entire school from departing on its scheduled walk. He keeps quiet, choosing to let the anger subside. At the end of the school year, he asks me to recite the poem that recounts the story of Mr. Sotiris. Everyone is moved by my recitation! I remember almost the entire poem to this day:

In the village everyone knows that old Mr. Sotiris
is very poor but honest, a good family man.
He has four daughters, a mate that passed away
and a son in foreign lands, very far away.
In our small village we have neither palaces
nor coaches, King, to be drawn by horses.
My four girls, not that they are mine,
have learned, since they were young, to live with honour.
And for dowries they had, King, their great virtue!

But when the dishonest traitor entered my home
and stole the treasure of my first daughter...
And when my son returned, King, from foreign lands
and learned how he had dishonoured the guileless virgin
"He will not marry her?" he asked, "Son, he married another!"

My son, in great pain and sorrow, raised up his head
looked at his sister and said "you've brought shame on us!"
and, like a small child, he began to cry...

After the son has a good cry, he kills the man who despoiled his sister. When he is sentenced to death for murder, Mr. Sotiris goes to the King to plead for mercy.

And when death takes both him and me, King,
how will four girls survive on the streets alone,
what will become of them without a father or a brother?
I ask for mercy, King — what else can I do?
since they have decided to take my son's head.

In the last grade, in 1901, I am trailing two years behind due to absences from all those times when my tuition was not paid. The school is now renting the konak of Yiannis Kazinieris, on the road to Nicosia, practically in Pano Kerynia. Rumour has it that the mariner has money problems. The konak has a large hall at its center and four large rooms on each side. All students fit comfortably here; my teacher Yiannis Hadjitzypris stays in an unused room, since he hails either from Karavas or from Lapithos — I don't recall which exactly. I am pleased that he is our teacher again for the graduating year. One day he comes to class with a big smile of his face and announces his engagement to the daughter of the well-known Daktylidaris. He takes us for a walk and we share in his joy. Now we are learning about the ancient Greek philosophers; I greatly admire Socrates and feel bad that my name was changed from the philosopher's to whom *"the religion of the Jews was revealed, and he perhaps believed in Christ, while he worshipped Zeus."*
He even teaches us a nice poem about Socrates that recounts what the philosopher did when he was satirized by Aristophanes:

He smiled calmly and stood straight up in his seat
[...]

and instead of leaving the audience in dread
he proposed to hear their ironies and bitter comments.
The crowd stopped laughing, respecting the superiority of Socrates
Oh offender of the clouds, the one whom you have offended has exacted
his revenge!

And his student, Plato, promised that

"I shall write all this, oh wise one, with a reverent pen
and my name shall soar next to yours unto the ages!"

For our graduation ceremony our teacher decides to stage
a theatrical performance, which he begins preparing at the beginning of the school year. The play is "Athanasios Diakos" and I
am given the role of the hero's sister, Eleni. Yet, this year, anger
abounds; everyone in Kyrenia is at each other's throats. Charilis,
the registrar's son, picks a few green almonds from a tree that belongs to a certain malikkis;[14] the malikkis's son, who is one of my
classmates, reports Charilis to the teacher, who then disciplines
him by making him go without lunch. He puts me in charge of
supervising Charilis because I do not go home to the village at
lunchtime. I stay at the school and make do with a piece of bread
and a few olives. At noon the registrar turns up, calls his son,
and takes him home. In the afternoon both teachers question me
persistently about whether the registrar actually set foot inside
the school. What difference does it make? Apparently it makes a
huge difference because no one is allowed to enter school premises without permission, not even the registrar at the Administration Building. Clearly the quarrel goes deeper than the excuse, a
handful of green almonds. The actual conflict is over who will be

---

14 Malikkis (Greek: μαλίκκης): A Greek adaptation of the Semitic words
malik or melik, malka, or melechis that mean "king," "prince" or "chieftain."
In this context it means "land owner."

elected Archbishop: Kyrillatsos or Kyrilloudi... [15] But I don't understand it; I find it all rather confusing.

What I do know firsthand, however, is how the biggest scandal of the year got started. Panayis, the son of Hadjiyiorkatzis, is sixteen or seventeen years old. He is the oldest student among us because he has difficulty learning and always ends up repeating the school year. One morning he goes into the room where our teacher is staying and notices a hemline under the bed. He yanks it and forces Pattisharou to come out of hiding. In the blink of an eye, every student in the school is standing around her while she, obviously frightened, tries to explain what she is doing in the teacher's room. She says that she came to bring the socks that the teacher ordered, and her hands tremble as she holds them up to show us. She claims that she hid under the bed when she heard noise. Panayis Hadjiyiorkatzis winks at us with meaning: Pattishiarou is known in Kyrenia not only for her knitting machine, but also for other things. But how does this incident become the talk of the town? And why do so many people become involved? Well, the other teacher, Stavrides – more than happy to oblige! – reports the incident in suggestive language in the newspaper that he publishes. The scandal becomes so enlarged that the School Board shuts down the school! [16]

My teacher is innocent – I'm sure of it, one thousand percent. He takes the case to court but the School Board will not allow him to continue teaching. While the trial is underway they temporarily replace him with Georgios Loizides, who taught for many years before going on to study law. A good but very stern teacher, he expects us to learn all the ancient texts by heart. I do not have a tough time of it; I learn everything rather easily and still remem-

---

15 Kyrillatsos (Greek: Κυριλλάτσος) means "big Kyrillos" while Kyrilloudi (Greek: Κυριλλούδι) capitalized here as "little Kyrillos."

16 According to "Rayias Newspaper" (nos. 57, 59, 60 and 61), the incident, which caused the scandal, took place on Saturday, October 13, 1901.

ber much of what I memorized back then. I am especially fond of the sermon that the Apostle Paul delivered at Areios Pagos:

"For as I passed along and observed the objects of your worship, I found also an altar with this inscription, 'To the unknown god.' What therefore you worship as unknown, this I proclaim to you…"

Although I am a good student, during final exams I stumble when the teacher asks me for the root of the word "gamos"[17] because the finals are held in public: School Board members, clergy, parents, everyone is sitting across from me! I blush with embarrassment and keep silent, but he insists.

"Don't you know, Costas Charalambou?"

"I do know, Sir… But I'm embarrassed to say…"

Loizides becomes enraged.

"You're embarrassed? They twist our language and give lewd meanings to words that express precisely and with dignity the milestones of human life and, instead of dignity we feel embarrassment? Impermissible!" he shouts.

He gives me a passing grade nonetheless. I receive my diploma but do not take part in the school play; Loizides removed me from the cast when he first took over the class. He gave the role of Eleni to my best friend, Yiannis Vrahas. Kotsios, the son of Captain Ttooulos, gets the role of Athanasios Diakos and does an excellent job of it. Meanwhile, I am left knowing all the parts by heart, especially that of Athanasios Diakos, which I remember to this day!

Why do you hold me bound? Why do you torture me?
Why have you brought me here, oh cruel one, in chains?
So viciously you have sought to ravage my entrails
and to enact the laws of the fiercest nature upon me.
For God have you no reverence or respect?
Look what time Charon has chosen to take me,
Now when branches are in bloom and the soil sprouts!

---

17 Gamos (Greek: γάμος): An ancient Greek word that means wedding; variants are used as lewd expressions in Greek.

The theatrical performance is held at the Club House, which is frequented by Kyrenia's wealthy and educated – today's Hotel Coeur de Lion. The play is a great success; everyone cries when they impale the hero and roast him on the spit. The proceeds of the performance go to Miss Marie for her studies at Arsakeio in Athens; she is studying to be a teacher.

My beloved teacher, the one who initiated the production of the play, is not at the performance; he is not even mentioned. Whereas, around the same time, across from our school, the wealthy merchant and landowner Yiannatzis Karalatzias steals the wife of Pantelis, a pitiful public servant who is renting Ttofaros's house. Many people see them together at his lemon grove in broad daylight; he holds her by the waist and lifts her up high in his arms. He is big and strong, while she is small and delicate. Yet no one speaks up. Other than being physically strong, Yiannatzis Karalatzias is married to the daughter of a powerful family of notables; he is not a poor teacher like Yiannis Hadjitzypris who is bullied, harassed, and unfairly accused for allegedly "offending the moral sense of his students!"

At last the court exonerates my teacher but there is no end to his misfortune. His fiancée breaks off their engagement and he falls deathly ill from shame and sorrow. In his case "exoneration is half a shitting!"[18] The injustice greatly pains me because, being poor, I am always humiliated by people for trivial things, too. One day I go to Hadjilambros, the shoemaker across from our school, to ask for some adhesive for my book, which has come unstuck. He looks at me fiercely:

"Come back when my daughter, Persou, goes for a shit and I'll give you some. Get lost! Scram!" he barks at me.

Right in front of me, on the counter, the container with the glue is full to the brim. What I am asking for would not have cost him anything yet... Be that as it may, I see malice even in my

---

18 "Rayias Newspaper," 1902, No. 97, 98, 99, 100.

schoolmates. Yiannis Kazinieris does not escape bankruptcy in the end; all his belongings are put on auction including the konak, where our school is housed, so we witness the entire process. "Going once, going twice..." While this is underway, my classmate Millarotos stares at Kazinieris's young son, Costis.

"Serves you right! They're selling off everything you own! Looks so good on you," he says while smirking tauntingly and striking his clenched fists.

The boy does not make a sound, but his eyes are as hot as burning coals and tears stream down his cheeks. I feel so bad for him; I know poverty. My heart bleeds for him!

On the other hand, there are also acts of kindness: One day I am taking our donkey, loaded with a huge sack of carobs, from the village to the storehouses in Kyrenia. Halfway there, the animal slips and falls. The sack is massive and I am young and helpless. Not knowing what to do, I start to cry. The son of Loumbas Stratouras happens to be passing by; he asks who I am and why I am crying. In a flash, he dismounts from his mule and instructs me to get a firm grip on the donkey's rein. He loads the sack back on the animal without any difficulty. I thank him and he smiles:

"Give my regards to your father; he's my uncle!"

At night I tell my father what happened and he begins to recount old stories about Loumbas Stratouras and his wife, who is my father's sister. He tells us about how they trade in wine and about how strong Loumbas is... He singlehandedly killed four of the six Yörüks[19] from Anatolia that came to ravage his herd. Father enjoys telling stories at night, around the hearth in winter and out in the yard under the stars in summer. This is how we also learn about his first wife.

"I would have gone far in life, if she had not died; she was such a hard worker and an excellent homemaker, God rest her soul!"

---

19 Yörüks: A group of Turkish people; some are nomadic and live primarily in the mountains of Anatolia.

His first wife was killed in a landslide on a mountainside where they were digging. She was buried alive! He also tells us how Thermia's first notable hounded him because he spoke out of turn. He had his people hang our father's mule and burn manure to drive away his bees. They also stole the hog that he was raising, took him three miles away to Panayia Glytziotissa by boat, slaughtered him, lit coals in a pit to make kleftiko,[20] and had themselves a feast. All this because, in a drunken stupor, our father had said that the notable was having relations with his mistress in the hollow trunk of an olive tree outside Karakoumi. Father also tells us about his big lucky break – the time he had found an ancient artefact. While he was in church on Easter Sunday, the neighbours took the opportunity to steal it; worse still, this caused his second wife, our mother, to die of sorrow. As a result of all this, he is twice a widower and we are orphaned of our mother.[21] He also tells us about the rock carrying that he has had to do all his life – rocks to build the hospital in Kyrenia, rocks for the wall of the cemetery, rocks for the town's first notable. This is how he ekes out a living, providing dowries for my sisters and money for our clothes, for one pair of shoes for each one of us but not always, and for my tuition, which he scrapes together albeit not regularly. Nevertheless, my father never gives up; he always comes up with the money somehow because I do well in school. The struggle for my father, and for all of us, is how to get ahead in life!

Getting ahead in life is easier said than done. All my sisters are

---

20 Kleftiko (Greek: κλέφτικο) is a typical Greek dish. It derives its name from the Klephts (Greek: Κλέφτες), which means "thieves." The Klephts were anti-Ottoman insurgents, who lived in the countryside when Greece was a part of the Ottoman Empire. Since they had to cook without being detected, they would place meat on coals in a hole in the ground, cover it up, and let it cook for hours, thereby producing no smoke.

21 The stories of Charalambos Catsellis are given in the books by Rina Katselli *Kyrenia: Through the Mouths of Elders I* and *II*.

waiting in line to marry after Polyxeni, to start their own families. My two brothers do not seem concerned about the future, but I am: What will become of me? My brother Glioris always says that "I must learn about the world." He left school and now runs errands for people, works the land, and earns a daily wage as a ploughman. In the summer, on Friday mornings, while it's still dark, he and I set out for Nicosia with the donkey loaded with produce from our fields. We wait outside Kyrenia Gate along with all the other villagers. At first light, when the Hodja chants the call to prayer from the minaret, we are given permission to enter to sell our goods; we cross Kyrenia Gate. Glioris is smart; he knows how to bargain, selling eggplants one shilling for one hundred. He buys white bread from Nicosia – as ordered by our father – and kousvos.[22] He can read a little but is good with numbers. My older brother Antonis is illiterate. He is an apprentice with Stavris Vottis, learning carpentry, but not very good at the craft. We do not go hungry. We eat whatever our father manages to grow on his land: fava beans, black-eyed peas, chickpeas, gourds – many brightly coloured orange gourds, fresh when they are in season or preserved in winter; sometimes we have to make do only with fried red gourds for weeks. We manage to obtain oil although we do not have olive trees of our own; even luxuries such as sugar, coffee and rice are not unknown to us. My sisters bake once a week. At the end of the week the bread is stale but then we fill up faster and with less. We have few clothes, almost no shoes, and when we do have them, we take very good care of them; we go barefoot both in summer and winter to save our shoes for Sundays and important holidays. Our father has oxen with which he

---

22 Kousvos (Greek: κούσβος): A round, dark coloured sweet derived from the process of blanching sesame for the production of tahini and halva – essentially, the shells of the sesame seeds, which are not very tasty but quite nutritious. Kousvos was sold cheaply and purchased primarily by the poor, who ate it with carob syrup.

ploughs not only his fields but also other people's, when we works as a day labourer. Sometimes my brothers take the oxen out to work, too. This happens when our father has a job carrying stones with the donkey: 25 para for each load and, in each load, two large stones on the either side of the donkey in the saddlebags, and one balanced on the animal's back. I hear about Loukas, a rock carrier like father, who left for the East. He worked hard for a few years and saved some money. He came back with approximately £100, which he lends out and earns interest. He lives like a king and no longer has to work. I see him in Kyrenia's coffee shops, dressed nicely, twirling his prayer beads. My father cannot do the same because he has a family. Even if he weren't concerned about us the boys, what would happen to his daughters? He can't go. But I can! I hear about Egypt: five shillings for the fare! After the graduation ceremony Georgios Loizides asks about my plans for the future.

"If I had five shillings for the fare, I would go to Egypt to work and strike it rich!" I reply.

He becomes angry; he says that young men should not leave their country. My father feels the same way and refuses to give me the five shillings. He could find the money if he wanted to, but he does not want me to migrate. He wants me to stay in Kyrenia.

"Something will turn up," he keeps telling me.

But what? I think about my classmates: Yiannis Vottis, Panayis Hadjiyiorkatzis, Kotsios the son of Captain Ttooulos, Yiannis Vrahas, Yiorkos Dkiolaris from Thermia, Demetros the son of Mihalatzis... Most of them have something to fall back on: family money, boats, a store already set up. Nothing big but at least they can count on a piece of bread. My friend Spyros, the son of Kyriakos Lordos, enrols at the Pancyprian Gymnasium because Volonakis, the school's headmaster, comes to Kyrenia in the summer with his sister to go swimming. He has a word with his father and convinces him to send his son to continue his education. But I have neither land, nor boats, and higher education is not an option. Opportunities for work for young men in our parts are not only hard to come by, but nonexistent! Almost all of Kyrenia's young men have migrated, most of them to Egypt, which seems to be our only hope.

CHAPTER 3

THE FIRST STRUGGLE FOR SURVIVAL

Kyrenia, 1902-1904

Unpaid Work and Humiliation

Barefoot and dressed in my only pair of cotton pants, I have a problem – not only are the pants too old, they are also too short. I have grown a lot recently. Luckily, I have not gained any weight so they still fit. My shirt is in better condition, even though the sleeves come only to my elbows. Father in front with me in tow, we arrive at a large stone-built two storey konak, like all the houses on the west side of the crescent of Kyrenia's port, directly across from the Castle. Goods of all sorts are stored on the ground floor: sugar, rice, pots from the East, rolls of European fabric. I follow my father inside, where we see an old man.

"Sit down!" he tells us.

Since there are no chairs, we sit on some sacks. I try to guess what they contain; I am concerned because, if they are filled with legumes, my behind will break out in hives. But their surface, from what I can tell by touch, is smooth and crunchy. Sugar perhaps? The old man paces up and down, glances toward the wooden stairs that lead to the upper floor, and winks suggestively.

"Wait until Mr. Costantos finishes his...business!"

I do not understand what he is implying and my father remains serious; he does not react to the old man's naughty gestures.

"All right, we'll wait," he says with a nod.

The stairs creak and a beautiful woman appears at the top; she is plump with an olive complexion. Her vest fits snugly around her shoulders, her silk waistband is tight, and her bosom spills out of her lace blouse. As she walks down the stairs, her full skirt inflates like a sail and her gold bracelets jingle. Black-eyed with arched brows, she looks at us and smiles.

"Hello!" she says as she exits, but the scents of rosewater and laurel oil trail behind her.

The old man motions to us; it's our turn to go upstairs where rosewater and laurel oil still hang in the air. The embroidered throws are rumpled on the divan. Behind the massive desk, Mr. Costantos smiles under his meticulously twisted black moustache. His hair appears to be freshly combed and his parting is immaculate, along with everything else on him: his black suit, his white shirt, his tie... He cheerily says "good morning." My father hesitates and lowers his head subserviently.

"Mr. Costantos, I brought my youngest son, like we said the other day..."

Costantos looks me up and down.

"Yes, I'll put him to work at the shop so he can learn the business," he says.

He looks at me again, thinks for a moment, stands up, opens the dresser against the wall, digs around inside, and pulls out a piece of clothing that he tosses at me.

"Here's a pair of pants..."

I catch it mid-air and manage to utter a "thank you."

"Take him to Nikolis Trooditis. At night he'll stay with us at the house; he'll do some chores, like we said..."

My father respectfully nods "goodbye." We go downstairs, cross half the port, enter the alley of Trypitis, come to Panayia Chrysopolitissa, cross Esso Geitonia, and pass the large wooden lattice door of the general store. To our right is Kamouza, a towering brown mass; Costantos's shop is directly across, on the main road that leads to Nicosia. Since I am confused about the most basic thing, I stop. My father turns back to look at me.

"Move!" he orders but I do not respond.

"Why are you standing there, Costis?"

"Nothing was mentioned about payment. How much is Mr. Costantos going to pay me?"

My father is startled, as though I had asked the most astonishing and impertinent question.

"Pay you…? Learn the job first and then have the gall to ask for payment. Let's go!"

Nikolis Trooditis, a plump moon-faced man from a village on Mount Troodos, is the manager of Mr. Costantos's store with a salary of nine liras per year and a detached room at the edge of the orchard at the boss's paternal home. He is young and ambitious. He reads; he is learning accounting. He wants to get ahead in life but the opportunities available to him in Kyrenia are very limited; he wants much more, much faster. As a result he is always irritated and takes his frustration out on me, his only underling.

"Boy, fetch pots from the storeroom at the port!" he orders and I bend over backwards to do as I am told.

I am wearing the pants that Mr. Costantos gave me but they are too big; they come up to my armpits. I tie them firmly with rope but they keep rolling down. Same with the legs… I roll up the hems several times but, by the time I carry the pots from the storeroom to the shop, they roll down again. I am terrified of tripping on them and breaking something. When this does happen, God help me, I stand as far as I possibly can from Nikolis Trooditis's rage! I wait anxiously for Sunday, my day off, so I can bring the pants to my sisters in Karakoumi. They tailor them to my size as best they can.

At noon I fetch lunch for the two of us from the boss's paternal home in Kyrenia – a large konak surrounded by a fertile orchard. On my second day I come upon the boss's father, old Malikkis,[1] in

---

1 Although the term malikkis means "landowner," here it is capitalized as "Malikkis" because it is used in the narration as a name, in reference to the man's station in life.

the yard; he is seething with anger. Two ploughmen are standing in front of him, struggling to make excuses.

"Well, boss, it's not like we went there to mess with a woman of honour; everyone knows that Theodora is loose..." one whispers.

Malikkis makes a large threatening gesture.

"You asked if you could go to her house, and she invited you in?"

"No... We tried to get in through the hearth's vent..." the other says, looking terrified.

Old Malikkis is fit to be tied!

"So you think you can jump any woman that you hear is loose? I pay you two liras a year! Can't you go about your business without messing with women that don't want you? Take off the vrakas[2] and the boots that I bought for you and get out of my sight!"

The ploughmen hesitate for a moment but the ferocity in old Malikkis's gaze leaves no room for negotiation. They strip down, taking off their vrakas and boots right there in the middle of the yard. The two men tremble; they do not know what to do with the garments. Should they leave them on the ground or hand them to the boss? Malikkis understands and motions to me.

"Costis, show them out and lock the gate!"

I do as I am told. When I return, I stand in front of him with the vrakas and the boots. What do I do with them?

"Give them to Flourentzou to have her store them away," he orders.

In the kitchen, fat Flourentzou takes the clothes and hands me a container with food and bread, wrapped inside a towel. Irini, one of Malikkis's daughters, catches up to me on the way out.

"I have an order for Nikolis," she says and stealthily hands me a piece of paper.

2 Vraka (Greek: βράκα): The traditional breeches of Cyprus that are extremely roomy; they are meant to be tucked inside long boots, just below the knee.

Nikolis opens Irini's order at once. My stomach is growling but I have to wait. He neatly folds up the paper, opens the container, and begins to eat.

"Why are you standing around? Store away the pots that you brought from the storeroom!" he orders with the first mouthful.

I get to work and forget my hunger; I stop only when he calls me. In the container there is as much food as he has left, half an onion, and a piece of bread. I am hungry and Nikolis's leftovers are not enough. I eat slowly so the enjoyment will last longer, there, in the shop's darkest corner. As I chew, my mind wanders back to the two ploughmen who were fired for messing with a woman. Meanwhile, Costantos has Hadjipetrena… Once a week she comes down to Kyrenia from her village, goes upstairs to his office and, at lunchtime, they eat together at Costantis Kotziama-nis's, the best eatery in town. I wonder whether old Malikkis, who is a principled and god-fearing man, knows this. Even if he does, it's clear that Hadjipetrena comes to his son of her own volition. Does the Englishwoman come of her own accord, too? I am not so sure… That girl has alabaster white skin, blonde hair, and spar-kling deep blue eyes. Her birth name is all but forgotten because she is as beautiful as an Englishwoman. Everyone calls her that but I do not know of any Englishwoman who is as beautiful as she is. She carefully looks at the two rolls of fabric that I have brought for her from the store.

"Tell Nikolis to cut only ten cubits of basma,"[3] she says to me in a low voice.

Periclina, her mother, intervenes.

"Tell him to cut taffeta, too!"

The Englishwoman sighs.

"But I have a nice dress, Ma!"

"That one's old. We'll give it to your sister and you can have a new one made," Periclina insists.

The Englishwoman motions wearily.

---

3 Basma (Greek: πασμάς) : Turkish word for a patterned cotton fabric.

"Alright, ask him to cut some taffeta as well..." she says and gets up off the sofa.

The Englishwoman always looks sad; she never laughs. I do not know how true this is but I have heard that she used to be a cheerful person until the boss made her his mistress. They say that the neighbour was paid to invite her to her home; as soon as the Englishwoman set foot in the house, the neighbour disappeared and Costantos appeared. He yanked her inside and locked the door. Did she scream or not? Was she able to scream but didn't? I don't know. But I do know that, since then, the Englishwoman measures her words, rarely leaves her house even for a walk, and always looks sad! Costantos sends her the best of everything from the shop along with his finest fabrics. I roll up the fabrics but want to be sure.

"One basma and one taffeta?" I ask.

Periclina becomes angry and sends me away. Luckily she does not hit like Nikolis. Costantos does not hit me very often but a beating from his hand feels worse to me. The worst beating I ever get from him is because of Potsiera. "Potsiera" is what everyone calls the pruned up, scowling creature with the patched up skirt that cleans the boss's office and prepares his special coffee. She simmers it on a small brazier downstairs in the storeroom, stirs in a thick white liquid from a can – "condensed milk" she calls it – and brings it upstairs to his office on a tray. I come in looking for the boss.

"Potsiera, is Mr. Costantos upstairs?" I ask.

She half-turns to look at me with a grimace but, before she opens her mouth, the boss appears at the top of the stairs.

"Upstairs now!" he commands sternly.

The moment I get upstairs, he starts to hit me.

"So you'll learn not to be disrespectful to women... Don't you know the woman's name? Don't you know it? Speak up!"

"I know it, Mr. Costantos, Sir!"

"What is her name?"

"Eleni, Mr. Costantos. Her name is Eleni!"

"Why did you call her Potsiera?"

"Everyone calls her that..."

Since the beating only gets worse, I realize that I should stop trying to explain.

"I'm sorry, Mr. Costantos. I'm so sorry, I will never..."

Eleni Potsiera simply looks on, neither pleased nor displeased. She comes upstairs with the coffee, waits for him to get tired of beating me, and then...

"Your coffee, Mr. Costantos," she says softly. She places it on his desk and heads back downstairs.

I follow her – a humiliated, beaten dog that has learned that no one calls her "Potsiera" to her face.

During this time my heart awakens. Her name is Dorothea and her father has a foreign surname. He works as an interpreter at the Administration Building. She is quite pretty. She wears a warm woollen knit dress and a cap from which two well-groomed braids emerge. One day she sees me eating in a corner at the store and smiles at me. I blush; my entire body tingles! Nikolis sees only a customer; he already knows what she wants because she always comes in asking for the same thing.

"My mother has sent me for half an oka of biscuit crumbs."

Nikolis glares at me.

"Damn you, boy! Are you still chewing?"

I swallow quickly and rush to serve her but Nikolis has already taken the container with the biscuit crumbs down from the shelf. While he weighs the requested amount, Dorothea keeps looking at me. I wipe my mouth and smile, but she sticks her tongue out at me. I know she means well so I do not take it badly. My insides crumble like those biscuits and my entire being sweetens.

At night, at old Malikkis's konak, the two servants Flourentzou and Agapiena stack up all the day's dishes for me to wash. The small bowls are easy enough to clean but I have a tough time with the large pots. I dip sponges in ash and scrub until they shine. Then I rinse them with lye. I am pressed for time because everything must be washed before dinner. While the bosses eat their dinner, I stand behind old Malikkis's chair. He walks into the dining room slowly, imposingly, grandiosely, and stands at the head of the table. I watch closely for when he is about to sit down, so I can push his chair forward. His wife inspects the table in case something is missing. Miss Efthymia is there and Irini comes in late as always; every evening she stands under the lemon tree in the back yard and chats with Nikolis in a low voice. She steps in as quietly as possible, hoping to go unnoticed. Sometimes she comes in after the prayer. Most of the time it's just the four of them for supper: old Malikkis, his wife and two daughters. His youngest daughter is away at a boarding school in Nicosia, and Costantos is rarely at home at night; he is usually out with friends or with one of his mistresses. Old Malikkis's other children are married, so they are at their homes. The dining room is spacious and the large fireplace is lit. From the window I can see the light in Nikolis's room at the edge of the orchard; two silhouettes are moving around inside. The second man must be Mattheos Kariolos. Also young, Nikolis's best friend is involved in shipping. He visits almost every night so they can talk. Both belong to the party that wants Kyrilloudi as Archbishop; as progressive supporters of Makrakis,[4] they are always talking about the war against injustice and the fight for social justice. Where is this justice? Where are the teachings of Jesus Christ and of Socrates that I learned about in school? Nikolis, a store manager with his own room and a salary of nine liras per year, is not satisfied; he wants more. He beats me, while I am the one doing the hardest jobs both at the shop and at the house without pay. "Costis, the oranges!" Malikkis's wife orders but I do not hear her.

"Costis! Costis!"

---

4 Apostolos Makrakis was a progressive theologian who, among his other activities, published the magazine "Logos" in Athens.

Alarmed, I snap back to reality, grab the fruit bowl with the oranges, and place it at the center of the table. The fruit is not premium quality; the oranges are small and misshapen because they take the good ones to market. They keep the rejects for the house and, if anything is left, they give it to the poor as charity. When Malikkis leaves the dining room, his wife goes into the kitchen to give instructions to the two servants. She sees what food is left and decides what will be given to the workers and what will be saved. As I am going back and forth from the dining room to the kitchen clearing the table, Irini finds an opportunity to strike up a conversation with me.

"Where did your mind wander off to?"

"Abroad! I'm thinking about how I might be able to leave."

"Leave? Go where?" Efthymia asks.

Overwhelmed with frustration, I cannot speak, so Irini answers on my behalf.

"I know! He wants to go to Egypt. That's what he told Nikolis when he first came to work for us. But he's still here!"

Irini and Efthymia laugh. I become angry and defensive.

"I'm here now but, one way or another, I will go overseas to work and get paid…"

I want to tell them that I want to make money, to do something with my life, to be someone, but I am choked by discontent. I start to cry in front of Malikkis's daughters. Thankfully, I have three dirty dishes in my hands and an excuse to run into the kitchen. In the kitchen a plate of food has been set aside for me; most of the time I eat what remains from the table, the leftovers. But it is always plenty and satisfying. I eat silently, carry out Flourentzou's last orders for the day, wash the remaining dishes, and walk down the long corridor to where the loom is. In the summer I lay down my bedding there because it's cool, but in the winter I bring it down into the dining room next to the extinguished fireplace, which retains its warmth. Once in a while there are strange late night visits, in which case I do not go to bed immediately; I have to

wait in the kitchen. Villagers bring ancient artefacts that they wish
to sell secretly, in defiance of British regulations.

I hear them talking in low voices, negotiating the price, often
making references to Lambousa. The curtains are always drawn. I
hear strange creaking – perhaps hidden compartments that I don't
know about, crypts that open and close. Ancient artefacts are free
for the taking! That's what everyone says without remorse, as long
as the British do not find out, because they want it all for themselves – they are so greedy!

On evenings when the Metropolitan of Kyrenia visits things
are very different, although again I have to wait in the kitchen.
The house is all lit up, every lighting fixture is on, the curtains
are pulled back, and the double doors at the front are wide open.
The elite come and go: rich captains, merchants and farmers not
only from Kyrenia, but also from the surrounding villages, including first notables and loyal supporters of the Metropolitan. The
Metropolitan of Kyrenia is a small, thin and pale man, who weighs
half an ounce; you can barely make him out inside his vestments.
It's no wonder that the supporters of the Metropolitan of Citium,
Kyrillatsos, mock him as "Kyrilloudi." Yet on most nights there are
neither obvious nor secret musafirs;[5] the house is quiet. I wash the
last dishes, eat the plate of food that Flourentzou leaves for me
and, at last, in a horizontal position, I review my situation: slave
boy, servant to all, beaten by all, without pay. I am expected to
be patient and to learn, but what am I learning? Nothing! Nikolis
is the one who keeps the shop's ledgers; he is the one learning
accounting, while I can't even look at them. How I am supposed
to learn anything? I am miserable and frustrated. I cry. I hear con-
versations in Turkish; it's the family of Abdulla Effendi, the Turkish judge who is renting half of old Malikkis's house. I do not
understand what they are saying; I know very few Turkish words.

---

5 Musafir (Greek: μουσαφίρης): A word in Arabic, Persian, Hindi and
Urdu that means "traveler"; in Turkish it also means "guest," which is the
meaning that it has here.

But the mumbling puts me to sleep because, thankfully, fatigue quickly overtakes me.

On Sundays, when the store is closed and I have the day off, I go to my paternal home in Karakoumi. It's a breath of fresh air, a sigh of relief, although I do not remain idle there either: I help my father with his chores and take the oxen out to pasture. My father is pleased that I am in the employ of the Malikkis's son; I am not, but I keep quiet. There is nothing I can do about the situation. Since Nikolis is not satisfied with his salary, he does odd jobs for himself, too. He often gives me money and, on Sundays, I travel around to the surrounding villages to buy eggs that he can send to Egypt. He is earning something extra. I decide to use Sundays for myself so I can earn a few pennies, too! In the summer, on Sundays, I pick carobs discarded by their growers — whatever is left behind at inaccessible locations such as steep riverbanks, or among spiny shrubs and nettles. The crop that I manage to collect is good; I sell it for four shillings and buy a young lamb. I watch over the lamb like a hawk and take it out to graze on other people's pastures since I have none of my own. On Sundays I bring it with me to Karakoumi. I no longer cry at night; I make plans! The lamb grows. I will sell it and save the money...

At Easter I celebrate with my family in Karakoumi. My oldest sister visits with her three daughters Athena, Eleni and Maria. She is pregnant again because she wants a son. The shop is closed on Easter Monday. Kyrenia and the surrounding villages are all but deserted; everyone is at the Chrysotrimithiotissa Festival except for the women of Karmi. They stay at the village and pretend to be men, making merry at the coffee shops, telling dirty jokes and uttering profanities. Early dawn, I am sitting on some sacks outside the shop when my old schoolmates pass by: Demetros Michalatzis, Spyros the son of Kyriakos Lordos who is home for the holidays from the Pancyprian Gymnasium, Kotsios the son of Captain Ttoulos, and my closest friend Yiannis Vrahas. They are heading to the festival and invite me to come along. Of course I want to go but how could I possibly accept the invitation? I am almost fifteen years old and have no money. How do I join in the fun? I confide in my friend Yiannis.

"How is it possible that you have no money, Costis?" he asks discretely.

"Honestly, I don't. Where would I get it?"

I reach mechanically into my pocket and find the money that Nikolis has given me to buy eggs, one grosi per dozen. Yiannis is waiting. I open my hand and there they are, three grosia…

"I have some but it's not mine; it belongs to Nikolis," I explain to him.

"Come on, Costis, that's just enough to cover your share. You've been collecting eggs from the villages for nothing for so long. Put in the money and let's have a good time!"

It is a huge temptation! And I give in…. I use the three grosia to pay for my share. I go to Chrysotrimithiotissa with my friends! We pass under the icon; we pray; we wander around the festival grounds. Vendors with carts, shamishi[6] makers, people that sell animals, butchers that slaughter them and sell meat on the spot. We buy meat, cut carob tree offshoots on which to skewer it, collect wood, and start a fire. An argument flares up next to us between men from Karmi and men from Karavas, as always. They're looking for any excuse, take offense at anything, swear at each other and draw daggers but, fortunately, zaptiehs[7] separate them in time. We watch the commotion in amusement then return to our souvla, which is now ready to eat, and to the jug of wine that we have bought. Feeling unrestricted and liberated I eat, drink, and have a good time. The fiddle and the lute players are making the rounds, passing by groups of people sitting under trees. They also come to us. I want to dance but discover that my legs won't

---

6 Shamishi (Greek: σιάμισιη): A popular Cypriot sweet; fried triangles made with semolina and topped with syrup.

7 Zaptieh (Greek: ζαπτιές): Turkish word for police officer.

hold me up, not from weakness or from the shivers of malaria, but from the pleasant faintness of alcohol. I fall flat to the ground and, while I try to sing with my friends, my mind drifts to Dorothea. Kotsios, the son of Captain Ttoulos, looms over me with a pocketknife.

"What's the matter, Costis? Shall I cut off your ear like they do to goats to see if you'll bleed?"

I pull myself together and stand up.

"No! Leave my ear alone!"

My best friend Yiannis brings the jug of wine to my mouth.

"Since you're already drunk, have some more. One who's already wet isn't afraid of water!"

"He's not afraid... He's not afraid of anything!" I concur and suck back more wine.

The wine goes down, heats up my insides, spills out of the corners of my mouth, runs down my throat, and trickles down my chest. Millarotos Hadjidemetris from Thermia starts bragging that he fancies Dorothea and that she's impressed when he rides around her house on his mare. Despite the inebriation I am overcome with anger, until I remember how she looked at me that day at the shop... I ignore him. Let him talk; let him do whatever he likes! I may be in a stupor from the wine but, from the corner of my eye, I notice that Nikolis is watching me suspiciously from a distance. Troodites knows my friends and has a way of extracting information by asking indirect questions. I have a bad feeling... The wine and its sweetness are fleeting. I've got it coming to me and it will be very bad, I know it!

Next morning, on Easter Tuesday, as I approach the store, I see him standing outside. Instead of unlocking the door, he just stands there. My heart is beating so hard that it's about to burst.

"Come here, you! Let's go!" he orders.

"Where?"

"You'll see!"

I have no choice but to follow him! We go around Kamouza,

enter Esso Geitonia, pass Trypitis, and come to the port. He stops in front of the storeroom; the boss's office is upstairs. It's very early in the morning so I am praying that Costantos is not in yet. But he is! He sits behind his desk, listening to Nikolis recount the events of the previous day in great detail. He knows everything, even that my share was exactly three grosia, no more no less. When Costantos stands up, he appears taller than usual...

"Is it true that the money you gave for the roasting feast belonged to Nikolis?" he asks and takes a few steps toward me.

I cannot lie.

"Yes, it is," I say.

I know I'm in the wrong. I nod affirmatively and do not look up again. Two slaps strike my cheeks so violently that they send me tumbling down the stairs. All day at the shop I do not raise my eyes, which are red and swollen from crying. I hide when Dorothea comes in to buy biscuit crumbs. I don't want her to see me. What's the point? This is no way to live!

With the first chance I get, I tell my father how unhappy I am. How long is this situation going to continue? My father advises me to be patient and promises to speak to Costantos about a yearly salary for me.

"If he doesn't give it to me, I'm leaving!" I tell him, standing up to my father for the first time. My father keeps his promise and speaks to Costantos.

He agrees to pay me 25 shillings for the third year, starting in May. It's not that I'm satisfied but it is something! It's better than nothing... Meanwhile, my lamb has grown but I do not want to sell it just yet; I decide to wait for a better price. The next time Dorothea comes to the store, I reach for the ladder so I can serve her. The ladder slips and, despite my efforts to hold onto the shelf, I fall to the floor among shards of broken glassware. Alarmed, Dorothea leans over me with concern. I blush as I look up at her; she blushes too. Millarotos can brag all his wants about impressing her by strutting around her house on his mare! Foaming at the mouth, Nikolis starts throwing threats around about the broken glassware. Silent and dignified, I weigh the biscuit crumbs for Dorothea, while Nikolis continues cussing. It's not that he's wrong; I realize that he has his own problems but he also claims to be a supporter of Makrakis. I never see him demonstrating any of the love of Christ or the social justice that this saintly man teaches... Since Nikolis does not act on Makrakis teachings, why does he claim to espouse them?

Kyrenia has only beatings and humiliation for me. In addition, the whole town is embroiled in endless arguments about politics and who will be Archbishop. Even families are divided over this issue. Old Malikkis is not speaking to his eldest son, Michalakis, who holds a prominent position with the British Administration. One day Nikolis sends me to his house with several fabric rolls for his wife. Michalatzena, a kind-hearted woman, looks at the fabrics while taking some sweet-smelling koulouria[8] out of the oven. She asks me about a particular roll, but I know that the boss's sisters are keeping that one at the house. They have made garments from it and refuse to return it because they do not want anyone else to have dresses with the same fabric, at least not until theirs get old. I make up an excuse.

"It's at the boss's house..."

A bright woman, Michaletzena understands and smiles.

"It doesn't matter," she says and asks that fabric be cut from the roll that I have brought.

I roll up the fabric and, as I am about to leave, she hands me a warm, large koulouri.

"Fresh out of the oven!" she tells me.

Back at the shop I slowly munch on my koulouri, enjoying the crispy sesame seeds, and the lovely aromas of mastic, mahlepi, cinnamon and clove. I offer a few pieces to Nikolis. He asks where I got it and becomes infuriated when I tell him.

---

8 Koulouri/Koulouria (Greek: κουλούρι/κουλούρια): Simit, a circular-shaped bread, which is typically encrusted with sesame seeds.

"From Chariti, the wife of Michalatzis? Have you no shame? Accepting something from her...? Don't you know that they can't stand the sight of her at your boss's house?"

I know but I do not care; the woman is nice and polite, a far better person than all those who dislike her. Nikolis tells Irini and she comes looking for me while I am washing the evening dishes. She is enraged.

"Get in here!"

I follow her into the dining room, where her sister Efthymia is also waiting to confront me.

"Tell me, don't we feed you enough? You're not satisfied with the food that we give you?" she asks.

I nod "yes" but that only makes her angrier.

"Why did you accept a koulouri from Michalatzena?"

I keep quiet and Irini throws out a "you're so ungrateful" at me. And they don't even know that I told Michaletzena about the fabric roll that they are keeping at the house!

"We've brought you into our home and you go to our enemies?" she adds.

I keep my head down but my heart is not pounding; these two do not give beatings. They just hold onto to their malice and leave me with the pain of humiliation. At that moment Costantos steps into the dining room, all dressed up and smelling of cologne. My heart starts pounding like a drum. Now I am scared! He beats and kicks hard enough to throw you five fathoms across the room. They tell their brother, he listens carefully, and then:

"What were you doing at her house?" he asks me.

"Nikolis sent me with basmas from the shop for her to choose," I explain.

The boss thinks for a moment.

"Did she?" he asks.

"Yes."

"Okay, get back to work," he orders. I don't think I have ever been so eager to wash dishes before or since...

A narrow escape because the boss places his clients and the shop's business above his family's bickering. He seemed pleased that Michalatzena bought some fabric – that's why he did not get angry with me and I escaped the beating. I scrub the large pot with a grin, thinking about how Irini must be ready to burst. I am dying to see the expression on her face so I return to the dining room. Costantos has left and, yes, while I slowly collect the dishes, Irini and Efthymia mumble to each other with scowling faces. My mere presence vexes them. The family's youngest daughter, Elenitsa, is sitting next to the light fixture; she has come home for Easter from the Kalogries School in Nicosia. She is leafing through a magazine and staying out of the dispute.

"So what are you going to do now?" Efthymia asks me.

"I'm going to Egypt to work because they pay well there."

"That's what you said last year and the year before that!" Irini says mockingly.

I do not respond; I just smile. Efthymia looks at me with consternation.

"Yes, but last year and the year before he was always crying; he doesn't cry anymore," she notes.

The youngest sister looks up from the magazine and examines me for a moment.

"Why don't you cry anymore?" she asks.

"I used to cry because I had no money. This year I have more than enough!" I explain.

And that is neither a fib nor hot air! I have 29 shillings in my waistband from selling the lamb. With my third year on the job nearly completed, at the end of April the boss will owe me 25 shillings more. When I ask for my 25 shillings, he tells Nikolis to settle up with me, but he gives me only 18.

"Why?"

"The six shillings are for the glassware that you broke, or have you forgotten?" Nikolis says.

As I am walking out, he points to the straw hat that he gave me to wear during the summer and to the box where I stored my few belongings under the loom, next to my bedding. I need neither but the fact that he asks for them is poison to me! I place the two items on the counter in front of him and feign indifference, for I no longer cry and whimper. The Hevedia docks in Larnaca on the 4th, 14th and 24th of every month, picks up passengers, and sails to Egypt. I have already missed the 4th and the 14th, but May 24 is only days away. I leave the store with two golden liras and seven shillings in my pocket! While I am leaning against Kamouza's brown mass, I hear someone calling my name.

"Costis!"

Kotsios Fieros is sitting at the coffee shop across the street. He is looking at me.

"Did you call me?"

"Yes!" he says as he approaches.

"I've heard that you're planning to go to Egypt. Is this true?"

"Yes."

"I'm going, too. Can you collect some eggs and halloumi so I can bring with me to sell?"

"Of course!" I agree.

Kotsios promises to provide me with assistance and companionship during the journey. He travels to Egypt often, knows his way around, and says that there is nothing to worry about as long as I am with him.

My sisters have baked barley rusks for me. My new cotton suit is not too bad. Even Millarotos Hadjidemetris does not bother me any longer, even if he does ride around the interpreter's home trying to impress Dorothea. If she is impressed by an idiot, albeit it one on horseback, I could not care less! I start making the rounds to collect eggs and halloumi for Kotsios Fieros, who promises to help and protect me during the journey.

CHAPTER 4

ECONOMIC MIGRANT

Egypt, 1904-1906

End of May: I am looking at the plains of Mesaoria from the window of the carriage as I depart. Golden, they are harvested by stooped labourers, each moving along in his swathe of land. I know the backbreaking labour of the harvest, how you move along reaping, drenched in sweat. I also know how small the payment is, and that makes me feel confident in my decision to go abroad.

Kotsios Fieros keeps telling me to stay alert because thieves will rob you in a blink of an eye. Larnaca is noisy – hotels, consulates and, at the port, the ship that will take us away. Everything is so different here than in quiet Kyrenia; I find it rather intimidating. I find a place where I can be alone, tear two strips of fabric from my kerchief, and remove my low boots. I firmly tie one lira under the big toe of one foot and one under the other; now both are safe. I put my boots back on and tie them very tightly. Thank goodness I had the foresight to leave only change in my pouch because there are a lot of people on board. The Hevedia is not a large vessel, 1,500 tonnes, but it is carrying more passengers than its capacity. The deck is packed.

Something tugs at me, stretching and hurting me, as I watch Cyprus vanish in the distance while the sun descends into the watery line of the horizon. Leaving is painful. Although my father did not want me to go, he said nothing – now I know how he feels. He wants me to do well at home, in Kyrenia. I want the same thing, too, but how does one get ahead there? Even my friend Yiannis Vrahas, whose parents have some money, is having a tough time.

He picks up odd jobs here and there, whatever he can get. He has
been hired to keep records of the carobs that are brought to the
storerooms – an easy job that pays well, but only for the summer.
He hopes to find something else in the winter. What can I hope
for? A slave at the shop, with Nikolis making my life miserable because his life is inching along, too, and a slave at Malikkis's house
saddled with all the chores that Flourentzou and Agapiena do not
want to do. All this for a plate of food and that only on weekdays.
On Sundays I must eat from my father's humble table in Karakoumi, feeling obligated to help there as well, since I cannot bear the
thought of owing anything to anyone. Never mind that my sisters
have to get married and I am incapable of contributing in any way.
Painfully aware of all this, my father did not try to stop me.

"Keep your wits about you where you're going, Son," he said
and I felt the poison of migration coursing through his veins as I
bent down to kiss his hand, early dawn, before I set out from the
village.

My sisters washed my bed sheet and clothes, two changes of
underwear and a second shirt. Everything I own is inside this
heavy cloth sack, including the barley rusks – not many, as many
as they were able to give me, offerings of love. Overwhelmed
with emotion, a "thank you, thank you very much" melted on my
lips. Glioris and Antonis waited until the last moment to say goodbye. No one cried, no one spoke, but we understood each other.
What was there say? The separation was unbearable then and it is
just as unbearable now on the ship, as I sail away from my homeland. I understand my father completely now, but what choice did
I have? It's not that I was hanging from a thread in Kyrenia; I did
not even have a thread!

Next to me on the deck, Kotsios Fieros is tying the baskets
with the eggs and the halloumi onto himself, carefully sealed as
they are with burlap around their bloated mouths. He is concerned about me.

"Costis, did you do what told you to do?" he asks about the two liras and I nod affirmatively.

He smiles with approval. Kotsios is not going aboard to work; he travels regularly back and forth, doing odd jobs and small-scale trading. We are surrounded by a motley crowd, which is firing hostile glances at me, or is it my imagination? I am even frightened of the monk sitting across from me, although a middle-aged woman is smiling at me with kindness. I recognize her: It's Periclina, the mother of the Englishwoman, the boss's mistress. She is travelling to see her daughter, who works as a maid at a wealthy home in Alexandria. I surmise that her enormous bundle is filled with the Englishwoman's hand-me-downs for her other daughter.

"Do you have a place to stay, Costis?" she asks.

I nod "no."

"Come with me. We'll find a place for you to sleep at the konak where my daughter works."

I am relieved to have secured my first night in the foreign land.

Having finished securing his baskets, Kotsios Fieros lies down and rests his head on his bundle; I do the same. Periclina checks the knot of her oversize bundle, sits on it as comfortably as she can, and crosses her arms. She seems determined to stay awake. I detect fear in her eyes in the way that she is glancing around at the other passengers. Further down, a group of merry Limassolians begins to sing. Darkness falls and fatigue forces even young women to sit down on the wooden deck, exposed as they are to the elements for the first time, without the protection of the four walls of their homes. Those of advanced years, both men and women, are calm and patient; they give me hope that the world is not as chaotic a place as everything on this ship. The first passengers to be gripped by seasickness rush to the ship's railing, hang their heads over the water, and empty their stomachs. I can clearly hear the sound of vomiting. I pray that I fall asleep so I can avoid the same fate. I feel relatively secure; my two liras are concealed under my big toes, inside my low boots. I feel around

inside my cotton pouch. After the last few trades and sales I made
before leaving I now have, beyond the two golden liras, one shilling and some grosia left, after paying for the carriage ride and the
ship's fare. I cautiously take the money out of my pocket and slip
it into my shirt; it's twice as safe there! I close my eyes and sleep
until I am awakened by a woman screaming for help... When I
open my eyes I see that everyone is pretending to be asleep except
for Kotsios, who is standing up and hastily fumbling around with
his baskets. Approximately three fathoms away, two people are
struggling on the ground, gasping, breathing heavily. The woman's
voice is throttled   someone sees to that. My heart is pounding!
What is going on? I know but I don't know... Periclina's silhou-
ette towers over me, remaining seated and frozen on her bundle.
Somehow the woman's screams find a way to escape and become
more desperate before they are stifled again. A powerful kick to
the leg startles me.

"Costis, mind my baskets. I'm going to take care of the scum-
bag, whoever he is!"

I sit up and watch the towering mass that is Kotsios Fieros leap
over the passengers on the floor. Someone shines a light and I can
see his huge hand descend on the two who are struggling. The
woman's voice tears the darkness without obstruction now.

"Don't be afraid, lady!" I hear Kotsios say and watch him yank
a man by the scruff of his neck.

"Scoundrel! Bastard! Do you really think you can go around
attacking women? Aren't you ashamed to wear a monk's habit,
pezevenk?"[1]

It's the monk whose gaze had even alarmed me! Kotsios is not
afraid; continuing to swear, he kicks the monk until he manages
to escape his grip. Kotsios does not go after him; he turns to the
woman instead.

"Come over here, where we are," he tells her.

---

1 Pezevenk (Greek: πεζεβέγκης) : Turkish word for pimp, procurer or
fancy man that is used as an insult in Cyprus.

From atop her bundle and without saying a word, Periclina wraps her right arm around the young woman's shoulder, while she tries to suppress her sobbing.

"That son of bitch... Looking to do his business!" Kotsios mumbles as he begins to secure his baskets again.

I stand up to help him. I want to tell him how much I admire what he did but cannot get a word out; I just fumble around with the ropes in the darkness. As I try to get back to sleep, using the sack with my undergarments as a pillow, I notice how protectively Periclina is embracing the young woman. I consider her lot in life: Her own daughter, the beautiful Englishwoman, was a good girl that never raised her eyes. Costantos set his sights on her, but she wanted nothing to do with him. Her neighbour Yiannou, Chlorou's daughter, invited the Englishwoman for coffee at her house. Not suspecting anything, the Englishwoman accepted the invitation and, instead of coffee, Yiannou pocketed five liras from Costantos, who was lying in wait. This is how he made her his mistress... God only knows how much bitterness and sorrow Periclina, a poor mother, has had to swallow! I fall asleep, clutching my barley rusks.

The Patriarchate of Alexandria

Next evening I eat my last rusk in the kitchen of the konak where Periclina's other daughter works. In the morning I have nothing to eat but I'm too embarrassed to ask for food; I thank them, take my bundle, and wait in the long spacious corridor of the Patriarchate. It has high ceilings and several doors on both sides. Fortunately, between the doors, there are chairs and several long and impressive benches made of dark wood. While I sit there waiting, I read the Bible verses written in large red letters high up on the walls, close to the ceiling. I also look at a crucifix and at a large photograph of the Patriarch inside a heavy, dark frame. I am not alone; at least fifteen young men around my age are also waiting here.

They do not have a choice; I do not have a choice. In order to work in Alexandria one needs a certificate from the Patriarch, or so they tell me. When two Patriarchate employees cross the corridor, we take the opportunity to ask.

"His Eminence is resting!" they tell us.

One young man is daring enough to ask for more information.

"Which means what exactly?"

The response is sharp and unyielding:

"Which means that he is resting…"

A while later, a good-looking, fair-haired monk walks past.

"The Patriarch?" the young man, who is sitting next to me, asks timidly.

The man in the habit stops and glances at us without saying a word. I notice his lips – they are red as cherries but do not open. The young man next to me sighs.

"Is he still resting?" he asks again.

The monk raises his brow.

"Oh, no! His Eminence is awake. Now he is taking his bath."

I fold my hands over my empty stomach in an attempt to stifle its embarrassing growling, as the monk disappears through one of the doors. When I look up again, I see him coming out with a newspaper.

"When will the Patriarch see us?" I ask.

He looks at me for a few seconds without saying anything. This time I notice his blue eyes and rosy cheeks.

"His Eminence is taking his breakfast; afterwards he will read the paper," he replies.

"When will he see us?"

"Afterwards! If he does not have a scheduled meeting with an official, he will see you. You have come for a certificate, correct? Then you must wait!" he says and dashes off, indicating that he cannot waste time on people who need certificates.

My stomach is out of control – the growling has turned to howling. I blush with embarrassment, grab my bundle, and run out to the street. I come to a piazza called Mohammed Ali Square, as I learn later. I buy some bread and a small cucumber. I do not want to spend too much money before I have secured a job. Nevertheless, hunger makes the bread and the cucumber as sweet as honey in my mouth.

"Boy! Hey, boy…" shouts a man standing at the entrance of a shop; at first I do not hear him, absorbed as I am in the enjoyment of my food.

"Boy!"

I finally turn toward him with my mouth full; he seems to be calling me. I bring the hand with the bread to my chest and look at him inquiringly.

"Yes, you… Come here!"

He is looking at me, examining me. I approach apprehensively, aware that my cotton suit screams "Cyprus" and "thousands of miles away from home." The man chats me up: "Who am I? When did I arrive in Alexandria? Am I looking for work?" He is the first clerk at the grocery shop, the largest business in the square.

"Come with me. I'll take you to a place where you can work!" *Without a certificate from the Patriarch?* I am about to ask but change my mind. Since he has not asked for it…

The Italian Inn

Fortunately, the short, portly and kind Italian man does not ask for it either! His large home has been converted into an inn — eight rooms, which are permanently occupied by eight French pilots who work at the Suez Canal. In another four rooms he accommodates short-term guests, typically also Frenchmen who work at the Canal. I tidy the twelve rooms, clean and make the beds; then I wash the dishes and shine the guests' shoes. The Italian has a heart of gold. Formerly a teacher, he speaks to me in Italian, teaching me the language. Before long I am able to communicate easily with him. I take the tray with his coffee and breakfast to his room. I knock on the door. As soon as I hear noise, I turn the handle and step inside.

"Buongiorno, Signore, il vostro caffe e pronto!"[2] Then I rush off to serve the eight pilots.

I work from dawn until night but, every month, I collect one golden lira as payment, and my sleep is deep and restful in the clean laundry room that smells of green soap. All is well at the inn except for 'the higher power' — forceful and loud, she shakes the inn with her shouting. She works hard and oversees everything but, strained by fatigue and responsibility, she takes it out on her poor husband. He puts up with her temper and outbursts stoically, never saying a word. After each storm, when things calm down, he approaches her with a timid smile and sings softly to her in Greek: "I was wrong, forgive me. Open your arms, hold me, kiss me…" The two of them kiss and make up but a very different tune plays when it comes to me… For the most trivial reasons she strikes my back with a broomstick. It's not that she beats me very badly — I am used to beatings — but summers in Alexandria are oppressively hot, making the fever from the malaria much worse than it ever was in Cyprus. I do not tell my bosses about the malaria because I am afraid that they will fire me. I hide in the laundry room, vomit bitter bile, and pass out, while the Italian woman keeps shouting because I have not finished mopping the stairs. She opens the laundry room door with a ferocious expression, with a torrent of Italian spewing from her mouth, with her broomstick raised… I am already trembling and burning up so much that I have no fear. Lights out, I faint! When I open my eyes again I see a hot cup of tea next to me, and the woman looking at me with sad, wide-open eyes. The tea makes me feel better. I explain to her that it's nothing, that I have had this since I was a child, a remnant of malaria. When the teacher comes in, I explain the situation to him, too. They are compassionate people; they feel for me! Not

---

2 "Good morning, Sir, your coffee and breakfast!"

that I escape the beatings altogether, but her hand is lighter now when she lowers the broomstick on my back.

Then a compatriot gets me thinking:

"Why are you working at the inn? I know a confectionary where you earn money and learn the art at the same time."

The confectionary is located at Sharif Pasha Square and the prospect of the learning the art of confectionary is tempting. The boss, a Greek man, promises to match my salary: one golden lira per month. I hesitate; the security that I have at the inn is an important consideration. I am torn, so I make up a story:

"Scusate, my father has taken ill. I have to go to Cyprus to see him. I can sail on the Hevedia on the 4th and return on the 14th. I need ten days leave."

"Go! Go!" says the teacher with the heart of gold.

Instead of sailing to Cyprus, I work at the confectionary but the Greek confectioner is almost never there. I learn nothing. I mind the shop and take care of all sales. When he comes to the confectionary in the evening, I give him the cash but he has doubts; he opens one of the glass jars with bonbons and counts its contents to check whether I have given him less money! I am offended by his lack of trust. At night I sleep in the confectionary's stifling back rooms, which leave me wanting for the inn's spacious laundry room. The Hevedia docks on the 14th of the month:

"I'm leaving tonight, Boss!"

"You don't like it here?"

What do you say to that?

"I don't want to become a confectioner," I tell him, making up an excuse.

The confectioner is already tight-lipped and, instead of loosening, his lips get even tighter.

"I'll pay you for the ten days," he says and gives me the money that he owes me.

With my bundle on my shoulder, I arrive at Mohamed Ali

Square. I salute the statue at its center. The inn's open door is directly across. I cheerfully greet my two bosses.

"Is you father well?" the man asks me.

Having forgotten my excuse, I am caught off guard; it takes me a few moments to recall the story.

"What? Ah, yes! Fine… He's fine!" I say and disappear into the laundry room.

I smile to myself, glad not to have lost the security of the inn. The 'higher power' is not fooled so easily, however:

"That crafty Greek didn't go to Cyprus to see his father; he looked for work elsewhere! He must have not liked the other place so he came back to us," I hear the Italian woman say and anxiety overcomes me.

What security can there be here for me now, when she knows that I have lied? To make things worse, I feel guilty for having acted underhandedly. And I pay for my sin; whether I like it or not, I start to look for work elsewhere, before the Italian woman has a chance to burn me.

Raml

An opportunity becomes available through Yiannis Themistocles from Kyrenia. I know him well because he was a regular customer of Costantos in Cyprus. The job that he has promised me must be good; I trust the man. He assures me that the salary will be the same: one lira per month. As the train travels toward Bacos Station I see fertile fields all around. Yiannis Themistocles tells me that he will not be staying in Alexandria much longer; he has arranged passage to Transvaal, where he will partner with Mattheos Kariolos. They are planning to set up a profitable business there. So Mattheos Kariolos, Nikolis Troodites's best friend, has migrated as well! We arrive at Bacos Station. Raml is Alexandria's most wealthy and beautiful suburb. Huge mansions, verdant gardens. We arrive at a store; I stand aside, while Yiannis Themistocles

waits out front for a man approaching on a donkey. He greets him
cheerfully.

"Stelios, my old friend…"

"Good morning, Yiannis. Welcome!"

Stelios dismounts; he is a man of a medium built, olive-skinned,
somewhat portly but well dressed. A boy around my age runs out
of the store, takes the animal, and leads it to the back yard. Stelios
and Yiannis Themistocles arrange a low table between them and
sit down.

"What would you like to drink, Yiannis?"

"Whatever's easiest," he responds.

"Two beers!" Stelios orders and two young men run around to
serve them.

Another young man, a fourth, comes out of the store with a
cart loaded with goods.

"Where's that order going?" the host asks while pouring beer
into the glasses.

"It's for Hassan Bey, Boss!"

"Good! Take it, but get back here quickly; I have another rush
order. Cheers, Yiannis!"

"Cheers!"

They drink and chat, but Yiannis Themistocles does not forget
me.

"I brought the young man that we spoke about," he says at an
appropriate break in the conversation. The other man turns to
look at me.

"Alright! He'll deliver orders and mind the shop. At night he'll
sleep in the attic with the others. The salary is one lira per month.
He'll go out with the others for the first few days until he learns
where the houses are. What is your name?"

I take a step forward.

"Costas Charalambou."

"Go inside and have a look around."

Inside I learn that the boss, a Limassolian, provides the mansions of the beys in the wealthy suburb of Raml with all they require. He delivers everything to their doorsteps!

All is well with the job, except for the army of bedbugs that torments me at night. I can't sleep! In the darkness I watch the others sleeping soundly, while bloodthirsty insects gorge themselves on their blood. I wonder how they can sleep, scratching only when the bedbugs overdo it or when they start on sensitive body parts. In the morning, not having slept a wink, I shake my bed sheet violently with disgust and go outside. Across from the shop, I see a man unlocking a huge shed filled with timber and carpentry benches. I approach and say "good morning." The man looks curiously at me.

"Are you new?"

I nod "yes."

"Why are you up so early?"

At the end of my tether, I pour my heart out to him about the bedbugs in the attic. How can anyone sleep in such conditions? The middle-aged man shows compassion.

"Where are you from?"

"I'm from Cyprus, from Kyrenia."

The man is stirred; his eyes light up.

"A fellow Cypriot then? My name is Aspris, I hail from those parts, too!" he says, obviously moved.

In our hearts reside the same places, our land, Kyrenia and her sea! But I am also thinking ahead... Seeing the carpentry benches I dare to ask:

"Could I...? Could I sleep in your shed at night on one of these benches?"

Aspris smiles.

"Of course!"

The door of the store opens and one of my co-workers runs out, asking if I know how to prepare a donkey. I do! In the back

yard I find the animal, saddle it, and bring it to the front. Wearing
a freshly pressed shirt, the boss is waiting there with a small riding crop; he says "good morning," gets on the animal, and departs.

"Where is he going?" I ask.

"To the houses to take orders. By the time he returns we will
have tidied up the store and prepared the first cart. Come…"

We organize the store and then load the cart either with a sun-
dry of goods or with coal. I haul it to Raml's mansions and unload. I have no complaints because the carpentry benches have no
bedbugs. I choose one, spread out a thick layer of wood shavings,
climb on top, and wrap myself in my bed sheet. It is quite comfortable but – best of all – there are no bloodsucking insects here.
Before falling asleep, I pat with satisfaction the attractive money
belt that I have bought to keep my golden liras, to which I add one
more at the end of each month. And there's also the letter from
my father on my chest:

"Dear Son, Mr. Costantos wants you to come home. He will
pay you as much as you are paid in Egypt. You will have the same
salary and you will be in your homeland. This letter is written on
my behalf by Pavlos Hadjicostis. I wait for your response so I can
close the deal. Your father, Charalambos."

Father wants me at home, not abroad. I add things up: I have
been in Egypt for a year and a half, seven days work, seven days
food, good pay, and every month one more lira, a golden lira!
What more could I possibly want? Ah, but I do want more! I miss
my homeland. When Aspris and I talk, Kyrenia rises up inside us.
We see her in each other's eyes. For me it's mostly homesickness;
I miss my father, whom I love and respect. I also miss my siblings
very much. All day I haul the cart back and forth, at times loaded
with coal, at times with other things and my homesickness grows;
so I weigh my options. I will have the same pay from Costantos
and now I will not be inexperienced; there are eighteen golden
liras in my money belt, nineteen at the end of the month! I will
be able go to the Chrysotrimithiotissa Festival on Easter Monday.

I will be able to pay my share for the roasting feast, no matter how much it is, because now I can afford it. I will have a good time with my old friend Yiannis Vrahas and the others. I will celebrate without the fear of humiliation. No more humiliation! I write "yes" to my father, write off Egypt, and sail back to Cyprus, to Kyrenia, to my homeland.

CHAPTER 5

RETURN TO KYRENIA

Kyrenia, 1906-1907

Caught in an Unfair Trap

I return home only to find myself trapped! The contract that Costantos had my father sign was not for one lira per month but for a total of thirteen liras over three years! A mouthful of bitterness – how do I spit it out? When spitting it out would be the same as spitting on my father's signature...This is not something I can do, even if my father keeps saying that everything is fine, that I should be patient and work hard, that I am slowly getting ahead in life. At least, at the shop, Nikolis shows some consideration for me now. He is quite curious about what it's like overseas and keeps asking: "How is it? Is it alright?" I show him my leather money belt, which I never part with and always wear flush against my skin, with the nineteen golden liras from my nineteen months in Egypt. Nikolis is irked because I had the guts to go abroad, while he remains stifled at Costantos's shop. Once in a while he opens up to me about his best friend Mattheos Kariolos, who migrated to Transvaal. He no longer raises his hand on me. I no longer get beaten but everything else is the same: I do all the work at the store, run around town with fabric rolls, fetch pots from the storeroom at the port, take care of everything that is required. At night Flourentzou still saves all the heavy labour in the kitchen for me. "Costis, do this! Costis, do that!" while she strains to bake bread for old Malikkis, rinsing the flour again and again, before she shapes the dough into small rolls.

The old man says that his sugar is high and that regular bread is harmful to him. I place the rolls in a separate basket on the table, close to his seat, and stand behind his chair waiting to push it forward when he is ready to sit down. While I stand there I question things: *Why does life have to be this way? Why must I be humble, subservient, abused, without a hope in the world?* My mind wanders back to what I learned in school – the teachings of Socrates, the teachings of Jesus Christ. I also ponder all that Nikolis keeps telling me about Makrakis. He says that, because Makrakis wants to see the true teachings of Jesus implemented, he is hounded in Greece, where he is a considered less than a louse and treated like a leper. In all likelihood he will be declared a heretic; his enemies will not be satisfied until they kick him to the curb. And because the Metropolitan of Kyrenia is a good man, who implements the true teachings of Jesus, they call him "Kyrilloudi"; they accuse him of all kinds of things because they want as Archbishop, unlawfully, the Metropolitan of Citium, Kyrillatsos, who is a Mason. Nikolis is certain of this, as is everyone else at Malikkis's house. I also have to carry secret notes back and forth between Nikolis and Irini; I know that they are love notes, not shopping lists. I understand that they are young and fond of each other, but I am astounded that Nikolis has the nerve to set his sights on the boss's sister! After dinner I clear the table and wash the dishes. I finish up, wait for the bosses to leave the dining room, take my bedding from the loom and lay it down next to the fireplace, which has consumed its logs but retains its warmth. I go to sleep. I am reliving the same nightmare because I cannot break the contract that my father signed on my behalf; I cannot insult his signature. And when I try to tell him how unfair the situation is, his response is always the same.

"We've been eating their bread for years; if we don't respect our bosses, who will respect us?"

This is his life stance – what can I do? I keep my head down and keep quiet. This is a dead end! My father does not understand the concept of being paid fairly for your work. He has worked for Malikkis as a day labourer for years. He holds him in high esteem but Malikkis, although fair with his workers when they are honest too, is quite stingy. My father is so fond of him that, at one point, he carried rocks for him without pay because Malikkis's house was on his way to another job. Sometimes Malikkis lends out money because he wants every penny to be earning something but always honestly, of course; he is not like the other one, the big loan shark Sovaros, who lends money to the poor only to pile up interest on top of interest until he can auction off their properties: "Going once, going twice..." Most of the time he ends up owning everything for peanuts. My boss, Costantos, also lends money but he is not like his father; he enjoys playing the tough guy. One day my brother-in-law Argyros comes in to the shop; the boss looks ferociously at him and starts shouting that he wants his money back. Argyros becomes distressed, his eyes start to water, his head hangs low. Argyros, who smashes even the largest rocks while building houses, pleads:

"Please be patient, Mr. Costantos. I will pay you back but I need a little more time..."

"More time, more time... That's what you all say!" he shouts, bringing my brother-in-law nearly to tears.

This is the first time that I've heard that Argyros owes money to Costantos. I reach impulsively for my money belt; I cannot hold back.

"How much do you owe, Argyros?"

"Nineteen liras."

I motion to him and we step outside, to a corner where no one can see us. I untie my pants, open the money belt, and take out the nineteen golden liras.

"Here, take it. Pay him back!"

Argyros goes back into the shop and I follow him. Now Costantos is saying that he does not want the money back right away; he claims that he simply wanted to remind Argyros of his debt. The truth is that enjoys humiliating people. Everyone knows that Argyros always makes good on his debts, that he is honest. He gives Costantos the nineteen liras on the spot! Costantos frowns, displeased because his money will no longer generate interest on top of interest; he needs to find another credit-worthy borrower for that. I take great pleasure knowing that my money has backed the boss into a corner – a small retribution for so much ill-paid labour in his employ. Moreover, I dislike those who profit from interest, albeit in accordance with British legislation, while the poor who need their help are treated unfairly. Every injustice and inequality is a thorn in my side!

And inequalities are everywhere, not only between lenders and borrowers, between rich and poor, between those who go hungry and those who have everything and their stomachs full, not only in our small town but everywhere in the world – poor countries oppressed by the large and rich ones that suck their blood. Great Britain exploits so many countries, including Cyprus. And we, its people – the majority of whom are Greeks – wish to be united with Greece. But Greece is on her knees; unjustly treated as she is, she cannot help us, and we are forced to remain separate from her. Even Matsoukas, who comes to Karavas-Lapithos for a short time, talks about this. His next scheduled stop is Kyrenia. The town is electrified; the standard is raised! A doxology at Archangelos Church, speeches, tremendous excitement... The young man, who wears a fustanella,[1] jumps onto some sacks of sugar outside Costantos's store; his forehead beams, his moustache is thick and manly, and his words move us to tears! I learn the poem that he recites by heart and remember it to this day:

---

1 Fustanella (Greek: φουστανέλα): A traditional skirt-like garment worn by men in many Balkan nations. A short version is worn by military units such as the Evzones in Greece.

My soul is a sea that cannot be touched by the wind
my desire is a chain that stretches as far as Polis.[2]
Night and day, like a bird drunk on the waves
I spread my broad wingspan, never resting,
sweet dream of my youth, dream of my life
Motherland, watered by tears and blood.
You, who look at me, you, who can see,
come, so together we can build that sweet dream!
Raising up our blue flag in our hands
for Freedom I shall fall in enslaved lands!

My heart swells whenever I recite this poem since – like my homeland – I, too, have been mistreated.

Matsoukas fundraises for the Greek struggle and we all give for the cause. I give from what little money I have in my money belt; even Nikolis readily makes a donation and he is a skinflint. Kyrenia cries out passionately for the Nation, for the enslaved lands, for Cyprus...

Matsoukas leaves to continue his mission elsewhere. The English Government takes my first teacher, Stavrides, to court; we all closely follow the trial and proudly observe his dignity on the stand, his confidence in addressing the English judge, who orders him to pay a large fine. The supporters of the Metropolitan of Kyrenia show no compassion for Stavrides because he published insults about the Metropolitan in his newspaper "Rayias"; they say that he deserves to be punished and that the fine will put an end to his conceit. In Kyrenia the arguments about who will be Archbishop flare up again. The Metropolitan of Kynenia arrives on a mule, escorted by two deacons. Malikkis receives him at the house, so I see him up close. He is indeed scrawny, his habits literally hang from him – no wonder they call him "Kyrilloudi"! Yet his eyes blaze through me like hot coals. Acknowledging the man's stand-

---

2 Polis (Greek: Πόλη): Short for "Constantinoupolis," which is Greek for Constantinople.

ing I withdraw; I bow down and kiss his hand with respect. Many people come to the house to see him, to speak with him. Malikkis informs him that the priest at Archangelos is against him. They invite the priest to the house and he does not come, so Malikkis goes looking for him. The two become embroiled in a huge argument, during which the priest removes his kalimavkion,[3] bows very low, and curses Malikkis! Everyone is mortified. The worst thing that can ever happen to you is to be cursed by a priest... Who will perform the burial rites when you die? Even notables, loan sharks and landowners die; no one can buy his way out of death. No one!

Every night I wait for everyone to leave so I can lay down my bedding and go to sleep. I work like a dog all day; I am tired. I keep pondering Aesop's fable "Cricket and Ant." I am an ant. I choose to be an ant. I want to get ahead with honest work. But the contract that my father was hoodwinked into signing is unfair. If it weren't for the contract, I would surely get ahead even in Kyrenia, because I am not afraid of hard work. But I am bound, caught in an unfair trap, due to no fault of my own. As I have said before: This situation is a dead end! A dead end, yes, but life has many turns and the wheel keeps spinning...

Life's Twists and Turns

Just as I am drifting off one night, I am awakened by footsteps upstairs. It's bitterly cold outside; a fierce tramontane howls from the unseasonably snowy mountains of Karamania across the sea; enormous waves break on Kyrenia's rocky shores; fingers and ears freeze; lips crack. Something is afoot on the second floor. The steps multiply... Flourentzou comes into the dining room, turns on all the lights without parsimony, and trips over me.

"Get up. The boss has taken ill!"

---

3 Kalimavkion (Greek: καλιμαύκι): The stiff cylindrical head covering worn by clergy.

I barely have time to store away my bedding when Malikkis's firstborn, the tall and regal Michalakis, turns up in the hallway! This is the first time that I have seen him cross his father's doorstep. They came to blows years ago for some reason and have not spoken to each other since. I am dumbstruck. Michalakis paces up and down as the first sobs are heard. The eldest son walks slowly down to the dining room, where he asks for pen and ink. He dwarfs Malikkis's other sons, Yiorkos and Costantos, who run around to fetch what he asks for; it's perfectly clear who the head of the household is now! No one cries but the wound of death is unmistakable on their ashen faces.

"So!" Michalakis says with a sigh and with determination.

"Are you sure?" my boss asks with uncertainty.

Michalakis does not deign even to look at him.

"I'm absolutely sure!" he lowers the pen into the inkwell and begins to write.

He runs out of paper and asks for a second sheet, then a third. He explains:

"Since the priest has cursed Father and refuses to bury him, we need three other priests to perform the funeral rites to cancel out the curse."

Yiorkos paces up and down.

"What if we asked him? What if we talked to him?" he proposes.

Michalakis slides the three sheets of paper into three envelopes and seals them.

"After everything they threw at each other...? Don't be a fool! Who's going to deliver these?" he asks, waving the envelops at his brothers, until he notices me standing in the corner.

"You, come here! Can you ride a horse?"

I nod "yes" and he gives me instructions. First I will go to Kazafani to give the first envelop to the village priest. I will deliver the second envelop to the priest of Bellapais, and the third to the priest of Ayios Epiktitos. How do I get to Ayios Epiktitos?

"Do I need to come back down to take the lower road to Ayios Epiktitos?" I ask.

"No, there is a shortcut – a footpath from Bellapais through the forest. Do you understand?"

I nod affirmatively and he hands me the letters.

"Give the young man two shillings for his trouble," he orders Costantos.

My boss furrows his brow and shakes his head.

"There's no need; he works for me. Get on with it!" he orders me.

How do I get there?

"The mare?" I ask.

The mare is at Michalakis's house; I knock on the door and ask his wife for it.

On horseback the tramontane pierces me like a sword but I reach Kazafani fairly easily; I know the way. Still groggy from sleep, the priest crosses himself. He says a prayer for Malikkis and praises God for treating everyone equally. The footpath to Bellapais is more difficult but I know the way, so I get there quickly. The priest of Bellapais knows Malikkis and has great respect for him!

"We have lost a pillar of our community. Eternal be his memory!" he says as he crosses himself.

I find the footpath to Ayios Epiktitos without difficulty but the stallions near Bellapais Monastery get a whiff of the mare. They break free and start to chase her. The mare gallops wildly to get away. At times she controls me, at times I control her... When she is in control I ride low on her neck, the only safe position because she can throw me at any moment. As I am entering the village I manage to get her under control – safe at last. The icy air freezes anxiety's sweat on my brow; it was a narrow escape from death. My mind wanders back to how my boss acted. Even on the day he father passed away he could not reach into his pocket for two shillings! Not that I'm dying for the two shillings; it's simply an indication of what his heart is made of...

By early dawn all of Kyrenia has gathered at Malikkis's konak; everyone is there, supporters of both Metropolitans bow their heads before death. Dressed in black and wearing a headscarf, his wife sits next to the body silent and still. But there is much commotion in the kitchen. Flourentzou and Agapiena, under the direction of Michalatzena, whom I have never seen in her father-in-law's house before, prepare pishies[4] and all the other dishes in the condolence meal. No meat is served but everything else is in abundance: fava beans for the workers, pilaf for the relatives. The halloumi jug is empty in the pantry. Three large jugs of red wine and several dishes filled with olives, enough for everyone – there is plenty of food, especially for the poor, whose stomachs are always half-empty. While they eat, most covertly slip a few olives or a piece of bread into the pockets. The funeral service performed by three priests is meant to cancel out the heavy curse of one; Malikkis is buried in accordance with Christian tradition.

(Years later, when they open Malikkis's grave to bury someone else, they see that his body has not decomposed; they attribute this to the curse and pray for him again so that his body can decompose and his soul can finally rest!)

The Great Defamation

Although nothing actually changes, after the funeral nothing is the same. Numbness at the store... Nikolis does not even glance at his accounting, nor does he order me around; nervous and restless, he keeps coming and going to the port. I wonder what is afoot but I have to stay at the shop to serve the customers. Yiannatzis Karalatzias does not come in as customer, however; he is Malikkis's son-in-law, married to his daughter Mirou. The moment he walks through the door, I stand up and offer to help him. No response.

4 Pishies (Greek: πσίες): Traditional Cypriot fritters.

He says nothing but examines everything: the rice, the sugar, the display. He scoops up goods with the measuring cup and lets them pour out slowly again.

"Nice!" he says.

He moves further inside, takes count of a stack of pots from the East, opens a large case of soap, takes out a bar, and smells it:

"Nice!" he says again and sighs contently.

He walks around a little more then runs his hand over the fabric rolls. Just as I am about to ask him what he wants, Nikolis races into the store. Short of breath, he bows deeply before him.

"Good morning, Boss!" he says and his voice trembles a little.

Yiannatzis looks at him and smiles.

"Good morning, Nikolis."

"Can I help you with something, Boss?"

"No, I was passing by and I wanted to have a look. Mind the shop now, you hear!"

He leaves at last and I learn from Nikolis that Yiannatzis has bought the store.

"And you?" I ask Nikolis.

"I'm part of the deal."

"What about me? Am I part of the deal, too?"

"No, the boss is keeping you. He wants you to pass by his office right away. He's expecting you."

Costantos tells me that he has sold the store and that, during harvest, he expects me to collect the yield of farmers who owe him money. He reminds me of the three-year contract that my father has signed, claiming that it is still valid. So I will be paid the paltry sum of thirteen liras for three years to work for a loan shark, taking food from the mouths of the poor, denying them the living they secure at harvest after so much hard labour! I hesitate but I am determined.

"Mr. Costantos, I can't…"

"Why not?"

"This is not a job I can do," I declare firmly but with the appropriate respect.

"Have you forgotten your contract to work for me for three years?"

He reminds me of the contract that was signed by hook and crook, by cajoling my father, who naively agreed because he felt beholden to the late Malikkis. *Enough is enough!* I think to myself, as anger rises up inside me. I raise my head fearlessly.

"Then you should demand the contract from my father, who signed it before I returned from Egypt, not from me!"

Costantos is used to raising his hand on me. The slap falls forcefully on my cheek, but this is not the time to bow down in fear. I have the nineteen liras from Egypt that I lent my brother-in-law Argyros, beyond the money that he owes me. I can leave for Egypt at any time and work there for one lira per month! I clench my jaw and, without even touching my cheek, I turn my back on him and walk out. I could have talked back, continued to argue but did not – not out of respect for Costantos but for my father's sake. My cheek may be on fire, but I feel as light as a feather. I pass Trypitis, Chrysopolitissa, the market; I go around Kamouza and find Nikolis standing at the door of the shop.

"Does Yiannatzis Karalatzias want me at the store, too?" I ask.

"Of course! I can't do all the work that you do around here," Troodites replies, seeming pleased to keep me as his assistant.

At the store it's the same work for a new boss, except that now the boss's brother, Mirtis, a short overweight man, is always coming and going. He confidently oversees everything but always keeps his hands in his pockets. When customers take out money to pay, he becomes flustered and his fists clench even more tightly inside his pockets. Money repulses him, so he points to the nearest surface.

"Put it there! There!" he says with his face turning red as he looks to one of us to come to his rescue. He orders us to collect the money and give change, if needed.

When young women come into the store Mirtis is electrified. He bends over backwards to serve them. He keeps circling around them, trying to brush against them. And he becomes despondent, if he cannot provide what they require.

"I'll get it for you... I'll get it! Pass by tomorrow and I will have it!" he assures them.

The real boss Yiannatzis Karalatzias, a tall strapping man, is almost never around; he is involved in trade with the East in partnership with Captain Ttooulos. Together they own Kyrenia's largest ship, which is operated by two other partners, Ttofaros and Stavrakkos Costantinides, both good and experienced mariners. Apart from that partnership, Yiannatzis Karalatzias owns much fertile land, carob groves and olive tree groves that he inherited both from his family and his wife's – land that Malikkis gave his daughter as her dowry. Yet he does not deal with any of that because his mother, the dynamic Karalatzinina, manages the labourers with an iron grip. Yiannatzis Karalatzias is married to Mirou and has a young son, his firstborn. So the boss drops by the store only to glance at the ledgers that Nikolis prepares. Once in a while, I run errands for him outside the shop. One day, before dawn, I load up all his hunting gear on the donkey and take it up to Pogazi Police Station. As I am trying to dismount, my frozen limbs fail me. When I try again, I fall flat to the ground! Then I look up and see both my former and my current bosses standing over me. They get off their bicycles and put on their hunting gear: high boots and wool pullovers under thick capes. I do my best to stand up, while the boss complains that I was not waiting for him at the edge of the forest. Luckily, the fireplace is lit inside the police station. I thaw out and keep warm until they return. Then I load up the donkey again with their superb rifles and other gear, along with the spoils of the hunt, and return to Kyrenia. They return on their bicycles; both are excellent hunters.

The change of ownership at the store has created a problem for Nikolis because he no longer has an excuse to visit the house of the late Malikkis. Along with groceries, now I deliver even more notes from Nikolis to Irini and vice versa. She claims that they are grocery lists that only he is allowed to open! I pretend not to know that they are anything but lists of fava beans, chickpeas, soaps and biscuits. Nikolis is my boss; I take orders from him at the store, so I have no choice. In any case, they are both young and clearly fond of each other.

At dusk, when the store closes, I head to the konak of Yiannatzis Karalatzias — a large, two-storey home in Pano Kyrenia which is surrounded by a nice, fertile orchard. The main entrance opens to a long hallway; a door leads to a large sitting room on the left and another leads to a room on the right, where they store produce from their fields. The kitchen is at the end of the hallway and the bedrooms are upstairs. At the back of the house a large pantry is used as a wheat granary; this is where I sleep. Fortunately, I have no contact with anyone in the house other than the boss's mother at dinnertime, a dragon lady in front of the hearths that shares out my serving of food. At her side, the young housemaid Anna never speaks or raises her eyes; she is always hunched over her work.

I spend time with Stephanis the ploughman and his wife; they live in the stable at the edge of the orchard. Nice people and good company until Stephanis suddenly falls ill and passes away — a twisted bowel, according to the doctor. And so I lose the little human contact that his company afforded me. At night I hear his wife's heartrending weeping, which tears me up inside. I think about how life is but, before I fall asleep, I turn to my own problems and take stock. No, my life is not satisfactory but I spend Sundays with my father and siblings in Karakoumi. Sometimes on weekdays, I visit my sister Polyxeni and Argyros in Pano Kyrenia; I play with their children, my nieces and nephews. A pittance of money but I am in my homeland and Nikolis no longer makes my life a living hell; on the contrary, we have become friends now that Mattheos Kariolos has migrated. I have no kitchen chores at night; no more dish washing! I am careful, keep to myself, never complain, and always follow orders. I am a worker ant, not a happy-go-lucky cricket that sings without a care in the world all summer long but dies of starvation in winter. Aesop's fable, which I learned in school, is always on my mind:

"The Cricket that sang incessantly in the woodlands
found himself unprotected in winter.
Nearly starved to death without provisions,
he went to the Ant miserable and downtrodden."

I want to be a worker like the Ant with my storerooms full and with a heap of money. I want to get married, to have children and my own home! My salary is small but it's something, and I have food to eat. There must be something better out there but finding it will take some thought – a lot of thought in fact. I fall asleep thinking about all this, time passes, and the year turns. It's now 1907.

I wake up to screaming and a great deal of commotion. It's not Stephanis's wife; this is something altogether different. The door to the granary bursts open and old Karalatzina storms in swearing.

"Aren't you ashamed of yourself, you little bastard? Did it even cross your mind what would become of the poor girl?"

Is she talking to me? Yes, she is talking to me! I leap up.

"What's the matter?" I ask.

The old woman brings her hands to her waist.

"What's the matter? You did your business, ruined the poor girl, and now you ask what's the matter?"

I do not understand.

"Me? What girl?"

The old woman swells inside her white nightshirt.

"Our maid, Anna, you scoundrel!"

Anna…? The silent maid, who is always hunched over her work and never raises her head? I have never spoken to her, not even to say "hello." What have I done to her? I am fully awake and my breathing stalls when at last I understand what the boss's enraged mother is saying. I react!

"No, I was sleeping! I was sleeping. I didn't do anything to her! Nothing!" I protest.

The old woman approaches me threateningly.

"You were sleeping? Let me pull down your underpants to see if you did it or not!"

She grabs me by the waist, determined to remove my underpants. I struggle, manage to break free, jump out of the window, while the uproar grows inside the house. I hide in the reed fields of Koronos River then head farther and farther up the mountain. I stop only when I am certain that no one is chasing me.

At first light, I try to convince myself that this is only a bad dream; but it isn't. I am still up in the mountains, still in hiding. I move about cautiously, crossing fields, wandering around in no man's land, as far away from footpaths as possible. I know that my father is working as a day labourer near the chiflik, on a field that belongs to Costantos. I decide to go look for him. He is already at work; I see him stepping firmly on the plough in order to plunge the coulter deep into the soil. I close my eyes, take a deep breath, and approach.

"Good morning, Father," I say and the pressure lifts off my chest for the first time.

No response. He does not even look at me, but I am not surprised; he is in the process of digging a furrow. I wait at the edge of the field, where he will have to stop. The oxen move toward me in their usual slow gait with my father behind them. I say "good morning" again.

"Good morning, Father!"

Instead of a "good morning" in return, I get the plough with its sharp coulter at the end! I raise my arm instinctively to protect my head but what about the rest of me?

"Get out of here, you scoundrel! Messing with your boss's maid..."

The crushing weight returns to my chest and this time it is unbearable. I make an effort to refute the accusation.

"No, Father…" but I stop because the coulter is raised against me once more.

This time I do not raise my hand to protect myself; I run! I run and run until I can run no more. I stop only when I am gasping for air. The severity of the situation is immense, if even my father believes the allegation! How do I escape from all this? My father has always been my protector, lifting me up on his shoulders as we crossed the raging rivers to safety. He always gave me his blessing at the beginning of each school year: I would kiss his hand and feel certain that nothing could ever harm me. Same as when I left for Egypt… Although he did not want me going overseas, he gave me his blessing and that was my protection. Now he raises the coulter against me! If my father believes the accusation then everyone else must believe it, too! They believe that I… My cheeks cannot bear the blush of shame, and the bitterness is so monstrous that it does not fit inside my chest. Where do I go? I wander about all day and, at night, I sneak into my father's stable to sleep because it's still cold. Only my brother Glioris seems to be clearly on my side. He secretly brings bread and olives from the house, just enough to keep me from starving. He tells me that my sister Polyxeni and my brother-in-law Argyros are willing to take me in, but I refuse to go. If I cannot cross my father's doorstep, there can be no home for me! Glioris also tells me that Yiannatzis Karalatzias has filed a lawsuit against me; he is taking me to court to force me to marry the girl that I supposedly ruined.

What choice do I have?

Vindication Without Reward

Standing hunched over against the wall of the Administration Building where the courthouse is located, I wait for my trial. I feel lost; I do not know what to do or how to act. All around me people with disputes are trying to reach some form of agreement, while lawyers run briskly back and forth.

"Costas Charalambou?"

The voice is familiar. I look up and blush, flashing back to my final examinations at school.

"What is the root of the word 'gamos?'" he had asked and I was too embarrassed to utter the ancient word, which has been turned into a profanity. And this made him angry. It's Georgios Loizides; he is standing very close to me, examining me with his eyes.

"I'm going to ask you to tell me the truth: Are you guilty of what they are accusing you?"

My mouth is dry but I muster all my courage to respond:

"No, Mr. Loizides. I did nothing to that girl!"

He shakes his head.

"Alright, come into the courtroom and have no fear!"

"Have no fear" is easier said than done. I drag myself into the courtroom on trembling legs. It was here that my teacher, Yiannis Hadjitzypris, also stood because of a false accusation; he was proven innocent but the scandal ruined him. It was here that Georgios Stavrides also stood when the British tried and fined him; also ruined by loan sharks, he has taken a job in Paphos, practically exiled from Kyrenia, while his wife and children do without the necessities of life, almost having to beg! What will become of me? My unexpected defender Georgios Loizides calmly approaches the stand and squarely faces the young woman, who is sitting across from him with her head lowered.

"So it was night and someone came into your room?" he asks.

She nods and a barely audible "yes" sounds from her lips.

"And that person was Costas Charalambou?"

She answers "yes" again in the same way. I am enraged; I clench my fists because she is clearly lying. But why?

"Did the man identify himself?" Loizides continues calmly.

"No, but I could tell who it was."

"In the dark?"

Again she nods her lowered head and answers "yes!"

"Can you tell me how many fingers I am holding up?" Loizides asks and holds up three fingers on his right hand.

The young woman raises her head and looks intensely at the lawyer. She does not respond.

"My fingers, young woman... How many fingers am I showing you?"

She opens her eyes wide, then squints, trying to focus.

"How many fingers am I showing you?"

Loizides's voice is authoritative; it forces her to speak up.

"I don't know! I can't see them, Sir... I can't see from a distance..." she admits and lowers her head again.

"In other words you are short-sighted, young lady, and even from a few steps away in broad daylight you can't see my three fingers. How then could you be certain that this particular young man came into your room in complete darkness?"

There's an upheaval in the court and the judge finds me innocent! Mr. Loizides smiles enigmatically at me as he departs, not expecting me to thank him not only for proving my innocence, but also for clearing me of the obligation to marry a young woman I do not know. But the shame remains; even if one hundred courts found me innocent, everyone would still believe that I am guilty, even my father, especially my father!

Sophocles Paphitis is found guilty on the same day. He has suffered the same fate, or almost the same fate, since he doesn't even break a sweat. His family is in Paphos, so he does not care. He taps me on the shoulder in a friendly way.

"Don't worry! They've accused me of indecent assault, too, against the wife of the Chief Justice. Me, her manservant...! See, I had just prepared her bath and was on my way out, when she undressed and rang the bell. Should I have gone back or not? I found the 'lady' sitting on the bathtub with her legs spread open, like her mother when she gave birth to her. She said: 'Sophocles, some hot water, please...' She was ordering me, goddamn it! Twisting around naked in front of me… I have blood; it heats up; it boils! And then they accuse you of indecent assault!"

"But I didn't do anything, I swear," I say with exasperation.

Sophocles pats my shoulder.

"Hey, don't feel bad. I'm certainly not going to stay here and put up with all this crap; I'm off to America. Are you in?"

"America?"

"Yes, America!" he says, nodding repeatedly.

I silently ponder his proposal for a few moments then ask for details, about the fare and the rest.

We talk on our way from the courts down to Koulas, where we lean against the brown rocks. I listen carefully; Sophocles knows everything about the journey to America. I do my calculations: The nineteen liras from Egypt that I have with Argyros, plus the two and change that I have from Costantos, makes just over twenty-one. Even when I add what I have earned from odd jobs here and there, it is not enough. If it were…

Nikolis appears out of nowhere with a smile on his face. Since he has his ear to the ground, he must know that I was found innocent in court; he probably even knows who actually raped the poor girl. Is this why he is greeting us in such a friendly manner?

"Hello, Costis! The boss said that he wants to set things right between you, since you have been found innocent. Shall we go see him tonight after I close the store?"

I am relieved; I feel light as a feather. If the boss believes in my innocence, then everyone in Kyrenia will do so as well, including my father. My father above all… I agree to go with him but Sophocles keeps at it; now he is trying to convince Nikolis to migrate to America, too. I can hardly wait for dusk; I am desperate to be cleared of the stigma once and for all.

In the sitting room, the boss has his firstborn on lap; he is playing with the boy, which is laughing loudly. His wife is sitting next to the lamp with her embroidery. Nikolis enters first and says "good evening." I follow silently. The boss greets Nikolis but when he sees me, the smile freezes on his lips. With a firm grip he hands the boy to his wife.

"Mirou, take the baby and go inside. There's something I need to do..."

His wife picks up their son, who has stopped laughing. As she walks past me, she stops for a moment and gives me a fierce look.

"You should have gone to one of your sisters to do your business, you little bastard, instead of ruining the poor girl!" she says and slams the door on her way out.

Startled and bewildered, I look at Nikolis. Am I there to make things right with the boss or...? Nikolis simply steps aside, making room for the boss to approach me. I wait for him to say something but he starts to hit me instead. What do I do? Do I hit back? How can I? And if do, what happens afterwards? I find the door and, just as I am opening it, I get the biggest kick of my life! It sends me flying five meters away from the stairs into the middle of the street. My breathing stalls; I am gasping for air.

"Ah... Ah..."

I stand up with difficulty, manage to get myself moving again, come to the reed field of Koronos, and hide there in immeasurable despair.

"America is a big country, liberal, with a lot of money, I tell you!" The words of Sophocles Paphitis are determinative. I add things up again: Nineteen liras from Egypt and two from Cyprus comes to twenty-one. Add to that what I have earned from odd jobs, I come up with a total of £27. It's not enough. If only I had ten more... Only my father can help, if he wanted to... He has land; he is credit worthy so he can borrow the money. In any case, the way things have turned out, what would he do with me here in Kyrenia?

I set my bitterness aside and send a message to him through Glioris. Father agrees. He borrows the money and I add ten more liras to my money belt. In my pocket I have the certificate in English that has cost me twelve shillings: "Costas Charalambou, born in the village of Karakoumi in the District of Kyrenia, Greek, Greek Orthodox, citizen of the Ottoman Empire." With this piece of paper I can travel to America! Two donkeys are loaded and ready to go in front of the house, one for me and one for my brother Glioris, who is accompanying me so he can bring the animals back. In the saddlebags are barley husks made by my sisters, a few olives, a sack, a bed sheet, and a few undergarments; it's not much but it is a little more than what I took with me to Egypt. I do not say goodbye to any of my friends or acquaintances. I am too ashamed to see anyone. I do not want to remind them of the shameful stigma, regardless of whether they believe I am innocent or not. And now with the acquittal I am doubly guilty in my father's eyes: He says that first I despoiled the girl and then fooled the court to avoid marrying her. I am in the yard, stalling for time.

"Come on, let's get going..." Glioris says.

No, I refuse to go like this. Something important is missing. Father knows that I am leaving today, so where is he? My youngest sister says that he left in the middle of the night to water the orchard. He never leaves the house that early. I know that he is avoiding me, but I refuse to go without his blessing. I simply cannot...

"Glioris, wait. I'm going to say goodbye to him."

The old man is leaning over a shovel, waiting for the water to fill the channel in his small field. He can sense me approaching but remains frozen. I hesitate; my heart is pounding.

"Father, I'm leaving... I came to kiss your hand and get your blessing."

"I don't give my hand to be kissed by children like you!" he says abruptly and bends down to redirect the water.

The water changes course; it flows into the next channel. Overwhelmed with frustration, I burst out: I boldly say what I have not dared say all this time.

"Father, I was unfairly accused! I never laid a finger on that girl! Karalatzias put this on me..."

I stop talking, take a step forward, and stand in front of him. The corner of his eye is twitching but he is still refusing to look at me. I am certain, however, that this is the first time he has considered the possibility that I may be innocent.

"Unfairly? You mean they lied?" he asks me.

"Yes! Unfairly! They lied!" I say sharply and take a deep breath.

He still won't look at me; he fixes his gaze on the mountain, which is slowly turning red with the first light of dawn. He looks at the sea and then, as if all his strength had suddenly abandoned him, drops to the ground. With his knees deeply lodged into the freshly watered soil, he bows down to the land then looks up to the sky. His hands let go of the shovel and rise up as high as they can, palms open.

"If it's a lie, may he be cursed by God and devoured by maggots!" he curses from the depths of his being and bends down to the ground again.

I wait for him to get up. I long to kiss his hand, to get his blessing, but he picks up the shovel again, leans on it, and casts a fleeting glance at me from the corner of his eye.

"Alright then, Godspeed!" he whispers softly and focuses on cutting off the water again.

I wait for him to finish but he keeps messing about with the soil and the water, remaining hunched over. As long as he is unsure about me, he will not allow me to kiss his hand. I depart without his blessing.

I will recount the end of this story now: In the following year a huge fight broke out at Chrysotrimithiotissa Festival. In the heat of the moment, they exposed Yiannatzis Karalatzias. They shouted out all the depravities that he has committed, including falsely accusing me and trying to force me to marry the poor girl that he ruined. My father was present but I was not; I was not able to enjoy my vindication. Worst of all, I was not able to kiss my father's hand. My father passed away in 1910, while I was in America. I never saw him again. However, I was back in Kyrenia when the strapping Yiannatzis Karalatzias fell ill. His entire body was covered by festering wounds. Flies sat on the wounds and laid eggs, which turned into maggots. They had to pulverize dried black-eyed peas into flour to put on the wounds to poison the maggots... My father's curse perhaps?

Chapter 6

The Long Journey

Cyprus, America, 1907

On the ship's deck to Athens I worry about my money belt, which is resting, firmly fastened, against my skin. I touch it every so often, making sure. I do not feel comfortable enough to even set down the bundle with my few belongings that I use as a pillow at night. Other than this I am calm, without the anxiety of the first journey. In any case, Sophocles Paphitis is with me. He comes and goes, serving up his English, making the ship his own. And we have an unexpected fellow traveller, Nikolis Troodites, although we do not see much of him. He is always in the ship's first class area. Irini is there with her mother and her sister, Efthymia; they are travelling to Athens. I want to ask him if he knew that Yiannatzis Karalatzias intended to beat me when he took me to see him, but I do not. It's all water under the bridge now. The fact that he has left his employ indicates that he has lost respect for the man. The ship keeps moving forward and there is nothing but sea all around; everything is behind me now, good and bad! Besides, we will need each other in foreign lands and Nikolis Troodites is a good friend; he is honest and smart. At Piraeus, where we wait for a few hours, I look after his belongings. He says that he is carrying something "very valuable." When he returns, his eyes are bloodshot from crying. It is clear that saying goodbye to Irini was painful, yet he must have known that their relationship had no future. How could he expect to marry Malikkis's daughter? I pretend not to notice. I stand next to him while the ferry crosses the Isthmus; he says nothing. I resolve to save not only my money, but also the rusks. At Aigio I buy a local koulouri like everyone else and eat it with my last few olives.

Patra is our last stop in Greece before the great journey. It reminds me of Kyrenia a little, except that its castle is high up, not on the surf. All Greeks travelling to America are assembled on the roof of a large building at the port. Officials lay down sacks for us for the night; we will sleep under the stars. It is a beautiful evening and most are in high spirits, singing and enjoying themselves. I do not share their enthusiasm, however; I feel anxious about the unknown that lies ahead. Nikolis is despondent about Irini, whom he has lost for good. In the darkness he pours his heart out to us for the first time. He speaks openly about their love, their kisses, their caresses, and other more daring things. He claims that they have refrained from taking the next big step in their relationship, but I have doubts. When one is in pain everything is magnified, perhaps even exaggerated. Who knows where the truth lies? I listen silently and, to my surprise, even the talkative Sophocles keeps quiet. He does not ask questions or make smart-arse comments. We are both mute witnesses to something beautiful that died before it had a chance to live.

Very early next morning we are awakened by loud voices. We are rushed into a large room on the ground floor that has many wooden benches and a few chairs. We sit on the benches; the doctors take the chairs. Everything is white: white walls, white counters, white doctor's coats. While we wait, I am troubled by a vague sense of danger, whereas Sophocles looks around with audacious curiosity. We form a line that enters through one door and disperses when it comes out of another. We are required to make three stops, each one at a doctor who does not speak Greek. The first doctor closely examines my eyes and folds my lids so far back that I think they'll come unstuck. The second has a stethoscope; he motions for me to open my shirt. The third forces me to reveal my private parts. I unbutton my pants and, although the sensation is quite unpleasant, I forget it the moment they hand me the paper and tell me to buy my ticket to America: £22!

One more thing out of the way! Outside, in the yard, I breathe deeply, feeling quite relaxed, until I hear Nikolis protesting angrily.

"How could I possibly have trachoma in my eyes?" he shouts.

Sophocles listens stoically and pats his shoulder.

"What is it?" I ask.

Infuriated as he is, Nikolis does not respond. He notices the paper in my hand and gives me a strange look. Sophocles whispers in my ear:

"They won't let him go to America. They found trachoma and syphilis..."

Nikolis grabs his things and walks away — tall, broad chested, and with a plump rosy face, round like the moon. Sophocles goes after him and I, feeling awkward, glance at the paper in my hand. I should not procrastinate; I should have the ticket issued as soon as possible.

At night, completely ready, I meet up with Sophocles who knows the town inside out by now.

"Patra is nice!" he declares.

"Where is Nikolis?"

"On the ferry back to Piraeus... Everything happens for a reason. You heard him last night..."

"You don't actually believe that Irini is going to marry him?"

"No, that's definitely over; Irini has been promised to a teacher. I told him to see a good doctor in Athens before he returns to Cyprus. In any case, why should he suffer? He's young and smart; he'll get over Irini. There's plenty of fish in the sea! So many young women in Kyrenia... He'll find someone to love, someone who'll want a husband."

So Nikolis is on his way back to Cyprus and we are sailing to America...

Back on the roof there is much discussion about the ship: the SS Celtic of the Hamburg-America Line, 9,000 tonnes, equipped with two stacks. Our imaginations aggrandize and embellish it but at dawn, when it appears at the port, well, it is pitiful! And its single smokestack puffs rather unconvincingly.

"Where's the second stack?" I ask a man in a merchant marine uniform.

He raises his brow with a devious look in his eyes.

"Ah, the second stack! Well, that pops out when the ship reaches the Atlantic. The Mediterranean does not require two stacks," he says and bursts into laughter, as he deftly climbs the ship's wobbly ladder.

All Greek immigrants board the Celtic by this ladder. I walk around on the noisy deck. The only quiet place is a makeshift pen, where some heifers chew without a care in the world, oblivious to their fate – our meat for the trip across the ocean. The sleeping quarters are below: rows of hammocks in stacks of six, one on top of the other. This is where we literally sink into sleep at night. The rows are dense and most hammocks remain unfilled. Why so many? The answer in Palermo... Begrimed porters carry coal on board for half a day, then Italians flood the deck, so many that I fear that there won't be enough hammocks. I speak the language, so I understand what the Italian next to me is saying. He is incensed because they won't allow his cousin to travel.

"Stronzi Americani! Non guardano la testa e guardano gli occhi!"[1] he says and bites his fingers.

Now there is literally no room on deck – if you dropped a pin, it would not find a crack to fall to the floor. Three thousand souls on board, too much weight for such a ship!

Our second stop is the Port of Algiers. I feel as though I am held within a large, secure embrace, yet there's a safety issue with the Celtic. The stokers go on strike and shut down the boilers. The ship cannot leave the port. Protests abound. The stokers as-

---

1 "American jackasses. They didn't look at his head but at his eyes!"

sert that the steam cylinders are not in good working order – they are not willing to lose their lives. Repairs are carried out and the stokers are convinced. After a two-day delay they fire up the boilers, and the ship departs. We cross Gibraltar. The azure of the Mediterranean is behind us, and the faded blue of the Atlantic Ocean before us. I look at the line that separates sea and sky – no trace of land in sight. I recall the mariner's laughter and start to fret. Moreover, the ship has not popped out a second stack! To allay my fears I keep to the daily routine. Famished at noon I go up to the deck and take a seat in a circle of ten passengers around a pot containing a broth, where a few legumes float along with flies. If the broth contains worms, it means that the day's menu includes meat, although I rarely chance upon a morsel. Speed is essential because, beyond the frantic race of the nine competing spoons, every now and then one of the ten passengers does not make it to the railing in time and empties his stomach into the pot. At which point, its contents are very unpleasantly enriched. Lying down is the only thing that helps when my insides start to churn.

The first few days are tolerable but, once the ship reaches open ocean, the situation becomes truly unbearable. I hang my head over the railing and empty what little food I have in my stomach. Then hunger obliges me to join the cycle of the pot, where I must battle with a spoon for a bite that reeks of vomit. I simply cannot bear it, so I return to the hammock. I would rather do without food, lose muscle mass since I have no fat, and chew on crumbs from the rusks. Some days I do not leave the hammock at all except to use the lavatory, and even that takes a lot out of me. I literally have to drag myself there and back.

One day, as I am about to take the first step to the lavatory, my foot lands in water. The hammocks are swinging violently back and forth; the ship is rocking ominously. Screaming from the women's sleeping quarters… An oddly quiet group of Italians enters; they gather their belongings and go. We are caught in a terrible storm and the steam engine cylinders are broken. The

ship is at the mercy of the waves! I barely have enough strength
to breathe. I hold on to one of the posts, where the hammock is
fastened, and allow myself to be rocked back and forth. I am in the
way of crewmembers rushing about with some peculiar-looking
pumps. They place them on the floor and pump feverishly to draw
the water, which is then dumped outside through long rubber
hoses. Louder than the women's screaming and the noise of the
pumps is the raging storm, which is made even more nightmarish
by the siren's constant deafening shrill. Why is it on? And for how
long? It seems to go on for forever! If only it would stop…

When the siren finally stops, I drag myself up to the deck and
breathe in plenty of fresh air. The sea has calmed down somewhat.
I lean on the railing next to Sophocles. He is not wearing his nice
clothing with which he could pass for a lord, but an old but well-
cared-for cotton suit. As always he is at ease, as though exempt
from what everyone else on the ship is forced to endure. He retains his usual self-confidence and knows exactly what is happening because of his English.

"Yes, we've been caught in a terrible storm for two days, the
cylinders are not working, and we have no radio. That's why the
siren is always blaring – it's calling out for help."

"Where are we now?" I ask, extremely concerned.

"Fortunately, a ship passed by and showed the correct course
to our captain."

I sigh with relief. Thank God! Thank God for what? The siren
starts up again, now at its highest intensity and with an echo.
Does the ocean create echoes? No, the echo is actually the siren
of another vessel to our starboard. I make out the markings of
the Austro-American Line on the other ship, where two sailors
with megaphones are shouting in our direction. What on earth…?
Suddenly the syllables choke in the sailors' throats and the crowd
identifies the danger. Thousands of mouths scream out in terror;
their ship is heading straight toward us! Its bow will thrust into
our side at any moment. Surely now we're lost! The sailors with

the megaphones shout again. With an ear-splitting creak, their ship makes a spectacular turn with seconds to spare. We avoid the collision, but we are drenched by waves taller than the Celtic's only stack. No one complains.

"In the nick of time!" Sophocles remarks, while wiping his wet brow with a wet kerchief.

A boat is lowered with our captain; he is on his way to the other ship to see his colleague. We all watch the friendly exchange between the two captains, when they meet high up on the bridge.

With a salute from both sirens we start to move again. Sailors are smiling and the ship is back on course, moving steadily toward its destination, as steadily as my spoon fights for food at lunch. I am determined to swallow anything that that pot contains, even if it's nothing but vomit! There is simply no other way: If I do not eat, I will die of starvation. I am drenched but do not care, not that I have a change of clothes in any case. The faster they dry on me, the better. At most, I change my underwear in the sleeping quarters.

Everything goes like clockwork until the butcher's hammer fails to deliver the fatal blow, causing the animal to go berserk. The bull jumps the enclosure, races through the frightened crowd, leaps over the railing, and throws himself into the sea. The siren again... The ship stops, a boat is lowered to capture the bull, and the butcher is left staring at the two or three animals left in the pen. Why is he shaking his head with such concern?

The reason is obvious: The terrible food has been short for the last three days. Three thousand hungry souls on board, three thousand empty stomachs... Blame it on the six-day delay caused by engine trouble and on the half-day wasted on a fruitless search for the runaway bull – no matter, hunger is hunger! A mob rushes to the lifeboats when rusks and canned food, stored there in case of a shipwreck, are discovered. The thick canvas covers tear as though they were made of paper. I don't move. First, I have no strength, and second, I think it's pointless. Never mind that it's not right!

How would we survive in case of a shipwreck? Such eventualities never cross Sophocles's mind, however; having managed to grab a rusk, he chews on his way toward me. He leans on the railing next to me.

"How many days has it been, Costis?"

I have been keeping count.

"Thirty one! The last three without any food whatsoever... We must be getting close, dammit," I respond, almost completely out of breath.

CHAPTER 7

AMERICA! AMERICA!

USA, 1907-1913

The first cry explodes out of the mouth of an Italian at the other side of the ship: "Americaaaaa! Americaaaaa!"

Fired up with excitement, everyone rushes to see the dark line on the horizon. Sophocles is among the first to have look, but I stay back. There's nothing left of me but skin and bone; I simply do not have the strength. There are moments when I even forget where I am, where I am going and why. The hours pass and, as the Celtic approaches land, the dark line changes. As it begins to take shape, something stirs inside me; I do not know what that is exactly, but it gives me an inexplicable boost of energy. I weave through the crowd. I ask and learn.

"Now we're approaching Sandy Hook!"

"Why has the ship stopped?"

"A special pilot is coming on board to navigate it into port."

We stop at Hoffman Island, where Public Health Service officials board to inspect for contagious diseases. Then we stop at a second island called Castigari.[1] We disembark and the hungry passengers race to buy some pies that are sold there. A war breaks out over who will get one first but, as it turns out, there's enough for everyone. The pies are devoured. Sophocles returns with one and with a flood in his mouth — it's truly mind-boggling how so

---

1 Castigari: After the transatlantic journey immigrants were processed at Castle Gardens (also known as "Castigari") located on Ellis Island.

much saliva can be produced after such a long spell of hunger. Mercifully, he gives me a piece.

"Here, Costis, have some…"

I take it! This is the first time that I have had food in my mouth in days.

"What about the quarantine?"

"Wait," Sophocles responds.

The hall is massive. Once the doctors examine the immigrants, the nurses pin one of three marks on their lapels. Those with the first mark are sent back to the Celtic; they have been rejected and must turn back. Those with the second mark are led through a door, where they disappear. The examination is quick: the familiar eyelid test, a glance at the chest, and a quick examination of the genitals. Those with the third mark, which is what I receive, are shoved outside through a large exit. I find myself on a pier among a large crowd of people. I see an empty spot; no one seems to want to go there. I do. As I stand there quite comfortably, a few others join me. I barely have time to exhale when a loud noise is heard… A massive lift is heading toward us! We rapidly disperse to avoid being crushed while the crowd laughs. I find Sophocles and, after a great deal of push and shove, we reach the pier's railing. A ferry is docked below; Sophocles explains that it will take us from the Public Health Service Island to Battery Place. More push and shove but I manage to sit next to Sophocles as the ferry departs.

"Make sure we stay together… We've made it, Costis!" he says in a quiet but triumphant tone.

Indeed, we are finally in America! But a question still lingers in my mind:

"So the others, those with the second mark who didn't get sent back to the ship, where are they held?"

Sophocles shrugs his shoulders. It's rare that he does not know something and, in this case, he obviously does not care. I ask the man next to me in Italian. He says that they will remain in quarantine until officials have determined that they are healthy. Then he adds angrily:

"Gli stronzi, guardano i nostri occhi e non la nostra testa!"

I recognize him! The Italian from Palermo has reached America without his cousin, who was rejected because of trachoma.

A sea of people at Battery Place; everyone ends up here not only from Castigari, but also from other Public Health Service islands. Policemen strike us indiscriminately with their shiny clubs and aggressively shout things that I do not understand. Obviously they want us to keep moving, but how do you move forward with so many people in front of you, blocking your way? Zero results, no matter how many blows they deliver. And why so much brutality after such a harrowing journey? This day was an ordeal for all concerned because, as I would learn later on, it saw the largest arrival of immigrants to America – 47,000 people were processed on that day in 1907.

Completely new surroundings and a sky bridge over our heads! This is the first time any of us has seen anything like this. We look up in astonishment, but the cops do not share our curiosity; to them it's just a delay and an excuse for more vicious beatings. We move further outside, where a vendor is selling pies. I buy one for ten cents. Its taste is so dreadful that it overpowers my hunger; I find it impossible to swallow. My first taste of America is not only terrible, but also accompanied by a painful blow to the back.

Sophocles and I on the loose in America… Our only hope for assistance is a reference letter for our fellow Cypriot Ttofis Hadjilambros, who has lived here for years. The short trips across the sky bridge and on the tram drain me completely. Calm and collected, Sophocles looks around and reads the address again: 6th Avenue, 40th Street!

"It's here but where, goddammit?" he says.

Barely able to breathe, I sink into despair. We have another look around and Sophocles is proven correct. It's right in front of us, but it is not a house like the ones in Cyprus. It's actually a café-restaurant below street level that smells of Greece all the same. My heart rests easy for the first time since facing the callousness of the police, even if the man in the restaurant is busy; he does not even look at us. We wait! At some point he finishes what he is doing and we hand him the envelope.

"Ttofis Hadjilambros? No, he doesn't live here. But he comes here almost every day to eat and collect his mail. Sit down and wait for him."

We sit and wait...

It feels wonderful to sit on a chair on terra firma again, without agonizing over the whereabouts of my stomach. I would not mind if I had to wait here for a week! The restaurant owner generously offers us something to eat and lets us spend the night, since the man we are looking for has not come. The makeshift bedroom is located further underground in the restaurant's stockroom, which is full of stored items and bedbugs. So there are bedbugs even in America! My mind jumpstarts and I begin to assess the situation: The year is 1907 and I am nineteen years old. In truth, I am a bag of bones, dressed in cheap cotton suit, the only clothing I own. I have nothing but nine liras and the hope for better days. I am equipped only with the desire to work and get ahead. With these thoughts I fall asleep on my first night in America.

Ttofis Hadjilambros arrives the next day; clearly, he is fully acclimatized to life here. He looks at the letter and examines us. Even Sophocles feels awkward so he keeps quiet. Finally, Ttofis Hadjilambros turns to me with a mocking smile:

"Well, well... Look what came to work in America!"

What can I say? You cannot take offense when you are depending entirely on someone's goodwill. And Ttofis Hadjilambros has both goodwill and a desire to boast. He brings us to Park Avenue and stops in front of a massive building on 42nd Street.

"This is the Belmont Hotel where I work!" he declares proudly.

We walk a little further and into another building. He opens a door on the second floor — two beds and two tables for all the necessities, while a huge closet stretches wall to wall on one side of the room.

"This is where I live!"

With someone else...

"They call me Mike but my name is Theodoros. I'm from Corinthos," the man introduces himself with a smile.

Ttofis Hadjilambros stretches out his arms.

"You can stay here with us as long as you like. There's plenty of room!"

"Plenty of room? Where?" Sophocles asks.

Ttofis Hadjilambros laughs and opens the large closet to reveal a comfortable bed.

"Both of you can fit in there; there's only half of the kid anyway," he says and we all laugh.

So America is this easy!

The Great Hunger – New York

In fact, it's anything but easy, as I soon realize. I am keen to work at the Belmont Hotel – Hadjilambros even gives me a recommendation. Since I am unable to communicate in English, they fire me on the third day. I sink in this first disappointment, whereas Sophocles lands firmly on his feet. Owing to his prior service at the home of the Chief Justice he speaks the language. He has an air of confidence about him and is dressed well – he looks as though he was born a lord! He is hired as a houseman at a wealthy home.

"You'll find work, don't worry," he assures me and pats my shoulder.

Even without English I have no difficulty recognizing Greek restaurants. I walk back and forth on streets and avenues, and learn to use the subway. By the end of the summer I have seen only the face of rejection, however; Greek restaurants are not hiring, because the owners bring their relatives from back home.

With the cold setting in, fear writhes in my chest like a sack of snakes. I was already used to the smallest amount of food but do not even get that anymore. Sophocles brings tea and sugar carefully wrapped in paper, as well as bits of stolen food from the house where he works. I boil water to make tea, chew on a dry piece of something, and get by. But I need money for the subway so I can look for work, and my nine liras are almost gone. The more my savings dwindle, the more my insecurity grows, while Hadjilambros pitilessly increases his jibes.

Sophocles is concerned about me. When he hears about the railway, he buys an axe and a shovel and takes me to the office where they are hiring labourers. While talking to the men in charge, he suddenly falls silent. His face drains of colour...

"What's the matter, Sophocles?"

They are accusing him of trying to take advantage of minor! Me, a minor...? I am nineteen years old! However, with what's left of me, I barely look fifteen. We get out of there in a rush and I start knocking on the doors of Greek restaurants again, while it gets colder and colder. When the snow comes I have a huge problem. My thin cotton suit is no match for such low temperatures. And the street kids make a bad situation worse; they chase me and throw snow at me when I sit breathless and shivering on benches. How do I escape this torture? Eventually my money runs out and Sophocles lends me $25 beyond the tea, sugar and leftovers, which are always free of charge. I continue to look for work.

Spring comes and the snow melts at last. I receive the first letter from my father; it may be formal, since it is written by someone else, but astonishing all the same. My innocence was proven beyond doubt and not in a court of law! Amidst all the excitement at Chrysotrimithiotissa Festival on Easter Monday, Anna – the silent young woman – overwhelmed by the injustice, did not simply speak up, but shouted at Yiannatzis Karalatzias at the church courtyard:

"Have you no shame, you lowlife? First you ruin me and then force me to accuse Charalambos Catsellis's boy?"

My father's letter may be a poignant apology, but I am certain that Yiannatzis Karalatzias has nothing to fear. He is a rich man; he will side-step the situation and continue living la dolce vita while I, the blameless, have been punished with starvation in America without my father's blessing! What good is vindication in Kyrenia to me now, here on the merciless streets of New York, where I cannot find a moment's relief from anxiety? I am still looking for work. I am down to one dollar and a few cents of the twenty-five that Sophocles has lent me. Unemployed for nine months, I am barely holding on to life with tea and leftovers. The depths of despair...

I chance upon Matsoukas delivering a speech on a boat on the Hudson River to a crowd of Greek immigrants. They throw donations at him while he recites. They are moved by his words but I do not have the strength to feel anything!

I drag myself to the subway, on my way to a place where they are hiring, without hope and with the heavy hand of an early death on my chest – an early death like that of Kalfas, whose fate chills me to the bone. Kalfas was a tailor in Kyrenia, a tall strapping man and a great dancer. At weddings everyone stood aside to watch him dance. He had perfect timing, vigour and grace. Carried away in the dance one time, Kalfas reached for his money; he gave some to the musicians and threw the rest on the ground. Coins everywhere! While the young and the poor scrambled to grab something, he – light on his feet, tall and straight like a cypress tree – continued dancing.

"I don't want to be a wage slave of the British or to carry their money!" he declared and laughed as coins with the picture of the British monarch clinked on the marble floor, amidst the commotion made by the kids and beggars chasing them.

Kalfas left Cyprus to work abroad and, when I was in Egypt, he came to Bacos to see me.

"I'm in Transvaal with Kkolis Bellapaisiotis. We have a vending cart there, but I'm leaving for America," he said.

When Aphrodite, his wife, learned that I was leaving for America, she gave me his address in Memphis, Ohio, although she had not received a letter or money from him for some time. I wanted to go see him, but Sophocles insisted that we send a letter first. He wrote a letter in English and we received the reply... While at work, the strapping dancer Kalfas went to a pit to dump ashes and fainted from the fumes. He fell in and died of asphyxiation! Another man nearly lost his life trying to save him but was pulled out in time. Kalfas is no more. Should I travel to a faraway place to visit a grave? What's the point? What's the point when I am standing over my own grave, a bag of bones in the expanse of America? I realize how truly close I am to suffering the same fate as Kalfas, but how do I hold on?

I am straining to hold on in the subway. The monotone sound of the wheels on the tracks suddenly vanishes along with the passengers. Am I still alive? My head is resting on something soft... a woman's face is looking down at me with kindness... the monotone sound returns and people glance sideways at me... I realize that I am still on the subway, lying down, with my head resting on the woman's knees. I try to get up, but she has no trouble thwarting my feeble effort. She says something in English that do not understand and I stay, sensing that it's for my good. When the train stops, she helps me to my feet and up to street level. She hails a taxi, pays the driver, and hands him a familiar piece of paper – my address, which I keep in my pocket just in case...

Although I am alone in the taxi, I feel comforted by the kindness of the rich woman, who brought me back from death's doorstep. I take this as a sign that I am not doomed like Kalfas. I gather my strength to get upstairs to the room. Theodoros, the Corinthian, is making coffee. He notices that I am in a good mood.

"Did you get a job, Costis? Is that why there's a smile on your face?" he asks.

I shake my head and crash land to reality. My mood turns.

"You weigh barely half a pound, kid! Why would anyone in his right mind hire you?" Hadjilambros says mockingly and bursts out into a booming laughter.

His jibe may be a stab at my heart, but a powerful slap to his cheek from Theodoros shuts his mouth.

"Shame on you! Don't you have any compassion? Isn't it bad enough that the boy hasn't found work all this time, do you have to tease him, too?" Theodoros says heatedly.

Holding his cheek, Hadjilambros looks like he is about to mumble something but bites his tongue. Theodoros is staring him down, making sure that he will not talk back. Then he turns his attention to the coffee, which he shares out into three cups. He offers one to me.

"Drink your coffee and get your things. I'm taking you to Trenton to get you a job. I'm off today."

My mind freezes. I fix my gaze on the cup, feeling very self-conscious while Theodoros looks me over; I am a mess and I know it.

"I'll buy you a new shirt on the way. You'll look better, don't worry," he adds.

Obviously, my threadbare, striped suit will impress no one. While I sip my coffee, the kind face of the woman on the subway melds with the serious, rugged face of Theodoros, the Corinthian, although they look nothing alike. I want to say something but I can't get a word out. I quickly finish the coffee and go to the basin to wash out the cup so they won't see me cry! This can't go on… Either something will come up soon or I will die a slow and sad death, not a quick and easy one like Kalfas.

The First Job – Trenton, New Jersey

I am wearing my old pants from Cyprus but my shirt is new, bought for me by Theodoros. We arrive at a shop that is both a confectionary and a fruit market. It sells a large variety of fruit imported from the four corners of the earth, even out of season. I wonder how everything is kept fresh.

Theodoros provides some background information: The owner is Greek, an Arvanites from Elefsina. I want to ask how he can be an Arvanites and hail from Elefsina at the same time, but I do not dare. According to Theodoros, his wife did not survive the journey. She died on the ship but his daughters are here with him. I listen but I am anxious. I am anxious to know the answer to the burning question: Will he give me a job? Ten winters weigh heavy on Arvanites's face. His lips are rigid, barely parting even to speak, but yes, he hires me for $9 a month including food. My heart is about to burst! I am saved. I have no idea how to thank Theodoros, who simply says "goodbye" and departs.

I work seven days a week, morning 'til night, mainly in the cold, damp and dark basement where snow from the river is stored. With a pitchfork I break up the snow into pieces small enough to fit into an ice cream machine. This part of the job is fairly easy but operating the machine is a gruelling task! I have to turn the lever nonstop until thousands of tiny crystals form on the cream inside the tin container. When it turns into ice cream, I place the container in the shop's fridge upstairs. Several containers are required on busy summer days. My hands are worn out from the constant churning but, when I finish in the afternoon, I mind the confectionery and the fruit market. While I wait for customers, I keep my hands in my pockets; I can't feel them because of the strain and the cold. The fruit market is a welcome change since my work in the basement is truly unbearable. The only good thing is the food. No more of the tea and leftovers that were so kindly provided by Sophocles; here I get real food, mostly legumes, but at least it's filling. I gain back some weight. With the specter of hunger behind me, I open my eyes to the world around me in Trenton, the capital of New Jersey. The subway entrance is directly across the shop; a few steps further, the tram offloads groups of young people,

mostly in my age group. Always well-dressed and in high spirits, they laugh and make noise – students at Princeton University
who come into town looking for a good time. Vending carts sell
fruit and peanuts on the street – most of them belong to Greeks.
One vendor, an old man, has permission to store his fruit in the
damp basement where I work, so it keeps fresh. He comes and
goes, frequently restocking his cart, mostly with bananas. He lifts
bunches out of the hay and places them next to an acetylene lamp
because the heat helps them ripen. Then he hangs them on the cart
for students to buy. The students are not only interested in fruit
and peanuts, but also in having fun. They pay double and triple for
the vending cart's lamp and take aim. When it shatters, their carefree, cheerful voices fill the street. I watch them from the shop.
I may be young, too, but I am neither carefree nor cheerful; I am
exhausted and weary from hard work. And Arvanites is a brood-
ing, ill-tempered man, who hits me at the drop of a hat. His two
daughters, ten and sixteen, are enrolled at the area's finest school.
They are well dressed, spoiled and overprotected. Overwhelmed
by the relentless torment, I feel alone; I need company. So my
mind embarks on fantasy trails: *When will I have children? If I have
a son, will I be able to send him to Princeton? Would he be carefree and
cheerful, not forced to ruin his hands on an ice cream machine? Would he
have enough money to pay double and triple for the vendor's lamp? Would
he take aim, shatter it, and be happy, making the vendor doubly and triply
happy while he waits for the next boy to pay him double and triple? Would
I speak to my son in Greek, but with Cypriot accent, so that even Greeks
won't understand what we are saying, just as Arvanites and his daughters
communicate with each other in their dialect and I have no clue what they
are saying?* My mind dreams, it travels far...

From afar I see the white apron of Nikolatzis Ellinas. To have a
fellow Kyrenian here is truly a blessing! A strap around his neck
suspends a deep tray with a white sweet, which he sells on the
street. He calls it "pastellaki." I am curious to taste it but do not
dare ask for a piece. One time, when he offers some to me, I blush

with embarrassment and say "no." Nikolatzis and I talk about Kyrenia; I also tell him about the torment of the ice cream machine.

"You should leave! Find another job," he tells me.

Find another job where? I got this one after nine months of unemployment, a bag of bones with one foot in the grave...

"Arvanites is taking advantage of you and you thank him, too? There are plenty of jobs out there," he insists.

"Where?"

"There are offices that find work for you. You pay them only 10% of your first month's pay. Listen to me... You look exhausted!"

"It's just my hands... That machine is going to be the end of me," I tell him, too ashamed to admit that Arvanites also hits me.

One morning, while I am holding the stick that I use to shove snow, I do not notice that the boss is behind me. He trips on the stick and falls. He gets up and starts to beat me awfully hard, but I do not move an inch. The specters of hunger and unemployment rise up before me. At least now I have good food, no matter how exhausting the work may be, or if I get struck from time to time. At night I lay down a rug in the dining room at the back, wrap myself in the thick bed sheet that I have brought from Cyprus, and sleep. I rest and gain strength for the next gruelling day. My hope is that, in the winter when it gets cold, my work on the machine will lessen because people won't eat as much ice cream.

Well, I could not have been more wrong! On Christmas Eve of 1908, I am forced to churn the machine for thirty-six hours straight. I can barely keep up with the demand. The old man comes to the basement to restock his cart with fruit for the third time.

"I sold really well, today!" he says, rubbing his hands with satisfaction and to keep them warm.

He examines his bananas. Some bunches are ready, completely yellow. He picks them up carefully then looks at me pensively.

"Are you still churning?" he asks.

"Nonstop since yesterday morning!"

"You haven't gone to sleep?"

I shake my head to indicate that I have not, since I don't have enough strength to speak. The container is heavy now, a sign that the ice cream is ready. I stop churning and take it upstairs. The boss is dressed in his nicest suit, same as his daughters, whose new dresses are adorned with frills and fineries. He orders me to mind the shop because he has to take his daughters somewhere. Thank God for the respite, otherwise I would not have been able to churn any longer.

He comes back quite late; I am so exhausted that I go directly to the back, lay down the rug, and shut my eyes.

God please help me fall asleep so I can rest, I pray. While I am trying to nod off, the boss comes in uninvited. I pretend to be asleep but, cracking my eyes open, I watch him pick up my trousers and slip his hand into a pocket. I know that that pocket is empty. A Cypriot twenty-piastre coin with a portrait of Queen Victoria is inside the other one. He finds it and starts to examine it, trying to identify the currency. Obviously he does not trust me. He is checking to see whether I have taken money from the till. A stab to my chest! Overwhelmed with frustration and disappointment, I prop myself up on my elbow using what little strength I have left.

"Did you find a bundle of dollars?" I ask with venom dripping from my lips.

He puts back the copper twenty, sets down my pants, and leaves. I lie down again and sleep finally takes me.

It's the end of January of 1909; having finished the last container of ice cream for the day, I go upstairs to put it in the fridge. At the door, Nikolatzis Ellinas is waiting for me with his tray. The container slips out of my hands and smashes a few ice cream glasses on the lower shelf. The boss beats me harder than ever before in front of Nikolatzis Ellinas! The humiliation is far greater than the pain, so much that I feel nothing. Getting beaten at the age of twenty in front of my fellow countryman is the same as being beaten with all of Kyrenia watching: my father, my sisters, my brother-in-law Argyros... I would rather be beaten in front of the President of the United States, in front of the whole of America, instead of Nikolatzis Ellinas. But what choice do I have? I approach him nearly gasping, trying to control my breath, and ask about the employment office. We never discuss the incident but understand each other. He gives me the details and goes back out to sell pas-tellaki. Nikolatzis plans to save a bit more money and then return to Kyrenia; he will start a small business there, make a home for himself, get married and have children. He is lucky because he is moving closer to his goal. When will I get those things? When?

I am torn: Should I go to the employment office first and then ask for my salary, or vice versa? I decide to leave at once because, if I go to the employment office first and Arvanites refuses to let me go, I am going to have problems. First thing in the morning, instead of going down into the basement, I ask for my wages: $90 for ten months! The boss is tight-lipped as always; he says nothing. He gives me $30 in cash and a cheque for $60 that, he says, I can cash at a bank.

On the train the terror of those nine months of unemployment looms large; it is crushing me. I forget everything I have suffered at Arvanites's shop and regret my decision. But the train has al-ready left Trenton; it's on its way to New York.

The employment office recommended by Nikolatzis Ellinas finds work for cooks and assistants – a ground floor office with writing on the walls in large letters that I cannot read because it is in English. But I can admire the artfully decorated cakes, some with two or three tiers, displayed on stands of various heights. A well-groomed, grey-haired gentleman sits behind the desk. I say "hello" and, as I prepare to serve up my minimal English, a young woman enters through a door at the back with a steaming cup, which fills the room with the strong aroma of coffee. She places the cup on the table, wraps her arms around the middle-aged man, and starts chattering sweetly in a language that is not English. She showers him with kisses and caresses. He smiles contently, answers in the same language, and takes a sip. The young woman leaves, and he has no trouble understanding that I am looking for work. He jots something down on a piece of paper and hands it to me.

"Kitchen boy... Kitchen boy... Dollars!" he says and holds up all five fingers on both hands.

I am in disbelief! Is it really this easy to get work as a kitchen boy for ten dollars a month? The man makes a gesture to indicate that I must take the train. I look at the paper, which must be the address of my new job, and take a first deep breath of relief.

"Thank you! Thank you!" I say repeatedly.

Before leaving New York, I attempt to cash the cheque but the bank will not accept it. After some back and forth, it becomes clear that Arvanites's cheque cannot be cashed because there is not enough money in his account. I feel as though I have been poisoned! For the slimeball to cheat me out of so much hard work...! And the cheque...? What do I do with the cheque?

Chappaqua

I keep looking at it on the train as I travel toward my new job. Do I keep it, or do I toss it? I sigh, having decided to toss it, but change my mind at the last minute. I slip it into my pocket. I have more pressing things to think about at this moment: I look at the address again as the train climbs the right side of the Hudson River, at times moving closer to the water, at times further away. With my minimal English I manage to read the name "Chappaqua." Is there really such a place? The train approaches the river again and I see steamships moving slowly ahead. Then the rail line travels through an area with tall trees.

"Chappaqua... Chappaqua..." the train conductor announces and the train stops.

There is such a place after all! And since it exists then the job must exist, too.

On the platform, as I watch the train depart, the fear that there may be no work rises up inside me. I must be 75-80 miles away from New York City but returning should be easy enough. Chappaqua is no larger than Karakoumi, although the homes here are large and well-cared-for and, instead of being near the sea, Chappaqua is next to the Hudson River. I attempt to communicate with a rail employee in English. He does not understand me. Fortunately, I think to show him the address that I was given at the employment office. His face lights up and he points to a road that leads to a lush green hill. While I make my way up through the tall trees, I am filled with so much anxiety that it feels as though I have been walking forever; in reality, the distance is small, less than a kilometer. The road ends at a property with a large building at the centre and four small ones on either side. This is not a house; it looks more like a hotel. In the front yard I see a fifty-year old man of medium build, rotund, and with an intensely rosy complexion. He moves his arms about rather awkwardly as he walks. I catch up to him and show him the paper without saying anything. He nods and shows me into the main building where a woman, no older than forty, smiles warmly at me. It has been a very long time since a human being has looked at me this way. A peculiar, sweet feeling settles inside me, as though I had been drinking zivana.[2] I follow the woman into a large, clean kitchen where three cooks are working; one is a tall and imposing black woman. Communication stalls again because of my English. A dead end... I am overcome with despair but one of the cooks leans out of the window and calls a boy into the kitchen. The woman says something to him and he starts speaking Greek to me, translating and explaining everything: The lady is the boss and her name is Mrs. Plenis. My duties are to clean the kitchen, to serve the staff, and to do whatever the cooks ask of me. In the morning, before dawn, I will fire up the boilers then collect vegetables from the garden at the back.

---

2   Zivana or zivania (Greek: ζιβάνα/ζιβανία) is a Cypriot alcoholic beverage.

"The technician will show you how to fire up the boilers to-morrow; Mrs. Plenis will show you the vegetable garden now," the boy says.

It's late afternoon and beginning to get dark. I look around with curiosity as I follow the lady down a narrow path to the back-yard. When I see an uprooted thorny bush blocking the path, I jump forward and push it aside to clear the way. The lady passes and smiles at me even more sweetly than before. I can sense that she is a good boss; I am sure that she is not one to give beatings. When we return to the kitchen, she asks the boy to tell me that I have made a very good impression on her, so much that she will give me a suit and a pair of shoes. The salary set by the employ-ment office is $10 a month, and I will start work tomorrow.

I can't wait until then; my heart is so full of joy that I throw myself into washing dishes after a plentiful and satisfying dinner. Earlier on, I had asked the boy:

"Are you really Greek?"

He is! His name is Nikitas and he is from an island in the Ae-gean. He has a rich brother here in America who is paying for his education. He explains to me that the main building is an ex-pensive private school and that one of the small buildings houses a kindergarten. Not only does Nikitas happily translate for me whenever I need him to do so but, when I show him Arvanites's cheque, he gives it to his teacher who, in turn, gives it to the po-lice. The police place someone at Arvanites's register in Trenton, collect $60 from his receipts, and send me the money! My sat-isfaction is indescribable, not simply because my hard work was paid in full, but because the man showed no gratitude; he did not trust me, and he beat me. With Nikitas at the school I do not feel alone; what is more, I receive not only care, but also essential help from Mrs. Plenis. Beyond the suit and shoes, she gives me a book with English language lessons for beginners. And she places me in her trust; I am always next to her at school events, doing whatever she asks of me.

"This is my boy!" she keeps saying to the other employees. When I finally understand what that means, I blush with satisfaction.

When 400 chairs need to be moved for parents and guests to sit on during school events, she gives me 50¢ for the extra work. I hope for many such events so I can move the chairs, even if my arms are sore at night. Mrs. Plenis also entrusts me with anything that she does not want others knowing about, like the time when we secretly buried some rotten hams. As we would later find out, however, disposing of the hams was a mistake since maggots were only on the surface. This is very common in cured meats – a cleaning would have sufficed and they would have been good for eating not burying!

"Oh well," she says and shrugs her shoulders.

I spend what little free time I have at the laundry room, which is my favourite place, with the six overweight laundresses and the somewhat younger ironers. Mary, the daughter of a laundress, is the prettiest among them! Drawn into their chatter, I gain confidence and start communicating easily in English. Nevertheless, I continue studying the book that Mrs. Plenis has given me. I learn to speak and read the language. My prediction that I would be treated well here is proven correct, even if I am often the butt of jokes, albeit not mean spirited ones. The first person I met upon my arrival, the fifty year-old, is sitting next to me in the kitchen. While we are chatting, he tells me in confidence that he and the others are planning an uprising and a hunger strike to demand better wages. I look at him with astonishment and declare that I am content. I have no intention of participating in such a scheme! I do not understand why everyone at the table starts laughing because I was dead serious. On the following day, when the fifty year-old troublemaker misses dinner, he orders me:

"Bring my food upstairs!"

After yesterday, I am beginning to dislike him.

"Isn't it bad enough that you're late, you want food brought upstairs to you, too? Come get it yourself!" I talk back.

The technician, who is sitting next to me, bursts out laughing again and gives me a friendly tap on the shoulder.

"Hey, stupid, that's the boss, Mr. Plenis. He was just messing with you yesterday. Take the food upstairs to him!" he comes clean. I am so mortified that I hope that the earth would swallow me.

This is how I learn who the boss is, albeit rather late. Mr. Plenis is a simple man, so jovial and hard working that I mistook him for an employee. Trembling, I bring his dinner and attempt to apologize.

"It's okay, boy," he says with a smile.

Now that I have learnt the language everything has become easier for me, but I also get myself into trouble. A man comes to the school looking for Miss Catherine, the piano player. I promptly respond that our piano player is a very nice old lady, whose name is not Catherine.

"What about Miss Catherine?" he insists.

"We only have one Catherine here and she is a waitress," I tell him and return to my work. The man lets out a screech and disappears.

Later, Catherine comes looking for me. She is red-faced and hostile:

"Why did you tell my fiancé that I was a waitress?" she asks aggressively.

"How was I supposed to know that you were pretending to be a pianist?" I respond pluckily.

I feel secure, so I am no longer afraid to speak my mind. And I truly care about the school. Pitch black at 3:30AM, on my way to the boilers in the kindergarten building, I see a shadow fleeing... I chase it! I catch up to Coco, a wealthy senior student from Cuba. He does not resist; with gestures he pleads with me to keep quiet.

"Please, don't say anything and I'll give you a brand new suit!" he says, looking rather frightened.

I do not understand what he is talking about but I let him go. At the door to the kindergarten I find Carolyn, a poor orphan that Mrs. Plenis is putting through school free of charge; in return she collects the laundry at the kindergarten. Her fearful eyes tell the story, without her having to say a word. Later on, while I am unloading snow in the kitchen, she comes in and tells the cook that she might kill herself, if something happened or someone said things about her. Obviously she means for me to hear. I smile at her and she sighs. Coco brings me the suit, the second one that I get in America; yet even without it, I would not have betrayed Coco and Carolyn. They are young and fond of each other. If only I could also... but I cannot. In fact, I am quite anxious because summer holidays are approaching fast. Where will I go when the school closes? Will I be left without work again? Mercifully not! When the regular students depart, disabled children arrive for the summer months. The clients may be different but the staff and the work remain the same.

At the start of the new school year, the bosses give me a raise. They are happy with my work. And they do not beat me, even when I drop the large urn with 40 quarts of milk into the deep snowy ditch and no one can get it out. It's gone for good but I still do not get a beating. I never get a beating! My salary slowly climbs to $40 a week; I could not have dreamt of earning so much money even in Egypt! Not wanting to spend money on a train ticket, once a month I walk to Pleasantville to deposit my entire salary and all extra earnings at the bank. Thank God I have food to eat, moreover, I never have to spend money on clothing. I send my father the money that he borrowed to help me come to America, plus a little more. Fortunately I was able to repay him in time, because he passed away in 1910. Losing my father may have emptied my soul, but entries keep filling my deposits at Time Saving Bank. Walking there is rather difficult in the snow but, on the way back, sometimes I chance upon the train that delivers milk to the village. The driver recognizes me and gives me a ride to Chappaqua. Every now and then, usually after a holiday, my co-workers and I walk to the village for a few beers. We feel like a family. Some young women are quite friendly with me, particularly a waitress who is always saying to me:

"I want nothing more than your dark eyes and black curly hair!"

Flattered as I may be, I am pining for Mary, the young ironer. I consider my options and take decisions. I do not dare take action myself so I ask Nikitas to speak to her mother on my behalf. Her mother, who is a woman of very few words, comes to see me.

"So you want to marry Mary?" she asks and I shake my head, feeling startled and certain that the big moment has arrived.

"It would be a shame, if you ruined your life on such a woman," she continues, and now I am even more startled.

"But she is your daughter..."

"Yes, and that's how I know... Do yourself a favour and look for someone better; she wouldn't make a good wife for you."

Her answer was sharp and to the point, but since I have not understood what she meant by all that, I am miserable. There's no consoling me. One night, while singing cheerfully on our way back to the school after a few beers at the village, we notice that Mary is missing. We start looking for her.

"Mary! Mary!"

After a great deal fuss, her mother speaks up:

"Stop calling her! Let her go wherever the hell she wants to go, and with whomever..."

Suddenly the picture starts to become clear to me. When we are back at the school, I stay up waiting for Mary, so I can confirm my suspicions. Close to dawn I see her returning with a tall man. Although I finally understand what her mother meant and I appreciate her honesty, my heart is broken all the same. I never set foot in the laundry room again.

As the end-of-the-school-year events draw near, I obtain Mrs. Plenis's permission to compete in the 10,000-metre race with the students. The physical education teacher has no objections but makes it clear that, since I am not a student, I will not be considered in the results. I do not mind. I throw myself into training; I run a distance of 300 metres with the wheelbarrow, which I use to carry snow from the storeroom. There I take a break, remove the thin cork covering, load the wheelbarrow with snow, and run another 300 metres with weight. Good training that makes good use of my daily chores. On the big day I leave the dishes behind and line up with the students for the race. I finish fourth! I take pride in my accomplishment, even if I am omitted from the results and my name is not mentioned anywhere. It does not matter – everyone knows at the school, especially my co-workers and bosses.

At the school closing ceremony, Nikitas, who has his ear to the ground, informs us that Mr. Plenis has sold the school and its grounds to a multimillionaire for $600,000. It will be turned into an asylum for physically challenged children. The regular students depart and, in the following three days, over 500 children arrive. It is inconceivable that so much suffering exists in the world... At Chappaqua Train Station the children with the most severe disabilities are placed in carriages. When they arrive at the school, they are given a bath and taken to their rooms. Many stay there for long periods of time, since they cannot walk at all, like a pretty sixteen-year old girl without legs. My heart bleeds for her!

Valhalla

On the fourth day after the closing of the school, my co-workers and I travel by train to Valhalla, which is approximately 300 miles away, toward New York City. There, a small house is in need of a good cleaning because it will serve as the temporary residence of Mr. and Mrs. Plenis, until their new school is built on the property. Mr. Plenis claims that the school will be ready by September, but we find this hard to believe; we are curious nevertheless. Over the summer months I work at the convalescent home in Chappaqua but visit Valhalla often. Mr. Plenis climbs scaffoldings and gives orders, and construction progresses at lightning speed!

This is due to the building method that he is using: First he pours columns to which he secures wire mesh, creating voids where concrete is poured. I am impressed and fascinated by his method. I enjoy watching the building process and learn a lot about pouring concrete, closed circuit boilers, wiring and electricity. In September, the new school is ready in Valhalla. Valhalla! That name makes an impression on me; it does not sound English. Another employee, who knows more, agrees.

"No, it doesn't sound English; it's Indian.[3] Indians used to live in these parts. This whole area used to belong to them!" he tells me.

At the beginning of the new school year, I leave the convalescent home and start work at the new school. But in the middle of the year, Fanny, the black cook, convinces me to leave. We go into business for ourselves, as partners.

3rd Ave, New York City

The space on 99th Street and 3rd Avenue in New York City is small. It has two rooms behind the kitchen, one for me and one for Fanny. We each contribute $400 and buy some cheap, second-hand tables. We open a small restaurant and serve made-to-order food such as steaks, potatoes and eggs. I work primarily at the front, serving, but also help Fanny in the kitchen. I learn a lot from her! She is a good cook but her specialty is bread; she can bake many types. Fanny also saves everything; nothing is ever wasted, not even the used grease from the frying pan. She collects it and makes soap using lye. Our business is not doing well, however. How do we get out?

Late one night, after Fanny has gone to her room, I am collecting the cash from the register and putting it in my wallet. At that moment one of the two men, who have been standing outside for some time, enters. He sits down and orders something. I smell a

---

3 In fact, the hamlet in question is named after Valhalla, a heavenly abode in Norse mythology.

rat... Fear sets in so I shout his order toward the kitchen to make him think that a cook is back there. Then, taking care not to be noticed, I cook and serve his order. He explodes in anger for no reason, shouting, throwing cutlery and dishes around, yanking the tablecloth. Not knowing how to react I just stand there, and then he suddenly calms down. He approaches me, apologizes, and taps my shoulder in a friendly way. On his way out, he embraces me in remorse. He is barely out the door when I slip my hand into my pocket. What I suspected all along is true: The 'gentleman' was a skilled pickpocket, who stole my wallet and the entire day's earnings with his phoney apologies and embraces. I decide not to chase him because he joins his friend outside. Two against one is not a chance that I am willing to take, especially since they are probably armed and would not think twice about killing me. On the following day Fanny and I dissolve our partnership. I have no hard feelings toward her because she has lost money, too, along with her hard work. Our things are placed in storage since we are not able to sell them.

Back to the employment office recommended by Nikolatzis Ellinas... Since I am now able to read English, I realize that on the walls are sayings, mostly humorous. One reads: "If you want to spit, don't step outside, spit in front of you." Conversing with the man I learn that he is French. He used to a great chef before he opened this employment office for cooks and kitchen boys. The exquisite cakes are his work! The same young woman and another interrupt us – they are his daughters, eighteen and twenty years old. They bring his coffee and shower him with affection. This time I am not anxious; in fact, I enjoy watching their interaction while I wait. When the young women leave, he looks at his papers and sends me to a girl's school in Stanford, Schenectady, near New York.

Schenectady, Stanford

I do the same work as I did for Mrs. Plenis as a kitchen boy, but now the salary is $20 a month instead of $40. The director of the school is nice. He takes notice when he sees me collect the discarded grease and mix it with lye, pour the mixture into moulds where it cools and solidifies, then cut soaps like Fanny used to do. Without having to ask, he raises my salary to $25 per month.

The students like me because, when I pick apples at the nearby orchard, I give them as many as they want, albeit without the director knowing because it's against regulations. The head cook is the only problem – an unbelievable character, with an enormous crooked mouth that nearly touches his ear. As cantankerous as he may be, his wife is doubly so.

"I cleaned the bathroom for my husband, not for you!" she shrills when she sees me coming out of the bathroom one day.

I apologize but she only gets angrier and makes a scene. A few days later I wake up from a strange dream, feeling certain that someone has died at the school. The dream is so real that I go down to the kitchen to ask if anyone is ill.

"Yes, the head cook's wife," I am told.

"What did the doctor say?" I ask with concern.

"We don't use doctors. It's against our religion," the head cook replies sternly.

"Even if you were to call a doctor now, it's too late. Your wife is gone," I declare with certainty.

The head cook runs to check on his wife and discovers that she has indeed passed away!

After that incident everyone looks at me strangely and with awe; they think that I possess psychic abilities! I try to convince them that nothing could be further from the truth, that I just had a dream, but they do not believe me.

Being an ordinary human without special powers, one day I faint at work. The director of the school calls a doctor, who comes to examine me in my room. The doctor notices my bank deposit book, picks it up, and starts to leaf through it. Obviously he is more interested in that than in me. He completes his examination and declares that I am gravely ill, claiming that I am consumptive and need to be in a sanatorium. I do not know why I fainted, but I am certain I am not consumptive. I have never spit up blood. I am certain that there is nothing seriously wrong with me but do not contradict the doctor; I keep quiet. As soon as he leaves, I hide my deposit book, get dressed, and return to work. Meanwhile, the doctor is waiting at the back of the school with a car, ready to take me to a sanatorium! Seeing that I am back at work, he becomes quite angry but there is nothing he can do – the director of the school has caught wind of his scheme. He can clearly see that I do not have consumption. The kitchen fills up with students. The girls are concerned about me. "Have I taken ill? Is something wrong?"

"I'm fine... Don't worry, you'll still get your apples!" I assure them, albeit quite moved by their concern.

I need a job for the summer, since the girl's school does not operate during the summer months like the Plenis's. Thanks to Nikolatzis Ellinas, who provided the contact, I return to the French employment agent. This time I declare myself a cook! Why not? Now I am skilled at the art of cooking, speak the language and communicate with ease.

"A cook?" he asks.

"Yes, a cook!"

The agent has no objections and immediately places an address in my hand.

Cook – Lower Bay, Hoffman Island

Cook at Lower Bay, Hoffman Island, one of the quarantine islands for new immigrants. The island may be small, one kilometer in diameter, but has all essential amenities, which are not few, in buildings that are up to four storeys high. There are four kitchens: one for doctors and nurses, one for staff, one for immigrants, and one for the young children of the immigrants. I am hired as the

cook and manager of the staff kitchen, with an Irish man as my assistant. The kitchen is spacious even though it's a semi-basement.
The job is not hard, and everyone is amiable and good-natured.
There are no particular difficulties. The immigrants never stay
long; they stop at the island for medical examinations and depart.
The ships that bring them always have gifts for us, mainly whiskey,
which vanishes in the blink of an eye. I do not drink but everyone
else does. However, when they bring mastic from Chios, the chief
physician gives it to me.

"For you, because it's from your part of the world!" he says and
this gives me great satisfaction.

When we are not working, my Irish assistant and I spend time
together. The man loves to bet! When I claim that I am a fast run-
ner, we bet $25 for ten laps around the island – 10 kilometers in
36 minutes. When the others learn of our wager, they take interest – it offers a break from our comfortable but predictable
routine. The chief physician acts as a referee. Watch in hand, he
signals for me to start. After the hardships of my youth and the
hunger of the first months in America, I now enjoy good living
conditions and a rich, healthy diet. At twenty-three, I am lean and
light as the wind, yet strong and healthy. I finish the 10 kilometers
in 33 minutes and, while my Irish friend is vexed about losing, my
competitive spirit soars.

"Do you know how to swim?" he asks while we gaze at the
water.

"Yes, I do!"

"How well?"

"I can swim from here to Brooklyn!" I brag.

"Come on!" he says in disbelief.

"Wanna bet?"

Of course he does! We place the wager and I lose. I give him
back the $25, but we bet another $25 for a distance of approximately 5 kilometers. I ask for a week to train and he agrees. Next
day at 3PM, as soon as I get off work, I head to the water for my

first training session. Yet, what I had no way of knowing is that there are strong currents in this area that pull you in the opposite direction. I fight the currents for hours until nighttime, when they finally come looking for me.

"Where's the Cypriot?"

Since some of my co-workers know that I went to train, they decide to take a boat out to look for me. Unfortunately a rope becomes tangled in the engine and the boat won't start! They shout out to me but I cannot hear them. In desperation, they throw life buoys and lumber into the water, hoping that the currents will carry them to me, but I do not see them. The chief physician jumps in; I hear him calling out to me, but he is no match for the currents. A lobster boat provides assistance and I am finally pulled out of the water, completely exhausted at 11PM. But the doctor is still calling out for help...

"There's someone else in the water!" I hear someone say on the boat.

The captain loses his temper.

"Are we going to be fishing people tonight instead of lobsters? Throw him a line and he can follow us!" he orders.

"Please, pull him on board. That's Hoffman Island's chief physician!" I manage to say before I faint.

I recall nothing more because it took me two days to recover. The chief physician had two nurses looking after me. I feel such gratitude that, as soon as I am back on my feet, I spend $8 on a lovely pipe, which I bring to him as a gift. No more wagers but also no more carefree time because big trouble docks at the island.

Cholera

Summer 1911: The Austrian ship Duke D'Ambrose and the Italian Moltke carry cholera. Instead of undergoing the usual medical examinations and departing, 7,500 people disembark and the island is placed under quarantine. No one is allowed to come or go – neither man nor bird, neither immigrant nor doctor, neither nurse nor staff member! The disease must be defeated at all costs. First they set fire to anything on the two ships that will burn: furniture, mattresses, curtains, doors, windows. Plumes of smoke rise up for days, while the two ships remain docked next to each other with their doors and portholes gaping – dark holes square or round, holes of all shapes and sizes. Everything is burned as a precaution. For our protection there is only garlic. First thing in the morning we rub our bodies with it; at meals we eat as much as we can and always wear gloves. Yet, week after week, instead of subsiding, the disease spreads. Every day people suddenly feel unwell; they start to shiver and shake, their complexions turn greenish then blue-black, and they become afflicted with diarrhoea. We rarely witness the final stages of the disease because the nurses swiftly transport those patients to Swinburne Island. No one returns from there; I do not even know where the dead are buried. We lose 30-40 people each day – immigrants who left Europe with dreams of a better life come face to face with death at America's doorstep. They waste away with shivers and diarrhoea on a rock island, before setting foot in the country that they believed to be a paradise. Many desperate souls jump in the water – some to drown themselves, some in the hope of swimming to the shore of their dreams but, unaware of the currents, also end up drowning. And some are no longer interested in paradise, in America, or anything at all… A mother from Crete loses her three daughters almost at the same time: nine, twelve and sixteen years old. Her heart is breaking but the woman does not utter a sound. She simply jumps from the tallest balcony, killing herself. I set down the basket with the bread that I am carrying into the kitchen to see what has become of the unfortunate woman. I watch as they collect her remains, the remains of the only person in her family that did not die of cholera! And cholera makes no exceptions… It strikes the staff, too. Two doctors and six nurses perish. Everyone wants to get off the island, especially the nurses, but quarantine is strict. Kitchen staff are decimated, the four kitchens merge into one, and I, the only cook untouched by the disease, am put in charge. I am tasked with preparing meals for 7,500 people! An impossible feat but ships deliver all the necessary provisions and the meat pre-cut, which I cook in large steam pots. Three hundred immigrants from Crete are assigned to me as assistants. They work very hard, thank God! And we organize ourselves quite well: Cards pinned on the immigrants' lapels show the three meals that they are entitled to each day. Upon their entrance into the dining room, the corresponding meal is marked on their cards so they cannot re-enter. Portions are measured if not parsimonious, since they are provided by the company which has brought the immigrants. One day a Cretan, who is still wearing his island's characteristic head-wrap, takes me into the semi-basement dining room, where tables are already set with bread at each setting.

"What is it?" I ask.

"You'll see…" he replies.

We lie in wait until five sticks with sharp ends descend from the skylights. They fish around blindly at first but, in a few moments, pieces of bread are dexterously airlifted. This is the work of Italians who, accustomed to larger rations of bread, have found a way to supplement.

"Now I understand why we never have enough bread," I say, shaking my head.

"Don't worry, we'll teach them a lesson!" the Cretan says before rushing out.

The lesson is taught with brute force. After the beating, the theft of the bread stops. Yet, big trouble starts elsewhere: Greek immigrants immerse themselves in the Bible, chanting and making improvised entreaties to Jesus and Mother Mary for salvation. Some Italians mock them, blood boils in the two hot-tempered Mediterranean races, and a huge brawl breaks out! The alarm sounds on the island, a military ship docks, sailors disembark and separate the two groups, albeit with great difficulty. While all this is going on I am working in the kitchen and can only hear the mayhem — profanities in Greek, Italian and English. I want to go outside to watch but I am tasked with preparing food for so many people. No matter how much help I receive from the Cretans, the responsibility falls on my shoulders and this is not an easy undertaking. At mealtime, everyone comes into the dining room silent, battered and bruised. They throw themselves into their food. I seize the opportunity to go outside and find myself before a true battleground. While the nurses collect the seriously wounded, the profanities are replaced by groans of pain in as many languages!

Cholera persists all summer, almost two months. There seems to be no end to the misery. When asked to investigate, a German scientist discovers that the island's septic system is connected with its fresh water supply, finally providing an explanation as to why the disease does not subside. A small detail that has cost so many lives... So many people have died for no reason! At last they also find a way to determine which people have contracted cholera using stool sample analysis. The healthy remain on the island and the sick are moved away. Eventually the island is free of cholera but the blame falls on the chief physician, who is dragged into court. After a summer of unimaginable hardship, instead of thanking the man, they bury him! My heart is in pieces from all that my eyes have seen — how could so much suffering fit into such a small space? During the ordeal I never thought of leaving like the rest of the staff. Every morning I rubbed myself with garlic and immediately got to work. Something deep inside me assured me that I would not perish on this island, that it was not my time. Now that the quarantine has been lifted, feeling at ease and having less work, I can't stand being here anymore. I look for work elsewhere.

Times Squares, New York City

Back to the familiar French agent and this time I land a job at the

heart of New York City, at Times Square Hotel, as cook/fryer for
$110 a month. The kitchens are located two storeys below ground
and I fry from 6AM to 8PM, sometimes even later: I work 14 to
16 hour shifts in insufferable heat. I get so drenched in sweat that
I have to remove my shirt, wring it, and wear it again. I make sure
to drink the beer and cognac that they are obligated to provide to
cooks, otherwise I would perish from dehydration. When I get off
work I go up to Times Square where, in winter, the temperature
falls to approximately -10 degrees Celsius. After I step out into
the freezing cold drenched in sweat, I have to travel to my rented
room, which is not nearby. Do I have blessings from Cyprus that
prevent me from catching my death? I don't know, perhaps! Conditions are terrible in all New York kitchens; no one is happy. Our
union, to which we pay $2 per month in dues, decides to strike to
demand improved conditions and better pay. The day is set and,
at the hotel where I work, everyone observes the strike except an
Austrian cook. When he attempts to start work, a Greek hits him
so hard that he tumbles down a flight of stairs. I leave the frying
pans; I am in a rush to get to ground level not only because of the
strike but because I am anxious to buy "Atlantis."[4] I open it immediately and read the latest news. It's autumn of 1912 and the Balkan Wars are underway. I am engrossed, fired up and, because of
the strike, have time to follow the developments closely. I devour
every piece of news about the alliances that Greece is forming
with Montenegro, Serbia and Bulgaria against Turkey, about the
Cretan representatives that go to the Greek parliament, about the
victorious battle at Sarantoporo, about Constantine – the succes-
sor to the throne – who, as commander-in-chief of the Hellenic
Army, marches on Turkish-occupied soil and enters victorious
into Thessaloniki. Long live Hellas!

But our strike in New York is anything but victorious; employ-

---

4 "Atlantis" (1894-1973) was a Greek-language daily newspaper, which was
published in New York City with national distribution.

ers catch wind of the union's plans – someone must have squealed – and bring staff in from California. We are all terminated: 300,000 cooks, assistant cooks and kitchen boys huddled outside employment offices, and all the jobs are taken.

A Period of Rest

I get a job as a cook at the home of a wealthy Jewish family. I am alone in the kitchen but that is not the problem... The lady of the house gives me one egg with which to make consommé

"I can't make consommé with one egg, Madam!" I respond, as I pick up the knife to cut some butter.

Her eyes nearly bulge out of her head! She grabs the knife, runs outside and sticks it into the ground.

"Don't ever do that again!" she warns sternly.

I manage, albeit with great difficulty, to prepare dinner with the miserly ingredients that she provides.

Late at night, as I am cleaning the kitchen, she comes in to supervise, concerned that I may eat some of the leftovers. I take great offense to this. While I wash the pots and pans I feel so miserable that I quit in the morning, without even asking for payment.

Someone offers me a job as a fryer with a salary of $90 per month.

"It's not a fryer that you want but a dishwasher," I reply and turn down the job.

I have enough money in my bank account, I know the language and the art of cooking; this time I do not panic, moreover, my living expenses are minimal. I am focused on the Balkan Wars and on what my namesake Constantine is doing. I admire his achievements; I admire him! Beyond what I spend on newspapers, I buy a 25¢ standing room ticket for the Hippodrome Theatre. What a spectacle! The acts are truly extraordinary; in the blink of an eye,

the stage is transformed to the bottom of the sea where mer-
maids swim. How do they hold their breath under water for so
long? I notice that they breathe through special tubes; even so,
they are quite remarkable... I am mesmerized! I keep looking for
work because, as time passes, I get tired of having nothing to do.
So I take a job as a dishwasher for $25 a month. It's better than
nothing.

West Point Military Academy

I stay there until, through a different employment agency, I get
a job at West Point Military Academy, next to the Hudson River.
The grounds are impressive. A beautiful garden, tall trees, training grounds, and three statues at the main entrance: Lafayette,
Washington, and the Pole Kościuszko. There are 900 officers-in-
training here, including many Japanese and the future President of
the United States, Dwight Eisenhower. There are approximately
a dozen cooks in the kitchen, but I am hired as an assistant, in
charge of vegetables. The kitchen sparkles since the chef insists on
having it mopped twice a day! Various events are held at the Academy in the summer and, as a result, countless guests come and go.
When the adjacent hotel fills up, I am given responsibilities as a
cook there. I am pleased to be back at my regular job, which I now
consider my career, but my joy is short-lived. A pan filled with
grease slips out of my hands and spills onto a lit stove. I throw
it as far as I can, but the spilled grease flares up, fire spreads in a
flash, sending everyone into panic. Some break their legs leaping
outside, including two cadets. Not only is the kitchen completely
destroyed, but also fourteen hotel rooms! This is the first time
that I have had an accident so I am gripped by fear.

"I don't want any of you saying who was responsible for the
fire, okay?" the German chef orders.

Before long, the fire marshal has all us stand in a row.

"Costas Charalambou... Costas Charalambou...." he calls out.

I step out of the line. My heart is pounding but he taps me on the shoulder in a friendly way.

"Don't be afraid. Just tell us what happened," he says very kindly.

I tell him the truth, which I also repeat to the representative of the insurance company. Despite their graciousness and that no measures are taken against me, my fear turns to guilt. I do not get fired but their kindness is killing me: What happened is my fault! And a co-worker compounds the issue:

"Do you know who told the fire marshal? The German chef, who ordered us to keep quiet... He wanted to report it himself. He thought they would give him a medal!" he tells me in confidence.

Was the chef two-faced or was he trying to avoid confusion by stopping people from giving their versions of events? This I will never know but suffer terribly knowing that I caused so much damage, even unintentionally. I am so distraught in fact that there are moments when I want to throw myself in the river and end it all. I simply cannot bear it! Since they don't fire me, I leave on my own.

Catskill Mountains

Since the summer is not over yet, I take a job for one month at a resort hotel on the Catskill Mountains. Nature is lovely there and the area is full of wild strawberries and wild rabbits. Whereas other employees set traps, catch rabbits and amuse themselves, I am fascinated by the construction of New York's new water mains – enormous pipes, so massive that trucks can drive inside. The beauty of the place consoles me; eventually I calm down and find myself again.

Casey, Scranton, Pennsylvania

With the summer over, the resort hotel closes and I return to New York City where I fall ill. The French agent calls me about a job so I go to the office with his cakes and daughters, who are fawning over him as always. I take his letter of reference for a job at Casey in Scranton, Pennsylvania. I gather my belongings and head to the train station. Work there will be regular and full-time – I am so happy that I forget my illness. What illness? I march into the kitchen, where I cook for parties of 600 to 800 people. I am working as a fryer but want to look at the menus even if my co-workers, mostly Italians, intentionally keep them from me. Not taking no for an answer, I look at the written menu that the chef delivers each day. I compare it to the day's dishes and quickly learn what's what. First I learn to prepare the dishes that are my specialty, the fried foods, and then I learn dishes of other specialties. I am happy and begin to have confidence in myself, but it costs me dearly. One day I have to prepare kippered herring – fish poached in milk – but the butcher, an Austrian man, delivers the fish quite late. I become angry!

"I said kippered herring!" I repeat sternly and glance crossly at him.

The Austrian ambushes me after work. He beats me so badly that it takes me three days to recover. I leave!

Atlanta

I find myself in Atlanta at the Dennis Hotel, the largest hotel in the United States with 2,500 rooms and 62 cooks in its kitchens, not including assistants. The executive chef is excellent. And I, an experienced cook, have no complaints. I am twenty-five years old, with a nice sum of money in my bank account, but I am not here to stay. Beyond stirring me up emotionally, the Balkan Wars have fired up my nostalgia. I add things up again and again: I paid back my father before he passed away three years ago and sent £30 to my sister Milia so she can get married. The time has come for me to settle down in Cyprus. And now I can do it! I can use my savings to start something in Kyrenia that will generate income. That way I can get married, have children, and live in my homeland! It is my destiny and my duty, as well as the destiny of every man on this earth: first for himself and then for his country!

CHAPTER 8

THE FIRST RETURN TO CYPRUS

Kyrenia, 1913-1914

Temptation in Alexandria

After six years in America my savings are just over $1,000. I take most of it in a bank draft, along with a few large and impressive $5 and $20 gold coins. I do not have much to do in terms of departure preparations. My clothing consists of three suits and a few undergarments. I buy a new hunting rifle from Macy's on behalf of someone in Cyprus. I sail at the end of 1913 – first stop Le Havre. I cross France by train and arrive in Marseilles, where I encounter the only difficulty of the journey. I am forced to wait there for ten days before I find a ship. My next stop is Alexandria, where I have to wait for the ship to Cyprus again. Early afternoon I am sitting at a Greek coffee shop, feeling rather dismayed, because I am having difficulty obtaining the required certificate from the Patriarchate for the rifle that I am carrying. Two compatriots approach me and introduce themselves; we start to chat.

"Are you coming from America?"

"Yes!"

"Where are you heading?"

"I'm going home to Cyprus to settle down."

"You're waiting for the ship then? Tomorrow…?"

"Yes, tomorrow."

The conversation is quite pleasant. Having been away from home for so long, I open up to them. I treat them to food and drinks, and they promise to help me obtain the certificate for the rifle. They ask to borrow £5 and I unreservedly lend them the money. When the conversation turns to more personal topics, one of them proposes:

"Would you fancy a woman tonight, someone pretty? The three of us can go to a good house, a place we know... What do you say?"

I say "yes" and we agree to meet at the same coffee shop early that evening. They leave and the waitress comes to clear the table. As she wipes it down she leans close to me, much closer than necessary.

"Don't go," she whispers. "They're planning to rob you!"

I am stunned but, by the time I get a hold of myself, the waitress has already left. She returns in a while but keeps her eyes on the door.

"You should leave immediately. Go to your hotel, lock the door, and stay there until it's time to depart. Where are you staying?"

I give her the name of my hotel. I want to find out more but she leaves and, no matter how long I wait, she does not approach me again. The wheels in my head start to turn... I recall the story of the three brothers who, like me, were repatriating to Cyprus with all their savings. At a port of call in Italy a conman lured them with merriment and women and stole their savings. They were forced to return to America to start slaving for money again. Feeling suspicious now, I decide to heed the waitress's admonition. A knock at my door late at night... I open nervously and see the woman from the coffee shop; she looks frightened again.

"I came to see if you arrived safely, and whether you went with them," she explains.

"I followed your advice."

"Thank God! Those two would not think twice about..."

"Thank you the warning."

"Don't mention it. Goodnight!"

"Please wait..."

I offer her money but she refuses it.

"I didn't do it for money. I did it because I feel awful seeing them rob people's hard-earned savings. Goodnight," she says and leaves, accepting no compensation for her good deed.

An Attempt to Settle Down

In Cyprus our small family property has been divided amongst my siblings, who are all married now. My eldest sister Polyxeni, who is married to the builder Argyros, still lives in her husband's house in Pano Kenynia. Glioris married Eleni from Kazafani. Milia married Karangiaouris, the carriage driver, and lives in Pano Kerynia. Styliani lives in Kazafani with her husband Hadjisophos. My youngest sister Eleni married Kemmames and lives in the same village, as does Parashiefkou, our half-sister from our father's first marriage. Antonis and his wife, Mariannou from Dikomo, live in our paternal home. My share of the family inheritance is a small piece of land in Karakoumi, next to the sea. I make the decision to stay at Hotel Akteo, which is rented to Panayiotis Theodoulou, a man who loves his work. Using thatch partitions covered with thick layers of gypsum, he has divided the large rooms on the upper floor into small but clean bedrooms. Downstairs he serves good food; he is a skilled cook! Certainly this is not a hotel like the ones in America, but I am not fussy. My main concern is what business I should start up in Kyrenia. Kyrenia has not changed while I was away; in fact, it's even more slow and quiet now. The arguments over who will be Archbishop have ended because Kyrillatsos was elected. Kyrilloudi is still the Metropolitan of Kyrenia, with his seat at Ayios Panteleimon Monastery in Myrtou. He travels with a mule to all villages in his district – from Morfou to Palechori, to Kyrenia and farther east, all the way to Kalogrea. Christodoulos Fieros, who is married to my godmother Polyxeni, the daughter of the first notable the late Hadjiglioris, is now mayor. Neocles Loizou from Gabon, who is married to Kyriakos Lordos's daughter Myrianthi, has opened a new general store across from Kamouza. He bought the property from Houstoun.[1] He is doing well, not because of the store, which is not earning much, but from the farmland in his wife's dowry. The only new building of note is the Severios School for Boys, built with a donation from the moneylender Severis. It is located on a hill just outside Kyrenia, on the west side of the Koronos River. Although the school no longer moves from year to year, students from Karakoumi still walk there like I used to do. Karakoumi is smaller; its population has been reduced to forty residents. There are few new houses in Kyrenia – only the ones that Kyriakos Lordos is building for his five daughters, all in a row on the road to Lapithos, and what my father's friend, Stavris Vottis, is struggling to build for his children on the west side of the Koronos River, near the sea. A carpenter by trade, he carries the stones to the construction site himself and builds very slowly. The first house is located near the sea, at the mouth of the river; the second is further up, and the third is on the Karavas-Lapithos road. The latter belongs to his eldest, Yiannis, who wants to change his last name from Vottis to Votsis, because he greatly admires Lt. Nikolaos Votsis, who sank the Turkish ship Feth-i Bülend with his torpedo boat during the Balkan Wars. The Balkan Wars may be over but everyone still talks about them. They say that now that Crete has been annexed to Greece, it is Cyprus's turn to do the same! Yet I see clearly that the British still hold the island tightly in their grip, despite all the shouting in Cypriot newspapers. Only "Rayias," Kyrenia's paper, is silent. I learn that it is defunct and that even the home of its owner and editor-in-chief, my first teacher Georgios Stavrides, is on the auc-

---

1   George Ludovic Houstoun came to Cyprus during the first years of British rule. He came to love Kerynia, bought a great deal of land there, and later settled permanently in a lovely home. He was born in Johnstone, Scotland, and owned shares in mining. He was considered eccentric but cared about Kyrenia, helping both the place and its people. He was the town's first British resident.

tion block, due to the interest on the fine imposed on him by the British in 1906.

I reconnect with old schoolmates and friends. I recount my tales of America, and they recount theirs – anything from politics to romance, how they are faring with the opposite sex. Late one night, Stavris, the son of Captain Ttooulos, and I are out for a walk.

"Do you see that window? If I whistle, Nikolis Aroureos's daughter will come out. She's waiting for me!" he brags.

Since I do not believe him, he whistles. The window opens indeed and the young woman inside nods affirmatively! Stavris leaves and I am astounded: *Do such things really happen in Kyrenia? Young women willingly having rendezvous with men...?* The fact is that it is still difficult to even look at women; only at weddings can one catch a glimpse. Intending to do just that, I go to a wedding in Bellapais with some friends: Panayis Hadjiyiasemis, Lellos Poeros and Christodoulos, who was raised by Captain Petroulios. Christodoulos is going to the wedding specifically for Eleni, Stavros Vottis's youngest daughter, who is around twelve or thirteen years old and has very dark eyes. He is really sweet on her but learns, at the wedding, that her father has regretted marrying her sister Styliani to Costas Adamou from Bellapais too young. Since he will not repeat the same mistake with Eleni, he is not likely to consent to an engagement. Christodoulos is distraught; his plans to marry are dashed. But I make no such plans. Once I have set up a business and secured my future, I will think about marriage and the rest. In the meantime, the burning question remains unanswered: *What line of business should I become involved with?*

I discuss the matter with Neocles Loizou and he introduces me to Efstathios, who is married to Loukas's daughter, Sevasti. Efstathios is a confectioner; he has a shop just up from Akteon, almost directly across the market. He learned the confectionary art in Egypt. He has bought all the necessary equipment but lacks the capital to start his business. I am cautious because I do not place much faith in what Neocles is telling me. I look to Pavlos Hadji-costis for a second opinion, a man whom my father has directed me to trust. Pavlos Hadjicostis confirms that Efstathios is indeed a skilled confectioner. No one knows how to make koufeta[2] in Cyprus; such products are imported from Smyrna by ship. I make my decision! I take the bank draft for $1,000 to the Ottoman Bank in Nicosia. The teller opens the bank vault, takes out the equivalent amount in golden liras, and weighs them while I watch.

"The weight in gold is accurate," he says, trying to prove to me that the liras were counted correctly, £1 for each $5.

He places the liras in a satchel and hands them to me. I am stirred; this is the first time that I have had so much gold in my hands! On the carriage ride back to Kyrenia I make plans for the business. The next day I find a lawyer to prepare my agreement with Efstathios. I will pay £130 for the equipment and buy the ingredients, and he will contribute his expertise to our venture. We will make koufeta. We agree on a £50 penalty in the event that either partner changes his mind and wishes to dissolve the partnership. The agreement is signed, and I rent a room directly across from the shop, at the house of Nikolis Kotsinos. I go to Akteon, settle my bill, and move my belongings.

The next day we start organizing the business. I buy ten sacks of sugar in clumps for three grosia less three paras per oka from Neocles Loizou. When I hear that there is a shipment of almonds from the East for sale at the port, I rush there and buy it for five grosia per oka. Then I find a woman to shell the almonds. I carry all the ingredients to the shop and secure them. At night, tired but tranquil, I sleep in my rented room feeling certain that my time has arrived: I have finally settled down in my homeland and found peace and tranquillity.

---

2   Koufeta (Greek: κουφέτα): Bead-like candy, also known as Jordan almonds, a form of dragée; they consist of almonds, which are coated with a hard outer shell made of sugar in various pastel colours. They are often used as wedding favours.

As it turns out, I have found neither peace nor tranquillity! Malietzis, the tax collector, comes to the shop to take possession of its contents in order to settle Efstathios's outstanding taxes.

"Everything in this shop belongs to me," I inform him.

He takes me to court and, when I present the legal documents, the judge rules in my favour. Efstathios is indeed a good confectioner. He makes koufeta with almonds, koufeta with syrup at the centre, koufeta with orange with a piece of orange peel, even sweet-smelling tiny ones with anise, with one seed in each. Our production also includes salted chickpeas, which we sell to children on Sundays; we even make first-rate Cyprus delights. Orders quickly roll in from all across Cyprus, even from as far away as Paphos. I personally call on prospective customers with samples and collect orders. I return to Kyrenia, prepare some attractive packaging, and begin shipping orders to their destinations by carriage. In Larnaca, right in front of us, the shop owner claims that our koufeta are imported from Smyrna – they are that tasty and attractive!

The more the business becomes settled, however, the more Efstathios becomes unsettled. He starts making a fuss about the price, insisting that we sell our koufeta for 32 grosia per oka. I go over our production costs: He puts 2½ okas of sugar and one oka of almonds into the machine, which brings the ingredient costs alone to 25 grosia, and that's not taking into account the cost of the labour of the woman who shells the almonds. Since our production cost is 32 grosia, he is essentially insisting that we sell at a loss. I propose a compromise: If he added one more oka of sugar into the machine, we could afford to sell at 32 grosia per oka. He agrees and we fill an order for Kasoulis, who has a grocery store in Pano Kyrenia. Since the order is quite large, now that I have enough of a profit margin, I give the client a discount. The man is so pleased that he thanks us repeatedly.

"See, now the customers are happy and we're also making a profit!" I say with excitement to Efstathios.

Instead of being pleased, not only does Efstathios return to the previous unprofitable measures of sugar and almonds, but also stops working the machines on a regular basis. The orders are late and I have a problem... Eventually I realize that he is intentionally messing with me, trying to force me to dissolve the partnership. His goal is to collect the £50 penalty. I hear that he owes money to Neocles Loizou, who has been pressuring him to settle his debt. Yet I show patience not only toward my partner, but also toward all those whose pettiness vexes me.

Solomonides the suvar[3] puts on auction a piece of land in Kazafani that belongs to my sister Eleni. She owes him £8 for purchases from Leptos's shop, in which he is a partner. Not wanting to see my sister's land end up in foreign hands, I attend the auction. Solomonides gives me a dirty look; he is certainly not happy to see me there. He was hoping that no one would be interested, so he could buy the land at half price.

"Come on bid on it, boy, let's see what you've got!" he says to me with irony.

I do not respond. I bid on the land but Hadjipetris, the tax collector, offers more and wins it in the end. For £8 my sister has lost one of her best parcels of land, without having bought £8 worth of goods from the store. The debt swelled because Solomonides charges interest on top of interest. A hard pill to swallow but, again, I show patience.

I am also patient with Tirnavos, the attendant at the tithe storehouses. Tirnavos is not his real name but everyone calls him that because he has a huge nose. He has made an arrangement with Efstathios to have lunch at the shop every day for half a shilling. Sevasti, Efstathios's wife, prepares the food. Tirnavos is polite and friendly toward me until the day he proposes that I marry one of his three daughters. Preoccupied as I am with the problems at the shop and with Efstathios's behaviour, I respond very courteously that I have no intention of getting married before my business is

---

3 Suvar: A mounted police officer.

secure. He takes this rather badly; from that point forward, he is always grimacing and being as testy as possible with me. One day Sevasti is late with his meal and, since I am preparing an urgent order for shipment to Paphos, I do not set the table for him. When he arrives at the shop and sees that his lunch is not ready, he storms off, only to return in a while, wiping his mouth.

"Now you can pay Costantis's restaurant next door where I've had my lunch!" he says to me.

I am furious!

"You think that for the half shilling you that give Efstathios I am obligated to serve you? Here's your lunch! Sevasti has brought it. If you had waited a few minutes, you would have eaten here."

Tirnavos storms off again, mumbling threats. Efstathios arrives. I tell him what happened, taking the opportunity to let him know that orders need to be filled as soon as possible. Making a big show of it, he brusquely shuts off the fire under one of the machines.

"I know what you're after! You want to learn my art but you've got another thing coming, because I'm not showing you a damn thing!"

I bite my tongue. Feeling disgusted, so disgusted that I cannot utter one word, I walk out of the shop with the packages, which are ready for shipment to Paphos. Tirnavos on the one hand and Solomonides on the other and, worse of all, my partner Efstathios... It is plain to see that Efstathios is provoking me so that I will dissolve the partnership; that way he will collect the £50 penalty with which he can settle his debt to Neocles Loizou. For £50 he has ruined a sure and profitable business, never mind that he has annoyed me to death. I simply cannot take any more pettiness, any more disrespect and dishonesty for £50! After all, £50 is approximately $250, two months salary for me in America. Not much! It's not I but he who has come out the loser in this situation because he will never get ahead in life with his mindset. I make my decision. I will dissolve the partnership and leave, if possible, on the same day!

When I return to the shop I make the announcement. Efstathios agrees. I pay his debt to Neocles from the £50, he buys sugar, and we fill the outstanding orders for 2 grosia per oka. We fill them at a loss but it's better than not filling them at all. I do not bemoan the fact that Efstathios does not have the money to pay me back for the equipment. I know that he is bankrupt because of his attitude and refuse to waste another minute. Since I have already made up my mind to leave, I want to leave as quickly as possible. Efstathios agrees to a hypothecation of the equipment and to repay me as soon as he can. I draft a proxy in the name of Pavlos Hadjicostis so that he can collect the payment from Efstathios on my behalf. Since the man had been in my father's confidence, I feel that I can also trust him. I leave the land that I inherited in the care of my brother Glioris, who is a ploughman. That way he can cultivate it so that it does not become overgrown, thereby giving the British the opportunity to seize it. I am ready to depart for America on the same day that I made the decision to do so!

CHAPTER 9

THE RETURN TO AMERICA

USA, 1914-1921

Spring 1914: I am sailing away from Cyprus with Stavris, the son of Captain Ttooulos. I lose a few days in Alexandria while I arrange his passage to Kenya. He has decided to go there for work, since he is no longer able to earn a living in Kerynia from trade and shipping, like his father used to do in the heyday of the commerce with the East.

Fortunately my return journey to America is quick and easy, without the adventures of the first one. I cross the Atlantic on the luxury liner SS Washington, a gorgeous ship, where I meet a pitiful, rag-clad young man – a deserter from the Hellenic Army. He is going to his sister, who – he claims – is married to Polymeris, although I am not sure that I believe him. When we arrive in America, the young man is completely clueless.

"I'll take you to Polymeris, don't worry," I reassure him.

I know of Polymeris; he is a wealthy Greek, who owns mines in Canada and the Athens Hotel across from Grand Central Station on 42nd Street, next to the Belmont Hotel. I recall being fired from the Belmont Hotel in 1907, my first job in America, because I was even more clueless and lost than this young deserter. I first heard of Polymeris when his partner, Drivas, was murdered by gangsters. The story caused a big stir; for days the newspapers were reporting on it, and I read everything that both "Atlantis" and the English language papers published on the subject. When we arrive at the Athens Hotel, Polymeris is not there, but we are given the address of his home – a mansion on Riverside Drive so luxurious that it takes your breath away. For the first time I see how much success a Greek immigrant can attain. The young man is indeed the brother of Polymeris's wife, who welcomes us and treats us to an assortment of sweets on a silver tray! When I get up to leave, she offers me $10 for helping her brother. I do not accept the money; I was happy to help an immigrant entering the chaos of America for the first time. I know how tough it is being in that position. You don't know where to go, you don't know what to do.

Paterson, New Jersey

This time I am not afraid of the chaos; I know exactly where to go and what to do. A visit to the French agent's office with his cakes and daughters, and I get a job as a cook/fryer in Paterson, New Jersey. The United States Hotel is large. The chef is Belgian and two of the four cooks are Greek. Although I am pleased about this, I quickly distance myself from them because they are at odds with the beverage manager, who is the owner's brother. Their fights are frightening. They throw dishes and break empty bottles over each other's heads! I make friends with Samiotis, the owner of the fruit market across the street, the largest in town. On August 13 the European War is declared; they are not calling it a World War yet, because the United States and other countries are not engaged at this time. Samiotis and I discuss the war, which is far away from us. I organize my life and start feeling in control again, more in control now because work conditions for cooks have improved. I have my room. I buy "Atlantis" and read the news. I go to the theatre, which I have always enjoyed. I especially enjoy watching a comedian who, with acrobatics and miming, brings audiences to tears of laughter. His name is Charlie Chaplin...

I get along with the Belgian chef, although he speaks of nothing but the stock market. I am completely in the dark on the subject and, at first, listen without even knowing what the Stock Exchange

is, or how you make and lose money there. When he asks to borrow $100, I give in to my curiosity. I ask and learn: Your first stock
purchase must be a minimum of $100. If you do not have the
funds, you can find a rich partner. If the stock you are buying costs
less than $10 per share, you must pay in cash; if it is more than
$10 per share, you have the option of putting down a deposit of
only 10% and trading with a margin account, otherwise they sell
off the stock and give you whatever is left. If the share price rises,
you can sell your shares at a profit. And you make money without
frying and frying yourself in front of a hot stove for hours – just
like that! Sounds good to me. I am definitely interested!

"Can I go to the Stock Exchange, too?" I ask timidly.

"Sure, anyone can go. Why don't you come have a look?" the
chef tells me. The Stock Exchange is on the same street as the hotel. Although the upstairs is rather small, it has a machine with a
board that displays share prices behind protective glass. I buy one
hundred shares of Cambrian Steel for $5 each, for a total of ap-
proximately $600. I pay only the required 10% deposit. In a few
days the price climbs to $135 per share and expected to go even
higher.

"Sell it!" the Belgian chef advises me.

I sell my shares and make $13,000 without frying or being
fried! Eventually Cambrian Steel stock rises to more than $300
per share. They split each share into ten, and the price rises again.
The reason for this is the instability in the market and the European War. With my earnings I buy $4,000 worth of shares in a
mining company for $1 each and pay cash. Then I return to the
hotel and, as I am changing into my work clothes, I get a call from
the stockbroker. My stock has gone up...

"Sell it," I instruct him.

I return to the Stock Exchange to collect $8,000 of which
$4,000 is pure profit. I have made $25,000 in record time! The
Belgian chef buys stocks in refrigeration companies and also
makes money. He is sweetened by the easy money and so am I! I

start playing the market on a regular basis, buying shares in Mexican oil and in the United States Motor Company.

One day, a shoemaker from Kyrenia called Pikriyiannis shows up at my door. He has come to try his luck in America. He is in the position that I was in when I first landed, no English and no skills. I help him get a job at a biscuit factory. I also buy him a hat and a few other necessities because winter is coming. But he picks up a bad habit: He keeps showing up at the hotel asking me for food. I set aside a few livers and a couple of eggs, signal him, step outside, and give them to him half-heartedly – not because I do not want to help him but because It's against hotel regulations. It's like I am stealing from the boss! I try to explain this to him but he pretends not to understand. At the factory where he is employed workers are allowed to eat as many biscuits as they like. When I ask why he does not fill up there, he says that eating so many biscuits turns his stomach. Pikriyiannis wants a job at the hotel where I work. Beyond that there are no vacancies, he knows nothing about hotel operations and does not speak the language. How can I help him? Impossible! One day, Samiotis holds up a bunch of grapes across the street and motions that I should go over to his shop.

"Hey Cypriot, come get some early grapes. I've brought them from abroad!"

When I go to his shop for my treat, he brings up Pikriyiannis in the conversation.

"What's the story with that compatriot of yours?"

"He's my friend. I'm trying to help him."

"Your friend, Cypriot…? The man does nothing but speak ill of you! He's even told me that you slept in stables in Cyprus and that's why they call you Catsellis.[1] He thought that this would impress me, but I'm not a conceited man. Do you know how much money I had when I set foot in this town? Ten cents! Someone gave me another fifty and I bought some celery. I went around and sold

---

1   The nickname Catsellis is derived from the word "catsella" (Greek: κατσέλλα), which means "cow" in the Cypriot dialect.

it. I bought some more, sold that too, and so on... After a while I got myself a sturdy bench, which I used to display my produce and to sleep on at night. Little by little I started making money. I opened this fruit market, which is now one of the largest and best in the city. With some brains, eagerness and honesty, a man can achieve a lot in this country!"

I greatly admire my friend Samiotis, a man so rich that he buys the German American Bank for $120,000. He is not conceited; on the contrary, he is so kind and considerate that he invites me to spend Christmas at his house so I won't be alone. I am upset about Pikriyiannis but not because I am ashamed of being called "Catsellis" – this doesn't bother me since it was my late father's nickname. In fact, I prefer it to Charalambou because it is unusual and easier to remember; it also serves as a memorial to my father. So I start introducing myself as Catsellis, even if my legal surname is still Charalambou. But the question remains: How do I cut ties with Pikriyiannis, a leech who demands his 'takeout' and expects me to find him a better job, but speaks ill of me all the same? I do not want to confront him. He is a compatriot and I feel sorry for him. So I look for work elsewhere; it's the only solution.

Albany, New York

An employment agency for cooks, not the one that belongs to the French man, sends me to Albany, the capital of New York State, as a cook/fryer. The move proves lucky in many respects. The large restaurant where I work is close to the Capitol Building, which houses the largest Legislative Assembly in the United States. Many members dine regularly at the restaurant. When meetings run late into the night, they order refreshments from us. We send mountains of sandwiches, along with beverages in the summer or coffee in enormous pots in the winter. The kitchen is only three steps below the large dining room so no more basements. The only difficulty I face here is accommodations. I am turned down the moment I mention that I am Greek. Eventually I learn that Mediterranean immigrants, Greeks and Italians in particular, live five or six to a room. No one wants them as tenants because they are noisy and dirty. My new boss phones a woman and gives me a reference. She lets me have a room in her house straightaway. Thank God! Thank God, the boss is also nice. His name is John Keeler and he is around fifty years old. He owns many other businesses beyond the restaurant, mainly real estate, houses and shops that he rents out. His wife is also illustrious; she holds a high-ranking position in Education. Sometimes she eats at the restaurant too. Keeler's office is next to the kitchen. He comes in frequently to supervise and chat with us. Some employees have been there for decades. The one we call "Silverman," because he cleans and polishes the silverware, has been there the longest. The oldest employee is a Dane, who has been cooking roasts in this kitchen for twenty years but does not know how to make an omelette. The boss is quite fond of him; he collects cigar butts from the dining room because he enjoys chewing them. Always overjoyed to receive them, the Dane takes the dish with the cigar butts and bows repeatedly while muttering "Thank you! Thank you!"

I really enjoy watching him; we all do. One time, when the boss brings the dish and the Dane happens to be in the washroom, I hide all butts except one, which I fill with cayenne pepper. When the unsuspecting Dane returns, he puts it in his mouth and starts to chew. His mouth is set on fire!

"That's the son of a bitch who did it," the boss says, pointing at me.

Fortunately my prank does not upset the boss; on the contrary, it compels him to recount more humorous stories and jokes. He tells us that he has discovered a way to stop the stoves from smoking.

"Where does the smoke come out from then?" I ask.

"From the rear ends of the cooks!" he replies and bursts into laughter with the rest of us.

"Do you know why they fired a cross-eyed laundress from the church yesterday?" he continues.

"Why?"

"Because she was eyeing Jesus the wrong way!"

I like that the boss is friendly with me since the only Greek at the restaurant is a waiter from Chios, a nice man. We become fast friends but he takes a job in Washington. When he leaves I am crushed not to have a compatriot close by, so we can talk about familiar things.

The well-groomed, bearded chef is French, Alsatian. He is excellent at his job. When the old roaster retires, he proposes that I replace him.

"I don't know the job. Roasts are not my specialty," I reply.

"Then I order you to learn..." the Alsatian insists.

This is my introduction to this specialty. I quickly learn when the roasts are ready, when they need a little longer and, most importantly, how to slice them into equal portions without waste. I enjoy the change. I watch and learn from cooks of other specialties too, because I do not want to be clueless like the Dane, who only knew how to cook roasts. There are many specialties at the restaurant. Other than the fryer and the roast chef, there is the poissonier in charge of seafood who prepares lobsters and oysters. The garde manger is in charge of cold meats, while the saucier is responsible for all sauces. Since I do not drink alcohol other than what is required to prevent dehydration, I give what's left of my share of beer and whiskey to the sous-chef in exchange for showing me new recipes. At this time cooks and kitchen staff are given a third of a day off per week. The chef asks if I would like to go on rotation, meaning to replace the cook who has time off. I accept because, by now, I am experienced in all specialities. When he asks me to butcher meat however, I freeze up:

"I don't know how... When I accepted I didn't think this was included in my duties," I tell him.

"Do you want to learn?"

"Yes!"

On a Wednesday afternoon, the chef takes me to the meat locker in the basement, which is kept cool with snow from the river. He pulls up a chair, sits down, and points to a whole animal.

"Take that one down," he instructs.

I unhook the animal, place it on the counter, and he shows me how to break it down. Two more Wednesday afternoons are required but, as soon as I know how to break down meat, I go on rotation. I roast one day and fry the next. I prepare sauces or cold dishes, or I am in charge of oysters and lobsters... Before long the chef comes to me with another proposal.

"Instead of rotation would you prefer to go on the night shift and work from 2PM to midnight?"

I have nothing to lose, so I accept. And with this arrangement I have my mornings free. I can relax in bed in the morning, take the newspapers up to my room, and read the latest news from the war. I am interested; I am concerned. Europe is a bloodbath!

Around this time, my landlady's sister — a rather unattractive, unmarried woman around thirty-five — starts to bring me the paper, even strawberries at times. She is very polite with me but when she argues with her sister the filthiest language explodes from her mouth. Fortunately I do not have to listen to this too often because I am hardly ever home; now that I have time, I play the stock market. It is near the restaurant; it occupies the entire ground floor of the Ten Eyck Hotel. Two brothers, who own a large company, ask Ford for $600,000 and the stock exchange is rocked! The more time I spend there, the bigger my stock purchases become. As an indication of how much money I invest, there are times when I owe as much as $76,000 on margin! Meanwhile, at work, the night chef is a difficult man. One day, at 1:30PM, while I am eating lunch before starting my shift, he orders: "Cut steaks!"

I refuse. I do not like being ordered when I am off duty and especially while I am eating. The chef angrily picks up the bench where I am eating and throws it away. The next day he is fired for his conduct and I replace him as night chef. Now I am in charge of all specialties. I enjoy managing the entire kitchen and expect everything to be done correctly. I do not mind that most nights I work past midnight, especially when the Legislative Assembly is in session and I must provide food and beverages. I send them hot coffee in large pots, mountains of sandwiches on huge trays, and that's not including drinks.

It is not always easy managing everything and keeping everyone in line, however; there are times when I run into problems. When a dishwasher decides to fry something for himself, I become angry and toss the pan. Next day, when I come to the restaurant at 1:30PM, I see stacks of unwashed dishes; the dishwashers are refusing to work. John Keeler points to me.

"At night that's the boss in the kitchen. It's up to him whether you can cook special meals for yourselves, or whether he'll even let you get back to work now. If he does not, you can all go home..."

I am startled for a moment; I do not know how to react. In the end I tell the dishwashers that they can get back to work but that they are not allowed to cook for themselves. The boss backs me up again when a checker makes a fuss about a supposedly undersized portion of mushrooms and bacon on toast.

"He's the kitchen manager... I can't do anything," Keeler declares and the checker says nothing more.

Our system in the kitchen is excellent. For every order three tickets are issued: one goes to the guest, one to the checker, one to the cook. The checker lifts up the cloche that the waiter points out, checks the order, and marks it on the waiter's number, so that the manager will know which waiters are selling well.

I get in trouble with the boss only once: Late, close to midnight, a waiter brings me an order for plank steak with an arrogant air about him. It's not that I do not want to make the extra effort, but the cooks are always complaining about staying past midnight. Preparing this steak, which is cooked and served on a special wood plank with its condiments and side dishes, takes time. Never mind the attitude of the waiter who brought the order...

"I'm not making plank steak at this hour!" I tell him.

"But that's what he ordered," the waiter answers, looking rather frightened.

"Well, he can change his order to something more simple, since he's come this late."

Indeed, the guest changes his order to a simple steak, but the next day the boss comes looking for me. He offers me a cigar.

"I don't smoke," I respond.

"What happened last night? Why did you refuse to make the order?"

"The waiter was curt," I respond.

"Oh! And I thought you worked for me, not for the waiter," he objects.

Despite my embarrassment, I manage to present the more serious reasons for my refusal such as the complaints of the cooks, who are forced to stay late, and that plank steak takes time. Keeler smiles.

"Alright, alright! I know you're doing a good job. Take this and every month you'll get more because last night you took care of Governor Smith!" he says and places $10 in my hand.

He seems pleased that, without knowing it, I refused to prepare the difficult dish that the governor had ordered at such a late hour. From this point forward the boss personally delivers my salary, which climbs to $180 per month. But the restaurant is also doing well. On July 4th, on Independence Day, Keeler comes to the kitchen late at night.

"Do you know how much we've done in sales since 2PM when you came on shift? $6,500!" he says with excitement.

Assistance to Compatriots

In the middle of 1916 I receive a telephone call from New York
that new arrivals from home need my help. The restaurant closes
at 1:30AM. After work I jump on the train and at 6AM I arrive
in New York City at the designated address – Pikriyiannis's room!
He is sitting on a miserable-looking chair, while the others are on
the floor: my friend Yiannis Vrahas and his brother Antonis, Alexis
Tsiakkouris, Christodoulos Anayiotos, Savvas Poeros and Evangelos, the son of Yiannis Keperis. With them are also two young
men from Famagusta, one from Larnaca, and one from Nicosia.
Ten on the floor... Christodoulos tells me that he is determined
make enough money so he can return to Cyprus to ask for his
girl's hand in marriage, the dark-eyed thirteen year old; he is still
waiting for her to grow up. Since he has come with a reference, I
help him and Alexis Tsiakkouris get on the train to Messina, near
the Canadian border, where they will work at a foundry. Everyone
else returns to Albany with me. I bring them to the restaurant and
ask the boss to hire them.

"If they're like you, bring them," he tells me.

They work as bussers and assistant servers, clearing plates
from the tables. I do my best to help them learn the job; I feel
responsible for them, especially the younger ones. Antonis Vrahas,
the brother of my friend Yiannis, is inconsolable because he is
away from the girl he wants to marry. My friend, who is engaged
to Cleopatra from Bellapais, is more patient. Most of them do not
stay at the restaurant long; they find better-paying jobs at facto-
ries in Pittsburgh. Sophocles's brother Stavris also arrives around
this time. He claims to have worked as cook at Kyrenia's hospital.
I give him a reference and he is hired as a cook in charge of vegetables but, as it turns out, he does not know much. The kitchen at
Kyrenia's hospital and the one at Keeler's restaurant vastly differ
in terms of quality. Stavris cannot manage. As night chef I am ob-

ligated to come into work early to finish his work, but the Italian cooks complain. Stavris is sacked. Evangelos Keperis, the eighteen year old, stays a little longer. He is smart, a graduate of the fifth grade of the Lapithos Gymnasium. The school does not have a sixth grade and he is inconsolable because his father was too stingy to send him to Nicosia finish his schooling at the Pancyprian Gymnasium. He quickly learns the language. He is not doing too badly; he works as a server and he is fast and hardworking. Bedazzled by America, however, he spends all his time and money at a billiard club, even if he remembers his father saying that "To learn to play billiards, you must buy the table a leg of gold." I try to deter him but, no matter how many times I go to the billiard club and drag him out, he returns. Since the club's owner is Greek, I ask him to ban him from the premises, otherwise the young man will be ruined.

"Although what you're asking for is a loss to me, Cypriot, I promise that he'll never set foot in here again," he assures me.

In the end Evangelos decides to leave. I lend him a suitcase and, as he is packing up his things, I try to impress upon him that he has to do his best to get ahead in life. He nods, assures me that he will return the suitcase, but I never lay eyes on it again, nor do I ever learn what became of him.

The Great Fall

Never mind what became of Evangelos! What will become of me? My own life going to the dogs... The European War has turned everything upside down and, by now, I am playing the stock market obsessively. What is more, I play large. I owe up as much as $75,000 on margin and buy 10,000 rubles for 13¢ each at a loss. With the Battle of Jutland things get even messier. Panic strikes and the Stock Exchange closes! I lose everything. I am left literally penniless. I write to Sophocles and he sends me $300. I play that money and lose it, too. I, who was trying to save Evangelos Keperis from the billiard table, cannot resist the worst form of gambling there is. I have no hope in hell of getting ahead in life; I am ruined. I am in such despair that there are moments when I want to die.

Late, past midnight, when I return to my room after work, the Canadian consular assistant and an officer in the Canadian army are waiting for me.

"Costas Charalambou?"

"Yes."

"Your country is calling you to serve!"

Since I am upset that King Constantine has been deposed, I automatically think of Greece. Greece is calling me? What does Greece have to do with these Canadians?

"Which country is that?" I ask.

"Great Britain, of course. You will serve in the Canadian Armed Forces. The United States and the United Kingdom have agreed that all United Kingdom citizens who live here must enlist in the Canadian army."

Now I am furious!

"I am not a British citizen. My passport clearly states that I am a citizen of Cyprus – a native – and I have no intention of serving England just because Cyprus is under British occupation!" I declare.

The next day two police officers are waiting for me at work; they inform me that I must present myself to the Canadian Armed Forces Draft Center for enlistment. It's three doors down from Keeler's restaurant.

"Okay, I'll go there tomorrow," I tell them.

Early the following morning I go to the draft center. A tall, heavyset Canadian is sitting behind a desk.

"Your country is at war and it is your duty to serve!" he commands.

"I have no intention of serving England!"

"Don't you know that you are a British citizen?" he asks and the same story starts up again.

"No, I am not a British citizen!"

"Are you not aware that Cyprus belongs to the United Kingdom?"

"No, it does not! It was simply rented from the Turks. I am Greek; my passport says that I am Greek Cypriot, a citizen of the Ottoman Empire, and I am only willing to fight for Greece or for America, because this is where I earn my living."

"If you do not enlist within 24 hours you will face the consequences."

"No need to wait 24 hours. Whatever you're going to do to me, do it now," I say and notice someone approaching with a notebook.

"If you were called by the United States, would you enlist?"

"Of course. I would fight for America because it provides my livelihood and for Greece because I am Greek. But I will not fight for England!" I repeat angrily and return to work.

The next day, John Keeler comes to the kitchen: "Is that right? You're not willing to fight for England…"

I ask where he has learnt of this, so he shows me the newspaper.

"It's in the paper! Don't worry, a law is being prepared to prevent the conscription of immigrants working in the United States," he says.

I am pleased, not because I have avoided the draft, but because many Cypriots are forced to go outside the borders of the United States to avoid conscription and have a very tough time of it. As luck would have it, the Canadian officer is having lunch at the restaurant and the boss is in a good mood. Just as I am about to start my shift he comes to the kitchen, pulls me by the arm, and brings me to him.

"Here's the goddamn Greek who's not willing to fight for England but for America!" he tells him.

A Volunteer in the US Army, Maryland

Desperate as I am, calling myself a good-for-nothing for not being able to resist the stock market, I keep thinking about dying. But how? The war is certainly one way... Since I have always associated war with sacrifice and death for the homeland, I prefer it; suicide is not my style. I present myself to the American authorities to enlist as a volunteer and they accept me. I give my friend Yiannis Vrahas and his brother Antonis my two suits and anything useful that I own. I pack up some mementos, three thousand shares of the bankrupt Emma Company in Maine, and ask them to keep them for me. I feel so relieved! My draft call arrives at the beginning of January 1918. At 8AM I am waiting for the train along with all other volunteers. My landlady's sister, the thirty-five-year old, arrives unexpectedly and pulls me out of the line. She kisses me and starts to cry! I am at a loss; it never occurred to me that the strawberries were an indication of her feelings, not that I would have ever gotten involved with her. After some back and forth with her, I board. I sit there watching the overexcited volunteers break windows and destroy seating, doing terrible damage to the train. I am going to war determined to sacrifice myself for the homeland, determined to end my life with dignity for something that is worth dying for...

     Camp Meade, Maryland, and the stern soldiers of the Bayonet Military Police... The neighbouring lands are sandy; it's windy and bitterly cold. They are not organized: For two days we are kept segregated before they finally make arrangements for us. I am placed in the 11th Division, which is named Lafayette, in the special mounted company of the Military Police. The 11th Division has 36,000 soldiers. Two companies form the Military Police with 121 men, including officers but excluding the doctor; Bull is in command. It's a tough life and exactly what is required in my case. At sunrise a high-pitch electronic whistle calls us to rise and

the day starts with an obligatory cold shower. At times it's difficult to get water to run because it is frozen inside the pipes. My
skin is covered with rupturing blisters; I am truly a sorry sight.
The doctor quarantines me for three days and calls another to
examine me. After much deliberation the two doctors come to
the conclusion that the blisters are frost burns caused by the icy
shower. They give me some medication and my skin heals. After
the morning shower we perform Swedish exercises in our undergarments. Breakfast is good, if you ignore the black cloud of flies
that surrounds us. Despite being shooed away, they keep sitting on
our food until we get tired of shooing and just eat them, thereby
ensuring that we have good luck for the day!

The daily grind starts with training with horses, animals so
wild that they make me long for the docile Cypriot horses, mules
and donkeys. Mercifully the exercises are easy in the beginning,
providing you do not lose your cool. We lie down on the ground
in dense rows that are very close to each other while the horses,
off the reins, walk over us. Most are terrified yet the horses do not
step on us, regardless of how little space there may be between
us. Then we take riding lessons: The trainer holds the rein and we
ride around him in circles until we can comfortably rise up from
the saddle, thereby preventing our legs from striking it. Then it's
time for obstacle training. We jump increasingly higher and higher
walls, and the training is so intensive that our inner thighs become
raw. Then come the guns: a revolver at the waist and a long gun
that hangs from our shoulders while we ride. In the end, our backs
are also wrecked from carrying so much rigid weight. And this
is not the end but the beginning! We are also taught to shoot on
horseback.

The sergeant snaps orders at us: "Stand on the side! Ready to
mound! Mound!"

God help you, if you're not in the saddle in time. One time
when I drop my revolver and lose a few moments, the Canadian

sergeant hurls insults at me, the worst of which is "goddamn Italiano." That one I cannot swallow so I lodge a complaint with the day officer.

"First of all, I am not Italian. I am Greek! I came here as a volunteer and I don't like being insulted in this way," I tell him.

The next day the Canadian sergeant is in the second line of riders with his stripes removed.

But the training only gets tougher: We practice standing on the horses with our guns ready to fire, and other such exercises that resemble dangerous circus acts. These are called "monkey drills." If you do not possess the agility of a monkey, you're in big trouble. Never mind that we go without food or water for hours with all our muscles taut to the max – if you are not able to stay focused and alert you can be seriously injured. As we are jumping a tall fence, the Polish rider ahead of me falls from his horse and the animal steps on his face. His jaw is mangled. And I, directly behind him, manage to jump to his side in a very narrow escape! My superiors commend me but the Pole's mouth becomes infected. It smells badly and he is hospitalized. Over the next few days, three men die during monkey drills. After a storm of protests, this difficult part of training is abolished. Yet we have already gone through it and our basic training is finished.

They ask who among the volunteers are not American citizens, and whether they wish to receive their citizenship. Since my arrival in the United States, I applied for citizenship three times but failed the examinations. In depth knowledge of American history and the Constitution is required... I read and learned a lot but it was never enough. Now, all who raise their hands are taken to Headquarters, where they are asked to raise their hands again while an oath of loyalty to the United States is recited. And just like that, it is done! We all walk away with our American citizenship certificates. Thinking back to all the times I was denied this piece of paper, I am delighted. Now that they need me as human filler in the trenches of war, they do not care whether I

KYRENIA'S LEGEND

169

know enough about American history or the Constitution. Costas Charalambou, American citizen! And as a brand new American citizen, I am penalized with four days in prison because, when I passed Headquarters, I forgot to salute the American flag. Regulations are strict and I belong to the Military Police!

We, the men of the Military Police, are assigned duties. We guard certain posts and on Sundays, during visiting hours, we check the gifts that family and friends bring. Not a simple task because they are always trying to smuggle in restricted items in clever ways. For example, we discover entire bottles of whiskey hidden inside innocent cakes. At the end of the first month I find out that we are paid a salary of $39 per month, but where do I spend the money? On Sunday, my friend Yiannis Vrahas and his brother Antonis come to visit. I am very happy to see them so I treat them. I show them my citizenship certificate and pay to have photos taken of us.

Finally orders arrive that our Division prepare for deployment! We are assigned the essentials: a revolver, a rifle, a horse, and a round dog tag made of tin with our names and numbers – this will hang by a sturdy cord from necks. My number is 3743457, a valuable ID should I be wounded or killed in the trenches of Europe. That way they will know who I am! First we are sent to the Medical Office for shots then ordered to run back and forth for some time. The injection hurts and none of us feel well. Some become violently ill and the whole thing turns into a huge disaster. Men drop left and right... They suspect that something was wrong with the vaccines, which may have been sabotaged by the doctors and nurses. Most of them are German Americans, who abhor the fact that we are going to war against Germany. However, this matter is never cleared up because even greater ruin befalls our Division: the Spanish Influenza. Most of us catch it and it is deadly! In the morning I wake up to discover that the men on either side of me have passed away during the night. There are so many deaths that 6,000 soldiers are brought in from California to replace the men we have lost. When we begin to recuperate at last, deployment preparations resume. The section's colonel arrives for an inspection and the officers whom we so fear line up before him – it's their turn to shake in their boots! We take great delight in seeing how much they fear their superiors. In November 1918, just as we are about to ship out, a ceasefire is called! Instead of heading to Europe, the volunteer division is dissolved. I am sorely disappointed. We are told that anyone with a profession can leave first but I keep quiet. I declare "none" because there's still a chance... Although I do not know whether there's any truth to the rumour, I hear that troops are being deployed to Russia to fight next to the White Guardsmen. I also hear that Greece is sending 18,000 troops under Paraskevopoulos's command. Early one morning, they have us stand in line and a young officer orders that all cooks step forward. I stay back, even though I had declared myself a cook when I enlisted.

"Costas Charalambou," the officer calls out, forcing me to step forward.

"Why did you not step forward earlier?" he asks.

"I did not come here to cook but to go to war and fight!" I answer and he smiles.

"The war is over and we should be pleased about that," he says.

He sends me to the kitchen that serves officers and doctors, approximately twenty-five people, and puts me in charge. I burst out in tears when I start to cook because I was not fortunate enough to die for my country! Next to me, an Italian pastry chef, who is beating eggs, is thrilled that the war has ended.

The young officer has two stars and is in charge of the kitchen at Headquarters. He is polite, treats me well, and manages to calm me down. His name is Vanderbilt – he is extremely wealthy, since he inherited his father's fortune when he died in the Titanic. His family owns the largest rail line, which stretches from Washington to California. He is engaged to the daughter of the American consul in England and has applied for a discharge. When he receives his discharge, he is over the moon, so he decides to throw a big farewell party. He comes to see me. I suggest a menu; we prepare a shopping list and I am off to Washington to do the shopping.

I travel first class on the train. The middle-aged man sitting next to me asks why I decided to serve as a volunteer in the United States Army.

"Because America gives me my livelihood," I explain.

He seems pleased with my response. When the train enters Washington he notices that I am looking around with curiosity.

"Is this your first time here?" he asks.

"Yes."

"Where are you heading?"

"First I'm going to see a friend from Chios that works at a hotel…"

He asks for the name of the hotel and, when the train stops, he takes me by the arm.

"Since this is your first time in Washington, I'll take you to the hotel to see your friend."

On the way there, people on the street keep saluting me. Not only am I surprised but also find myself in a tough spot; I am obligated to respond to all military salutes and now I cannot do so because the middle-aged man is still holding my arm. When we arrive at the hotel, we go to the basement to see the timekeeper. He seems quite startled and, after my fellow traveler departs, he asks: "Are you Greek?"

"Yes, I am."

"How do you know him?"

"I don't. I just met him on the train."

"He's one of the most famous senators in the Congress," he says and informs me that my fellow traveller is Senator King!

Now I understand why all those salutes earlier on… I am delighted to see my friend; I do the shopping and return to the camp to cook for Vanderbilt's farewell party, which is a great success. As I am finishing up in the kitchen, the young officer and his fiancée come to thank me.

"Look me up when you get out of the army. I need you!" he says and hands me his card.

The next officer in charge of the kitchen has three stars; he comes in and inspects everything.

"I am in charge now and expect everything to be done right," he declares.

I have a sneaking suspicion that there will be trouble with him. Indeed, his authoritative approach annoys me more with each day's passing.

"You will make waffles today," he orders so forcefully that I can't hold back.

"I don't know how to make waffles!" I respond.

"Then go to the kitchen of the section next door and the cook there will teach you," he insists in the same tone.

Now I am really riled up! All the discontent from the past rises up before me…

"I came here to serve in the army not to learn to cook!"

"You will do as I say!" he insists.

But I dig in my heels…

"I cannot learn to make waffles."

He brings me before a court-martial made up of three judges. At the centre sits the colonel-military judge, a man who knows me well. Fortunately, he does not take the incident seriously because if you are charged, there is no saving you.

"This is what you've brought before us? And if we charge him who's going to cook for us today? Well, what has he done?" he asks.

The officer recounts the incident and the colonel looks at me with a smile.

"Tell me the truth: Do you know how to make waffles?"

His friendly demeanour makes it impossible for me to lie.

"I do."

"So why didn't you make them?"

"Because he ordered me in a very abrupt way."

He shakes his head. "I knew it...When you come down hard on Greeks, they dig in their heels. Go on, make the waffles."

I gladly prepare the waffles but the officer is infuriated that I was not punished for my insubordination. He is really gunning for me now...After everyone else is discharged, first he has me serve the four days in detention for not saluting the flag then take inventory of the kitchen equipment.

I am discharged on November 18, 1918. I receive $60 along with some commemorative medals and photographs. In one photograph, an aerial shot, the men of the 11th Division form the bust of Lafayette. In another photo, all the men of the Military Police are standing in line. One medal is bronze: an eagle with its wings spread out and with the year 1917-1918 above the inscription, "Presented by the City of Albany to C. Charalambou." Another medal depicts a shield on either side of which stand an American in civilian clothing and a Native American. "For Patriotic Service World War – Assiduity" it reads. On another, a winged female figure with rays emanating from her head carries a shield and a sword. On the back an axe with the initials "US," the phrase "The Great War for Civilization" and a list of the allies: "France, Italy, Serbia, Japan, Montenegro, Russia, Greece, Great Britain, Belgium, Brazil, Portugal, Rumania, China."

I add things up: I have served in the army for ten months and twenty-five days more or less. Because of the hardship that I endured during that time, everything that had compelled me to enlist was forgotten; but now that I am back in civilian clothes I must face my failings again. What am I? I am nothing! I have very little money – only what I received from the army and I still owe $300 to Sophocles. Vanderbilt comes to mind and, since I have his card, I get on the train and arrive at his house in New York, on River Side Drive. I double-check the number on the card and stand in front of the gate. The luxurious railing around his property alone is worth more than the houses of all the notables of Kyrenia combined. The garden makes the mansion in the distance look like a beautiful palace. I recall my time at Malikkis's house where I was subservient to all, beaten by all, humiliated and oppressed... Fears from the past rise up to suffocate me! Foolishly perhaps and definitely irrationally, I cannot take another step; I turn around and walk away.

Return to Albany

I go to Albany and timidly walk into Keeler's kitchen to see what the situation is there. The Alsatian chef tells me of the hardship that his son is facing as a mechanic in Alsace. He went there as a volunteer, fought in the war and faced its torment – the true torment of war! The man is in tears as he shares his pain with me. Although I see many familiar faces among the staff, I cannot muster enough courage to knock on the boss's door to ask for a job. Fortunately, as I am standing there chatting, Keeler steps into the kitchen as always.

He looks at me and says, "Goddamn Greek, why are you still standing around? Why haven't you started work yet?" and he gently shoves me behind the counter.

As I learn later on, he had requested my discharge twice because he needed me at work. I do recall being asked repeatedly if I wished to be discharged but – having had no knowledge of his request – I responded "no," underlining that I was happy to serve. Again the only difficulty I face is finding a room. My old landlady wants me back because – she says – I am quiet, clean and tidy. Since the room is temporarily occupied, she gives me a reference for another rooming house. When I return from work late one night, I turn on the gas but it's not working. The meter indicates that it's empty, which means that I must insert a coin. I do not have one and I am so tired that I lie down in the dark, forgetting to shut off the valve. When someone puts in a coin later on, the machine starts up automatically. By the grace of God, the landlady notices that I am not up at the regular time in the morning. When she finally decides to check on me, she opens the door to my room and finds me unconscious, nearly dead from gas inhalation. I spit up black tar for the next three days. My old landlady has an available room at last so I move back to her house. Now her sister is reserved – no more strawberry or newspaper deliveries to my room. But there is a young student from Canada living there, blonde, short, not bad looking. She makes a habit of coming to my room for a quick chat when she hears me come in late, since I am working as night chef again. One day I find a ring in the washbasin and take it to her.

"Does this belong to you?"

"Yes! Where did you find it?"

"It was in the washbasin."

"Thank you but... I've been meaning to ask... Why don't you ever ask me to sit down?"

"I don't want you to get the wrong impression..."

She seems upset by my response.

"I'm old enough and responsible for my actions!" she tells me.

I show her to the only chair in my room. She often visits when I get off work but, one night, she calls to me from her room:

"I'm not feeling well tonight so I can't come to your room. Why don't you come to mine and keep me company for a little while?"

Despite my hesitation I go to her room, only to find her reclining in bed in her most beautiful lace nightgown. She certainly does not look sick. During our chat she says to me: "The only two Greek words I know are 's'agapo' and 'fili.'"[2]

My back is up... Realizing that I must tread carefully in this situation, I go downstairs, bring some fruit up for her, and say

---

2 S'agapo (Greek: σ' αγαπώ) means "I love you" and fili (Greek: φιλί) means "kiss."

"goodnight." Not long ago two men from Mytilene became involved first with their landlady and then with her underage daughter. The police charged them and there were dragged into court.
They only escaped prison and deportation because the mother's
testimony saved them at the last moment. They paid a hefty fine
beyond the shame. I know of many others who have met with
worse, immigrants who ended up returning home with incurable
diseases that they contracted from women. I will not get caught
up in this. I am extremely careful because I am focused on settling
down and starting a family in Cyprus; this will no longer be an
option for me, if I ruin myself this way. I do not need this kind of
trouble on top of everything else.

The stock market, which remains a constant temptation, is my
main trouble… New regulations have been recently instituted and
it's no longer pure gambling like it was in the past. I am doing my
best to control myself; I play with small amounts of money. I do
not have much to spare anyway, even if my salary is up to $275 as
night chef, in charge of seven cooks. Everything is more expensive
now than it was before.

We have a cook from Andros at the restaurant, but he is not the
sort you would want to be friends with; he steals. He steals a lot!
He splits raw chickens and flattens them against his bare chest,
buttons up, and exits tall and proud through the front door, in
keeping with the restaurant's regulations. He fills up his chef's
hat with eggs, bends over, secures it on his head, and smuggles
them out of the restaurant in the same way. One day, while his hat
is filled with eggs, he is stopped by the manager, who is the boss's
brother-in-law.

"'Remove your hat when you're leaving the restaurant,' he
said to me," the cook from Andros recounts and describes how he
walked out of the restaurant as cool as a cucumber. "What would
have happened if he had taken off my hat, Cypriot?" he whispers
and bursts out in a roar of laughter.

I am in a tough spot – I do not want to turn him in because

he is Greek. Luckily he is a cook on rotation, so he is not on my shift every night. And making friends with him would not be wise, even if he is the only Greek at the restaurant.

Loneliness

My friend Yiannis Vrahas has decided to return to Cyprus. He has saved some money through hard work at the Pittsburgh foundries, where he went with Tsiakkouris. He is engaged with Cleopatra from Bellapais and feels that the time has time for him to start a family. I bid him farewell but he shows up at my workplace at midnight. He tells me that all his savings are gone and that he has no choice but return to Cyprus because his fare is paid for and his trunk has already been loaded onto the ship. I phone the boss at home:

"What on earth do you need money for at this time of night, you son of a bitch?"

I explain my friend's predicament to him and he instructs his brother-in-law, who is in charge, to give me $100. Yiannis takes the money and sails for Cyprus. As it turns out, his savings were locked up inside his trunk all along. Having forgotten that he put the money there, he discovered it upon his arrival in Cyprus. I learn of this in a letter, which he sends to thank me. I am happy for my friend but my heart is heavy.

Loneliness weighs heavily upon me and now, after my friend's departure, I feel even more alone. I meet two Cypriots, one from Larnaca and one from Lakatamia, who have purchased the lovely Boston Confectionary for $10,000. I really like them and do my best to support them. I invite my co-workers to their confectionary and treat them to milkshakes and ice cream. At this time there is a shortage of sugar, so I ask the boss for eight barrels, which I bring to them so they can make cakes and chocolates. With Christmas approaching I lend them $300 on top of everything else. But they are neglecting their business to the point that, when I go

there in the mornings and see a mess, I pick up broom and mop
to clean. To keep from declaring bankruptcy they secretly sell a
large order of boxed chocolates, which they ship to Buffalo. The
factory representative catches wind of this and they are nabbed.
The Larnacian's fiancée, a woman from Mytilene, comes to tell
me what has happened. Seeing her in tears, I am compelled to
post bail for them. They barely escape prison. But something is
fishy... At night, when I get off work, I am surprised to see that
the confectionary is closed. I ask around and learn that they play
cards at a club that belongs to a Greek. I am livid! I leave work
early, around 11PM, and go to the club. I knock on the door. A
small window opens.

"Is the Larnacian here?" I ask.

"Yes, he is."

"Tell him that someone's looking for him, but don't tell him
it's me."

"Okay."

It's very cold, the ground is covered with snow, but my blood
boils while I wait. He comes to the door and, before he even has a
chance to ask what I want, I start to beat him. We slip and fall but
I refuse to let go – I am foaming at the mouth! Cops take notice,
pound their clubs on the ground to alert each other, and quickly
surround us. They separate us and push us against the wall. Fortunately they recognize me because cops regularly drop in at Keeler's restaurant at night. I treat them to sandwiches and anything
they fancy, as per the boss's instructions.

"So you're the one making trouble? Go on, get out of here!"
they say and let me go.

Next morning I see a lawyer and file a lawsuit against the two
Cypriots for the money I lent them, a total of $3,000. I had not
asked for it earlier because I thought they were trying to get ahead
in life. And I learn the worst of it: The Boston Confectionary is
mortgaged three times! I persist however and, in the end, manage to recoup $1,000. But it's no consolation. I am deeply hurt

by this situation. *Is there even one human being that treats another with honesty?* I wonder.

Silverman, the man who polishes the restaurant's silverware, is a classmate and childhood friend of the boss. Since the boss is very fond of him and holds him in high regard, Silverman has a free rein at the restaurant. If he dislikes someone, he has a word with Keeler and that employee is sacked the following day. We all do our best to get along with him and it is not difficult because Silverman is truly easygoing. He has the manners and comportment of a saint, and I have genuine respect for the man. One night the cook from Andros goes downstairs to use the washroom and finds Silverman dead with his face in the toilet! He puts him over his shoulder and carries him upstairs. Ambulance, autopsy... It's a heart attack and, although the police say that the body should not have been moved before they were on the scene, this was not a crime. John Keeler asks us where Silverman lived but no one knows. After three days of searching and asking around, we learn that he lived in a workers' building. When they enter his apartment, they discover mountains of tablecloths, cutlery, dishware, anything you can imagine – everything lifted from the restaurant since all of it bears the boss's emblem. They also find three bankbooks with deposits at three different banks: $20,000 at the first, $12,000 at the second, and $6,000 at the third. We calculate that, on his salary, he would have had to work 178 years to save that much money. It is obvious that the money came from a lifetime of selling stolen goods. A huge van is required to transport everything back to the restaurant; we all stand on the sidewalk watching the porters unload. The boss watches for some time then looks at the busy avenue and whispers to himself: "I will never trust anyone again!"

He appears to be quite hurt, as hurt as I am by my fellow Cypriots. I am certain that he has lost all faith in mankind.

I have certainly lost all faith in mankind but not because of the poor who are selling black market alcohol during the Prohibition. They have poverty as their excuse. An Italian cook buys a suit, a tall hat and a doctor's bag, which he fills with bottles of liquor of all sorts. He goes around selling the liquor and remains above suspicion by pretending to be a doctor. At times he even comes to work with the bag and dressed this way; he greets us as he comes into the kitchen. Another Italian, who managed to buy 100 bottles of gin before alcohol was prohibited, sells them at a huge profit. His only dream is to return to his village in Italy in a rented car, so he can show his fellow villagers that he has made money abroad. And his dream comes true! He sells the gin, returns to Italy, and makes a show of his prosperity.

But what are my dreams? This is my fifth year working for Keeler, who always shows how much he appreciates me. While the accountant pays everyone else, he personally delivers my wages in an envelope so that the others won't know that he is giving me something extra. Whenever he sees me on the street, he gives me a ride in his car anywhere I want to go. When a fire destroys the kitchen and the restaurant closes temporarily for repairs, he recommends me to the club where he is a member. Beyond my salary, I collect an extra paycheck from there. When his restaurant opens again, I return as night chef. The Alsatian chef that I am fond of also returns at this time, but there's trouble brewing with the Italian in charge of seafood, a small but very hot-tempered man. Near the kitchen there is an area where they bake bread and do laundry – next to that is a small room, which cooks use as a change room. While I am changing there one day, the Italian starts to make fun of my socks, saying that they are cheap.

"Hey, spaghetti eater," I tell him, "did your feet know what socks were back in Italy? And now you think you can get smart with me?"

He becomes upset but the real problem is elsewhere... Even though he is married, he has fallen in love with a pretty checker that I speak to with ease. One day he approaches me: "I'll give you $10 if you tell her that I love her and that I want to marry her."

Having nothing to lose, I agree.

"Tell him that my heart belongs to someone else," the young woman responds.

I pass on her response and refuse the $10 he promised me. Even so, the man clearly dislikes me, mostly because I speak with the girl that he fancies. That night he refuses to prepare an order of oysters for me. Anger flares up between us.

"I won't leave this place until I slice you up and stuff you in barrel!" he threatens.

This gets me thinking... No Italian ever jokes about such things. One day, when Antonis Vrahas came in drunk and knocked over the sandwich bread, the Italian lost his temper and threw a knife at him. Mercifully he missed and the knife was embedded on a rail of the wooden staircase. When I tried to remove it, and it was not easy, I saw with how much skill and force it was thrown. At a hotel two streets away from the restaurant, two Italians got into a fight. One pushed the other's head onto the butcher block and chopped it off with a meat cleaver! A proper decapitation... In light of all this, I decide to have a word with the Alsatian chef about the threat. He smirks and pats down his elegant goatee – I am expecting him to fire the Italian, but he is pretending not to hear me! I do not like this; now I am both nervous and upset.

A Greek restaurant owner has been asking me to come work for him for some time. His restaurant is also in Albany. He is a nice man but miserable because he married an American woman who does not speak Greek.

"I'll give you some advice: Don't marry a foreign woman because you'll be miserable, no matter how hard you try to make it work. You go to a Greek household and can't speak your language because she thinks you're badmouthing her," he complains to me.

At his restaurant I reconnect with Stavris, Sophocles' brother, who has learned a little more about cooking by now. His brother-in-law Kritsos also works there. Back in Kyrenia Kritsos wore a vraka and worked as a technician at Paronakis's flourmill. Every day when he got off work, he would adorn his vest with a flower and walk about proudly with his arms folded over his chest and with his hands tucked under his armpits. I was a tormented flower at the time. But now in America, which had no love for me at the beginning, I am a chef with a big salary and he a simple kitchen assistant. He clearly resents me, so he is constantly bad-mouthing me. When I forget to put a case of chicken in the fridge, he takes the boss down to the basement to show him what I have done. I become aware of it because I happen to be going down to the basement at that moment. This upsets me so much that I cannot stand working with him any longer.

Pittsburgh, Pennsylvania

I find work at a restaurant owned by a Greek in Pittsfield, Pennsylvania. The salary is good, better than at Keeler's, but the restaurant is not up to standard. The Greek's prices are high and he takes advantage of his clientele. The situation is unbearable but, truth be told, the problem is inside me... I am discontented and always fearful – the temptation of the stock market will not loosen its grip on me. I continue playing small amounts but the more my earnings grow, the less I trust myself. At some point I give in: I bet everything I have saved since my discharge from the army, only to have it be blown away by the fickle winds of the stock markets again. Now what? Do I start at the beginning? What beginning since it's now 1921 and I am thirty-two going on thirty-three? Do I start at the beginning again? And for how long? Until I die? The Italian with the 100 bottles of gin comes to mind. He is back at his village, having arrived in a rented limousine and basked in the admiration of his fellow villagers. What are my ambitions? Do I have any? I feel so weary that I feel the need to do something drastic, to set a goal like the Italian had done. I start thinking about going home. Wasn't this always my goal and the goal of every immigrant? I am no longer considered young and it has been three years since my discharge from the army. I feel that I want

to return to Cyprus, that I *must* return to Cyprus. There I have
the land that I inherited from my father, along with a few other
parcels that my brother Glioris bought on my behalf with money
I sent him. Most of those parcels also belonged to my father but,
when my sisters found themselves in a bind, I bought them to
prevent the land from being sold to moneylenders, who snatch
everything for pennies. All additional parcels of land are next to
the one that I inherited in Karakoumi. I have sent money to all
my sisters including Polyxeni, to help her build a home for her
daughter Athena, who is getting married. I do not take any of this
money into consideration, nor do I wish to be repaid. But I am
counting on what Pavlos Hadjicostis has collected from Efstathios
on my behalf, and on what I have saved since my discharge. Surely
I will find a way to earn a living in Kyrenia and, if things get tough,
I can always count on my skills as a chef. The road to America is a
familiar one, and now I am an American citizen! I no longer need
to worry about survival and my ambitions are simple and human.
All I want is to settle down in my homeland with a secure livelihood and to start a family. Enough hardship, enough wandering
around in faraway lands! Back in Kyrenia, with the money that he
has earned in America, Yiannis Vrahas is building a ship in partnership with the Phytos brothers. Alexis Tsiakkouris has also invested
in this venture. Yiannis Vrahas is trading with the East and earns
a lot without breaking his back. "I assure you that Cyprus is like
America now in terms of money," he writes to me. He says that he
is planning to build a second ship and urges: "Come back, Costis,
you will not regret it!"

At the same time Polyxeni writes to me that the parents of a
nice young woman would consent to our engagement, should I be
interested. "What am I thinking?" she asks. What am I thinking indeed? I deeply long to have my own family and home! This is why I
have worked hard for so many years – so I can save money, return
to Cyprus, get married, and be a master of my own household. I
discuss all this with Alexis Tsiakkouris, who is still in America; he

has an unmarried sister-in-law in Cyprus. He shows me her photo
and hands me a watch. I will deliver the watch on his behalf and
use this as an opportunity to meet her. If I like her, I can ask her
parents for her hand in marriage.

I'm fired up! I pack everything and go to see Sophocles to pay
back what I owe him, approximately $500. He has not decided to
repatriate yet but America is finished inside me. I cannot bear the
loneliness any longer! The moment I set foot in Cyprus, before
I do anything else, I will look to get married. To this end I buy a
gold watch and a couple of other pieces of jewellery for my future
fiancée, whoever she may be, as well as two new suits for myself.
I sell my stocks at absurdly low prices, pay my ticket, keep some
cash, and take the rest of my savings in a bank draft – a total of
£1,131, everything I have saved since military service. This time
everything is paper; gold coins are no longer in circulation. In any
event, this is enough capital to start something in Kyrenia, especially since I am not returning with big dreams or great ambitions.

CHAPTER 10

THE REPATRIATION

Kyrenia, 1921-1927

The SS Washington, 40,000 tonnes and sturdy, quickly crosses the Atlantic. A brief port of call at Plymouth in England, and then we dock at Cherbourg in France. I disembark and take the train to Marseille. During the forty-six hour train ride I witness the true destruction of war. Cities, villages, everything in ruins... Even the train is a wreck – battered cars and a rusty, disintegrating engine that breaks down. Repairs take half the night. I encounter the same misery and destitution of war at Marseille; while I wait there for a ship to Alexandria, thieves break into my hotel room, open my suitcase, and steal my army jacket and a canvas belt that I really like, both mementos of my military service. Gone for good! Fortunately, they are not able to break into my trunk, which is solid and has very strong locks. Yet it is plain to see that the thieves, impoverished by war, are in need of basic things; they are not professionals.

I spend five days looking for a ship to take me to Alexandria. At last I find the Japanese SS Ame Maru, which makes a nonstop journey. A small number of Turkish officers board in secret and, when we encounter a Greek military ship en route, they hide in the cellar since Greece and Turkey are at war.

In Alexandria the familiar Hevedia line has a ship to Cyprus on the 4th, 14th and 24th of each month, as always. The closest date is the 14th; I depart and the next day I am in Famagusta! I arrive in Cyprus on the Feast of the Assumption, on August 15; I am thirty-

three years old and my hair is thinning at the temples. During the
transatlantic crossing I grew out my moustache so much that now
I am able to curl up the ends according to fashion.

The ship docks and I set eyes on the Port of Famagusta, which
– they say – is the most commercial of all Cypriot ports. Small,
miserable, no activity; it's practically dead! *Why on earth did I come
back to this wasteland?* I wonder. Misgivings rise up inside me. Almost regretting my decision, I start to cry! During the trip I kept
company with a third-generation potter from Famagusta, a skilled
craftsman, who is also repatriating because there was no market
for his line of work in America. He is certain that in Cyprus he
would earn more making pots above ground, instead of wasting
his youth washing pots and dishes underground in American restaurants and hotels. *It makes sense for him to return*, I think to myself.
He chose between being a simple dishwasher in America versus a
craftsman-potter in Cyprus, whereas I am an experienced chef,
who has left behind a salary of almost $300 a month and an army
of cooks and assistants at his beckon call! Where will I ever find
such work or pay in Cyprus? I explain my situation to my new
friend but he does not know how to console me. He brings me to
the small hotel, or rather the rooming house, which his mother
operates, where I will spend the night. When the woman hears
that I am from Kyrenia, she recounts all she knows about a terrible accident that took place last month: An old balcony at the
port collapsed, unable to withstand the weight of the people on
it. Many lost their lives; many more were injured. The dreadful
news sinks me deeper into gloominess. Early next morning the
kind woman puts out olives, halloumi and bread for our breakfast.
Happy to be back at home, her son has an appetite but I, feeling
low, can't get any food down. As I prepare to depart, I take out
money to pay for my stay but the woman will not accept anything.
I thank her, lug the trunk while her son carries my suitcase, and I
take the carriage to Nicosia.

I stop at the heart of Makrydromos at the High Life Confectionary, which belongs to Pavlos Hadjicostis. The waitress there is very pretty: a Russian refugee, a victim of the Revolution of 1917. Before Pavlos and I have a chance to greet each other, a man comes into the shop demanding £50. Pavlos tries to dodge him but the man insists. After some back and forth, Pavlos turns to me:

"Do you have £50 on you?"

"I do."

"Give it to me!"

I give him the money and, when he settles the invoice, he throws the receipt on the ground with fury! Obviously his business is not doing well. We sit and talk for a while, and he suggests that I buy the hotel across the street. But I cannot think – I am anxious to get to Kyrenia as quickly as possible, so I ask about a carriage.

I find myself in front of two malnourished, ailing horses and Stavris, the carriage driver, a man with harsh features that map out life's hardship. I get on the carriage and we get on our way. From my fellow travellers I learn the details of the balcony accident, which took place exactly one month ago, on July 16, on the eve of the Feast of Ayia Marina. Five British warships docked at Kyrenia's port, where they organized drills and sea races while everyone in Kyrenia watched – even people from nearby villages came to have a look. The port was so full of people that many squeezed onto the balconies of nearby homes for a better view. After the drills and races ended, an inebriated sailor pushed one of his mates into the sea; then a third sailor pushed the first, and a huge fight started. Many more jumped in the water to battle it out fully clothed. Hearing the disturbance, Kyrenians in nearby homes stepped out on their balconies again to see what was happening. And on the balcony of Hadjicostis Hadjipetrou, the man sitting next to me recites, dragging his voice:

Five and twenty bodies stood,
not knowing that safety they had none,

rotten and old with so much weight
the balcony became sword, knife, Charon!

A poem composed by the cook-poet Mavroudis, who turns any major event in Kyrenia and the entire district into song – all my fellow travellers know it by heart; they recite, correcting each other's mistakes. This is how I learn that the balcony's centre beam broke, causing people to fall to the ground. Among the dead were Hadjistyllis, his daughter-in-law Efrosyni, Philippina and Evgenia Pashina, the skilled loom weaver. Many others sustained injuries such as broken limbs, and some were left with permanent impairments. My heart feels even tighter now, not only from listening to all this, but because Stavris is mercilessly flogging his animals which, already weak and ailing, can barely walk in the oppressive summer heat. And the situation is made worse because the large gravel, which paves the road, hinders the movement of the carriage instead of easing it; every piece of gravel becomes a small but considerable obstruction to the wheels, which require additional force to roll. At each obstacle the driver takes it out on his unfortunate horses, flogging them pitilessly until, at the slope of the passage to Ayia Ekaterini, one falls and drags the other down almost immediately. Savvis gets off the carriage and, although both horses are on the ground, flogs them to the point that I can no longer stand it. We all get off the carriage and tell him that we will walk for a while in order to reduce the weight. Fortunately, the passage is a straight road through the mountains. Just before the turn of Phinitzia[1] we get on the carriage again, feeling confident that the downhill road that lies ahead will relieve the poor animals somewhat.

At the turn of Phinitzia I set eyes on Kyrenia and my heart leaps! All is forgotten – all that was good about America, my pro-

---

1 Phinitzia (Greek: φοινιτζιά) means "palm tree"; the name is derived from an actual palm tree, which stood at that location.

fession and my large salary. I am home at last! The weight on my
chest lifts and my soul feels as light as a feather!

I decide to stay at Hotel Akteo again but now the owner is
Pavlos Hadjicostis, who spends most of his time at High Life, his
confectionary in Nicosia. The hotel is neglected; in fact, it is rundown. The renovations that Theodoulos Panayiotou carried out
in 1911 have aged: peeling and crumbling gypsum on the room
dividers upstairs, frayed almost dilapidated furniture. The large
room on the ground floor that serves as the dining area is in the
same condition and the food is poor because Theodoulos, who
was a good cook, is no longer here. One long table is provided for
all guests. The server is the son of the stonecutter Fakalas, Michalis, who is slow – poor thing. He is dressed in a dirty shirt, a frayed
vest, and a discoloured vraka. Barefoot as he is, with his enormous
feet black with grime, he bounces in with a large platter. He places it in the middle of the table and we serve ourselves: the Turkish
director of the Post Office, the members of the Criminal Court
whenever they convene in Kyrenia, and the occasional wandering
tax collector. None of this matters to me; I have a place to stay.

Late afternoon, when the heat has been softened by the sea
breeze, I meet with friends at the port. At one point Yiannis Vrahas takes me aside:

"You know, I've told people that you've brought £10,000 from
America!"

"Me?"

"Yes, from your job and from the stock market... And everyone believed it!"

I smile because I know he means well.

"All I have is £1,131, no more no less," I say and explain that I
lost all my money in the stock market.

"What's wrong with saying that you've brought £25,000 even?"
he insists.

"I don't like fooling people."

On the afternoon of the following day I dare cross the threshold of Keperis's coffee shop, which is near Koulas and frequented by the well-to-do. I sit off to the side. Savvis, who works for Severis, looks sideways at me.

"So did you bring lots of money from America?" he asks.

I say nothing; I feel that I am out of my depth...

"Have you learned a skill at least?"

"Yes, I cook!"

"Hmmm, so you went an arse and came back an arse! What kind of job is cooking?" he says mockingly and returns to his game of backgammon.

The son of the late Hadjiglioris, Yiannakos, whom my family has appointed as my legal representative in matters of inheritance, is also there — I had sent him a power of attorney from America. He asks me to come work for him as a cook. My mind wanders back to Keeler's restaurant, where I had seven cooks under my command and a salary of $275 per month. I am certain that no one here has a clue what type of cook I am... I take the time to explain but neither the lawyer nor anyone else at the coffee shop understands.

"Thank you, Mr. Yiannakos, but I'm not ready to start working yet," I reply.

Christodoulos Fieros motions to me and I approach him.

"Is it true, Catsellis, that you've brought back all that money?" he asks in confidence.

"What money?"

"£10,000!"

"No, Mr. Fieros, I have only £1,131 and I'd give you £1,000 to collect interest, if you like."

"Sure, bring it!" he eagerly agrees.

Next day I receive a message from Pavlos Hadjicostis about the hotel on Makrydromos. I am interested, so I go to Nicosia to look further into the matter. The hotel's owner is Loizos, the son-in-law of someone called Tserkotis. I am fascinated by the man's eyes, which are different colours: one is blue and the other one amber. Loizos offers to sell me the business for £300 including furniture and equipment. This figure excludes the rent, which is paid separately to the landlord. Pavlos confirms that this is a good price, I agree to the deal, and we shake on it. On the third day since my return to Cyprus, I am already taking inventory at the hotel. During the process, however, I realize what terrible shape the place is in – this is a third-rate hotel, with furniture so old that it's good only for the trash. At some point, Pavlos drops in from the confectionary across the street, so I take a short break. We sit down while Loizos prepares coffee for the three of us.

"Catsellis, now that the deal is done, I'll tell you what we're going to do: We'll hang a sign outside that says 'Pavlos Hadjicostis – Manager!' You'll put me in charge and you'll see how much money we'll make!"

I really do not like what I am hearing, on top of what I am seeing at the hotel. He is essentially proposing that he would be the boss and I his employee! I recall my father's advice to trust Pavlos but that's a whole other issue... The reality is that I have regretted my decision to buy the hotel, but there is nothing I can do now. I have given my word, and a deal is a deal! I return to taking inventory.

Just as I am about to finish with the inventory, I come to a fancy photo of Venizelos on the wall; Loizos charges me £3.50 for it, an inflated sum, but that's not all...

"Take it down, I don't need it," I proclaim.

"Why? Do you think it's expensive?"

"No, I don't support Venizelos. I support King Constantine!"

"Is that so?"

"Yes!"

Loizos, a fanatical supporter of Venizelos, becomes quite angry.

"Either you take the photo or leave everything. The deal is off!" he shouts.

How could I, a long-term supporter of the King, ever agree to such a thing? Enraged as I am about the deal, which stinks as I now realize, I seize the opportunity...

"Okay then, I want neither the photo, nor the deal!" I declare.

I pick up my hat and leave. I do not stop at High Life; I go straight to the carriage and catch it as it's about to depart. It's the last one to Kyrenia for the day. On the way to Kyrenia I take decisions: No more hasty business deals and no more listening to other people! From now on, I will weigh everything very carefully, form my own opinion, and make up my own mind. When the carriage arrives in Kyrenia, I move out of Akteo and in with my sister Polyxeni in Pano Kyrenia. I do not want to give Pavlos, who manages the place, the opportunity to pressure me about Loizos's hotel or anything else that would benefit him. If I keep this up, I am going to find myself in worse trouble than I had with Efstathios and the confectionary. I resolve that I will not be pressured into anything ever again!

The Engagement, 1921

Polyxeni is pressuring me to get engaged, however; "It's time," she keeps saying. Although my sister is right, I make it clear to her that this, too, will be entirely my decision. I visit Petris, Alexis Tsiakkouris's father-in-law; his house is at the port, near Trypitis. I bring the watch and a few other things on behalf of Alexis, and we chat about what is new with him. It seems that Alexis has written to them that I might be interested in their daughter, Marie. The young woman enters with a tray. I take what she is offering and look her over; she appears overly excited and coy, far more than appropriate. I leave without any further discussion. I recount the encounter to my sister Polyxeni and ask about the other young woman that she had in mind.

"I'm going to have a word with Stavris Vottis because I think he wants to give you his daughter!" she says.

The young woman that my sister Polyxeni is referring to and Marie are cousins; their fathers, Stavris and Petris, are brothers. I do not have high expectations about the match because I have heard a lot about this particular young woman. She is twenty years old, pretty and modest. There are many suitors. In 1913, when she was barely thirteen, my friend Christodoulos Anayiotos went to a wedding in Bellapais to see her. I remember the occasion but not the girl. At the time, her father would not consent to her getting married at such a young age, not wishing to repeat the mistake he had made with his other daughter, Styliani. Later on I learned, however, that the reason he had not given his consent was because the man who had raised Christodoulos intended for him to marry his niece; not wishing to ruin the other young woman's prospects, Stavris Vottis would not consider him as a suitor. When it was all said and done, Christodoulos managed to turn the bitter into sweet. He got engaged to the niece of Captain Petroulios, who had raised him with all that a young man could ever want in life. The daughter of Stavris Vottis is a friend of Triada; one of the Phytos brothers, who are shipbuilders and good athletes, asked for her hand in marriage. Michalis Pelekanos was also among the suitors – some the father did not approve of and some she did not like. Her parents love her so much that they want to give her a husband of her choosing, so they ask for her opinion every time someone proposes.

My sister arranges a visit to their house in Kato Kerynia, in the outskirts of Kyrenia in fact, at the eastern bank of the mouth of the Koronos River, a little further from Alakatin. The moment I set foot in their house I feel that my chances are slim. My sister and I take a seat, and her father begins to ask me about America. I speak about my work there, underlining the fact that I have only £1,131 in savings and that I am determined to marry, have children, and settle down in my country. I am thirty-three years old and it is time! Stavris Vottis, the son of Hadjiparaskevas, is a man of few words. He motions to his wife Despinou and she calls her daughter to bring in the tray with the sweets: Eleni! I know her name because one of her suitors has composed a verse about her:

Even when Eleni gets old
her eyes will be as dark as coal!

As I wait for her to enter I think that, should we marry, God willing, we would celebrate our name days together on May 21, on the Feast of Constantinos and Eleni. Eleni enters with the tray. She truly is quite pretty, with a fair complexion and large, dark eyes; she is dressed stylishly but modestly. She serves my sister first, then stands in front of me. The tray is between us. She is perfectly calm; there is no agitation in her whatsoever. Sensing her sizing me up, I begin to feel anxious. Her mother follows her back into the kitchen, where I can hear them talking amongst themselves. I am sure that her mother wants to know whether she likes me. I pretend to be calm, although I am bound up in knots on the inside. Her mother returns; she glances at her husband with meaning. He nods slightly but I can't tell whether the response is positive or negative. Stavris and Despinou, who are among the most loving couples in Kyrenia, communicate without words. Stavris looks me straight in the eye.

"I agree to give you Eleni, if you agree not to take her abroad. I have no intention of having my daughter migrate," he tells me.

"I agree," I reply and breathe a sigh of relief.

But her father presses the point: "Do you give me your word that you will not go abroad again?"

"I do."

"Never?"

"Never!"

"Hmmm… And what are you looking for in terms of dowry?"

"Nothing!" I say with my joy sky-high for being accepted as their son-in-law.

"Nothing?"

"Nothing!" I confirm.

Stavris sighs.

"I have built a house for my daughter on the other side of the river, directly across from the sea; it is rented to Dr. Ieropoulos. Her entire dowry is in place."

"Okay," I say and ask about the engagement rather impatiently.

We decide on August 29 but then realize that that's the Feast of the Beheading of John the Baptist, a day of fasting and perhaps not auspicious. I say that I do not mind since I am not superstitious. My father-in-law agrees so we set the date. We also set a date for the wedding in one year's time. Two years is customary but, since I am older and the bride is twenty, there is no need to wait. Until the wedding, they will provide a room for me at the house of their eldest son Yiannis, on the Karavas-Lapithos road. As unreal as all this seems, this last detail eliminates any remaining doubt inside me: No more matchmaking, I am now engaged! Everyone is smiling, feeling relieved.

Eleni and her mother set the table with meze and drinks that they bring in from the cellar. Now that my anxiety has dissipated, I notice my surroundings: a sofa with patterned throws, a large carved chest, finely embroidered curtains on the window, cleanliness and order everywhere. I also recall noticing upon entering that the stables and toilets are at the edge of the yard, separate from the house. Suddenly I am overwrought with embarrassment; my entire body becomes tense... Who am I to come into such a home and marry such a young woman? Realizing how incredibly lucky I am, I surmise that my father-in-law has agreed because of the £1,131 that I have brought from America, not because he is after money but because he is concerned about his daughter's wellbeing. He does not want her to face any hardship. Eleni comes from good families on both sides. Her mother hails from the Hadjiyiangos family, which is rooted at the east slope of the river, just beyond the old walls of Kyrenia – from the family tree of Charalambos Economou, who fought for the rebuilding of Archangelos. I know that as a young man Stavris, the son of Hadjiparaskevas, and my father worked together as day labourers for Mesut Effendi. Later Stavris became skilled at carpentry but did not limit himself to that; not only does he farm his land, but also finds time to cut, chisel and carry sandstone to his properties. His brother Kel Panais, who is a builder, slowly constructs the houses that he is building for his children. Stavris makes the windows and doors himself. Rumour has it, however, that the brothers also discover valuables in the fields… Kel Panais might come across some gold coins, which he would separate from the cob with the tip of his trowel.

"Stavris, I've found another," he might say, as he throws it to his brother.

There may be some truth to the rumour, since this would explain how Stavris has managed to acquire two additional pieces of property. Yet, above all, Stavris is a frugal man, who manages his money so well that some say he is very stingy. In the interest of economy, the vraka that he wears every day is purple, coloured with half the dye. And he has the work ethic of an ant. How else could he have built three homes for his three oldest children one after the other? The first house on the Karavas-Lapithos road belongs to Yiannis; the second, which belongs to Styliani, is almost directly across from his house but on the opposite riverbank; the third, the one built for Eleni, is further down, where the river meets the sea, west of Xylogiofyro. These houses are spacious and comfortable, unlike those on the east side that were built for rayahs[2] living under the fear and injustice of Ottoman rule. And there is even a small shop on the parcel of land above Styliani's

---

2 Rayah: A word of Arabic origin. In Ottoman society, the rayah, which literally means "members of the flock," included Christians, Muslims and Jews who were 'shorn' (i.e. taxed) in order to support the state and the associated professional Ottoman class.

house that is promised to Costis, his youngest. By the time Costis is ready to marry, whenever that blessed and joyful day comes, a fourth house will have been built there as well. So let them think that the man is stingy; his family wants for nothing! He has sent his youngest Costis, who is seventeen years old, to Newham's English School in Nicosia. He does not penny-pinch on important things but is parsimonious when it comes to unnecessary expenses and his own needs, which he sacrifices for the welfare of his children. In any case, Stavris Vottis has had more than his share of pain when it comes to children. He has four that are inseparable and five that are deceased:

> 45.Vasilios Stavrou Hadjiparaskeva 1.1.1883
> (died on 21.1.1883)
> 82. Ioannis Stavrou Hadjiparaskeva 29.5.1884
> 151. Maria Stavrou Hadjiparaskeva 28.9.1887
> (died on 10.9.1890)
> 218.Theophanou Stavrou Hadjiparaskeva 12.6.1893
> (died on 14.2.1895)
> 349. Styliani Stavrou Hadjiparaskeva 14.11.1895
> 410. Paraskevas Stavrou Hadjiparaskeva 27.1.1898
> (died on 12.8.1901)
> 511. Eleni Stavrou Hadjiparaskeva 27.1.1901
> 598. Costantinos Stavrou Hadjiparaskeva 9.10.1904[3]

Yiannis is married to Mirou, the daughter of the shoemaker Polydoros, whom I know because his workshop used to be across from the elementary school at Archangelos. Styliani is married in Bellapais to Costas Adamou. And now Eleni, as much as I still find it hard to believe, is engaged to me. She wanted to be a teacher

---

3 Father Yiannis Paphitis, "Record of Births in Kyrenia from the Year 1880 until the Year 1905," (pgs. 3, 5, 9, 13, 16, 23, 29 and 34)

but her parents did not give their consent; instead they sent her to Phyllou, the best seamstress in town, to learn to sew. She stays home, helps her mother with the housework, and embroiders. In the summer, she is bold enough to go swimming with her friends within a wicker enclosure directly across from Akteo, while old Hadjiportolos serves as the strictest of guards.

On the following day I move from my sister's home into Yiannis's, who is now my brother-in-law. I am engaged! I feel rather strange as I'm walking toward the port from Koulas. Michalakis Pelekanou, who has a grocery store in a space that he rents from Hadjitelemachos, stops me. He motions to me and I step inside.

"Tell me the truth: Is it really a done deal?"

"What?"

"Did you get engaged to Eleni, the daughter of Stavris Hadjiparaskevas?"

"Yes!"

I can see that something inside him is about to burst. He paces back and forth a few times inside the store.

"Okay! Okay!" he says in the end.

I am perplexed by his behaviour until I learn at the port later on that he fervently wanted to marry Eleni. When he sent a matchmaker to make arrangements, her parents gave their consent but she turned him down. This must mean, of course, that Eleni and I are engaged because she actually wanted me as her husband! I am at once pleased and awestruck... She actually likes me! At night, when I spend time with her and her parents, I try to conceal how awkward I feel around her. And when there's a wedding in Karakoumi, they allow her go with me. Fiddles and lutes so I muster the courage...

"Would you like to dance, Eleni?"

"No!"

"Why not?"

She looks at me for a few moments, "Because it's not right. We're not engaged yet!"

I am both displeased and pleased because she wants everything done correctly and at the appropriate time.

Father Phinikarides from Prodromos is about to perform our engagement without a dowry agreement since I have no demands; yet my father-in-law does!

"If you get engaged to Eleni, you will not migrate. You'll stay in your country. You have given your word!"

"Yes!" I confirm once more.

Eleni and I are engaged.

Plans for the Future

So now I am in Kyrenia, having given my word to stay here permanently. I will get married, start a family, and settle down at last! But it's not that simple: How am I going to make a living here? And what is Kyrenia? Since in 1913, when I left, only one new house has been built, that of Yiannakos Demetriades, the first notable, the son of the late Hadjiglioris. The Administration is still housed in the same wooden shacks north of the Castle. The market – a series of arches on one side where the butchers are, and three plain walls – is an enclosed square courtyard, where vendors sell produce and other goods; at night it closes with a large, sturdy lattice door. At the hospital, which is the best-built of all government buildings, the same two English nurses serve still, Miss Atthill and Miss Trey. Yet there has been change in the Archbishopric: Kyrilloudi has been Archbishop since 1917, when Kyrillatsos breathed his last. In the district of Kyrenia, Metropolitan Makarios Myriantheas has decided to move the seat of the Metropolis from Ayios Panteleimon Monastery in Myrtou to Kyrenia. To this end, he finishes the construction on a small hill

with vineyards, west of the river, half a mile from the sea, near the
Severion School for Boys. The School for Boys also remains un-
changed, except that two grades have been added above the sixth,
something similar to the first two grades of gymnasium. Now the
mayor is Charilaos Demetriades of the well-known family of the
notable Hadjiglorios. Ioannides is the judge, Ieropoulos the government doctor, who is renting my fiancee's house, and McDonald[4] is the District Commissioner. He is married to the daughter
of V.S. Petrides, a Greek who lives in England; as a result, the
governor speaks some broken Greek. And so in Kyrenia, which is
more a village than a town, there are roughly 350 houses, 1,500
Greeks, and approximately 500 Turks of whom almost all live in
Pano Kerynia. There are ships but hardly any trade. With the end
of the World War all European goods, which are transported in
large ships, go directly to the Port of Famagusta. There is no longer demand for the goods from the East that Kyrenia's ships once
imported, and the war between Greece and Turkey makes things
so difficult that what little trade remained at the port of Kyrenia
has also vanished. Many ships are docked at the port; other than
the one in which my friend Yiannis Vrahas is a partner, Mitsides
has one, and the Vrahas family owns another in partnership with
Captain Panais and the Keleshis'. Unfinished at Proti Tsiakkileri
lies Savvis Severis's ship, dead before it was born – a skeleton for
children to climb upon and play. The Phytos brothers, the two
craftsmen that masterfully built the ships' interiors and tholepins,
have left. Danezis, who came to Kyrenia from the East, builds
small fishing boats and barges for the transport of carobs from the
orchards. I learn that some activity was created with the arrival
of Russian refugees after the October Uprising, but they have also
left Kyrenia in search of better opportunities elsewhere. Two or
three Britons live here permanently, with Houstoun being the
first. They employ a few locals, thereby supporting four or five

---

4 Eldred McDonald, District Commissioner of Kyrenia 1912-1927.

families, but this does not improve the overall situation. Only the
moneylenders are prospering by giving loans to poor farmers and
charging interest on top of interest until they break their backs.
They seize their land, put it on the auction block, and buy it for
pennies. Consequently, the moneylenders are the largest landowners, who end up renting to farmers the land that they took
from them. And that's not all: The district's entire carob, oil and
wheat trade has come under their control, since they also seize the
farmers' harvest as a repayment of their debts, although most of
the time this covers only the interest. The lawyers are not suffering either, since they can count on the trials of indebted locals. A
few landowners farm the land themselves, such as Kyriakos Lordos. Shop owners such as the Leptos family, Christophis Kestas
and Neocles Loizou are not faring too badly either. Beyond the activity generated by locals, the arrival of approximately one dozen
government employees has also created some change. And in the
summer months people from Nicosia come here to swim, looking
for a break from the heat. Using wicker partitions without a roof,
Petros Vrahas has sectioned off a rectangular stretch of beach below the Akteon Hotel and put old Hadjiportolos in charge. Wom-
en bathe within that enclosure, even locals, since they do not run
the risk of being seen or of tanning, thereby making themselves
unattractive. Even Eleni and her cousins go there to swim and
cool down in the summer months. Women from Nicosia, who are
more liberal, sometimes leave the enclosure, causing young men's
blood to boil – not those of my generation, however, since almost
all of the men in my age group, now in their thirties, are married
with small children. My schoolmate Spyros, the son of Kyriakos
Lordos, has graduated medical school. He is married to Marit-
sa, the youngest daughter of the notable Hadjiglioris; he is doing
the best among us. My brother-in-law Yiannis Vottis is married to
Mirou, the daughter of the shoemaker Polydoros; in elementary
school I had teased Spyros that Mirou was his fiancée and we got
into a fight. My best friend Yiannis Vrahas married Cleopatra from

Bellapais, and his brother married Athinou, the daughter of Had-
jistillis from Karavas – the girl that he was pining for in America.
Neocles Loizou, who is married to the daughter of Kyriakos Lordos, the sister of Dr. Spyros, has bought Karatzias's shop and is doing well because he enjoys his work. Mattheos Kariolos has settled
down with Panio, a refugee from Strantza; he met her during his
travels in the East and brought her and her parents back to Kyrenia. An incurable lover of the sea, he insists on trade and shipping.
Christodoulis Anayiotos, who is married to Marie, the niece of
Captain Petroulios, has also opened a grocery store. Some clubs
and associations exist but they are barely surviving. The younger
men, who have not migrated, are involved with athletics. With the
help of the Metropolitan of Kyrenia, they have founded an athletic
club named "Praxandros"; they are getting some regular exercise.

   I also get regular exercise by cultivating my land. While I was
away, I gave power of attorney to the lawyer Yiannakos Demetriades, so he could manage my affairs. Of my father's land my share
was 2½ skales,[5] along with an orchard of half a skala with access
to water. This is approximately the same as what all my brothers
and sisters inherited, except Antonis. He gave some money to my
siblings for a little more land and kept the family home since,
married as he is to Mariannou from Dikomo, he is the only one
who still lives in Karakoumi. I did not receive any compensation
for my share of the paternal home; I let my brother have it. But
I sent money for the purchase of 1½ skales from Paraskevas, the
father of the muhtar[6] of Karakoumi, and for 1½ skales from another villager, along with 5/7 of the village's running water. I also
bought my sisters' land in Karakoumi but not Antonis's. I own

---

5 Skala/skales (Greek: σκάλα/σκάλες): In Cyprus a "skala" is a unit of
measurement used primarily for land.

6 Muhtar: In Turkey and some Arab countries, the muhtar is the head of a
town or village. The term is used in Cyprus as well.

approximately twenty skales altogether and running water. I rise at the crack of dawn and, with the help of two labourers whom I pay by the day, I clear away stones from my land. During all those years that my brother Glioris was cultivating it, not only did I not receive any money, but I also sent him money for its cultivation. In the beginning I was certain that, with me managing it, the land would yield a profit; but I soon realized that my brother was right. Farming is essentially a dead end. The olive and carob trees do not yield a crop every year, and the olive fly further reduces oil production. Lemon and other orchard trees yield a good quality harvest when cared for, but there are no buyers for the produce. There is no possibility for export and, when it comes to local sales, what can you expect when Kyrenians grow what they need for their families in their backyards? It's plain to see that I cannot support a family from farming, at least not with the amount of land that I own. So what do I do?

With the £1,000 that I have collecting interest with Fieros, I could make a start as a moneylender and make a comfortable living. But do I want to make a living by suing, seizing and selling off the properties of the poor, or by taking their harvest to pay off interest? I neither have the heart, nor the desire; in fact, this is something that I detest to the depths of my being! For a short time I consider opening a shop, but so many of my friends and acquaintances have gone down that road; moreover, I have no interest in this line of work. Yiannakos Demetriades's proposal to hire me as a cook is not even worth considering. How much would he pay me and what type of cooking would I be doing in his house? Although he means well, he made the offer because he knows nothing about the culinary arts or how the kitchens of large American restaurants and hotels are organized.

I keep pondering all this as I remove stones, knowing that this land will feed neither my wife nor my children. Although it is difficult to pinpoint exactly when the idea first dawned on me, I start thinking about building a large hotel, where I could utilize my skills as a chef. Why not? They are no such hotels in Cyprus. And this would certainly solve all my problems. I have no options regarding the location; I have given my word to my father-in-law that I would stay in Kyrenia and marry Eleni. As I remove stones the idea matures inside me. I like it more and more! I would be master of the kitchen in my own hotel – a real hotel like the ones in America, a far cry from the pitiful ones in Cyprus.

I look for a site and find a suitable location: out of town to the west, high up, above an old quarry, a pristine stretch of land with nothing but savory and wild flowers – tulips, cyclamens, thorny brooms – near the dilapidated church of Ayia Varvara! Beneath is a spring with clean water, while the sea is approximately 200 to 300 metres away. The land looks onto Proti Tsiakileri with Savvis Severis's unfinished ship, then to the tithe storehouses, to Chamberlain's Catholic church, and finally to Kyrenia with Archangelos Church – bright white with its bell tower gleaming against the sky, which is blue most days of the year. This area to the west, approximately one square mile or more, belongs to Houstoun. Everyone says the man is eccentric, even Britons. The Administration brought a case against him for not farming his land since the law states that, if you do not cultivate your land for a certain number of years, the government will seize it. When Houstoun appeared in court, he declared that he intentionally does not cultivate his land because everything that grows there is beautiful and unique, and because he uses the land as a grazing pasture for the sheep that he has brought from Scotland. Houstoun always wears a monocle and, when asked about it, he replies that looking at Kyrenia with one eye more than suffices! Many stories circulate about the man, yet he was the one who built the Anglican church near the Castle and the police station at the passage of Ayia Ekaterini. He employs a few hapless locals and Kyriakos Lordos still manages his kitchen despite all the money that he has made over the years – this is, in

fact, why he has been nicknamed "lordos."[7] Kyriakos Lordos is still
his regular cook not because he needs to work, but as a favour to
Houstoun. He started working for him when he was very young —
a barefoot, indigent orphan that supported himself this way. Having no other option, I meet with Savvas Christis from Thermia, a
lawyer who studied in Athens, and instruct him to write a letter
to Houstoun: "Dear Sir…" I enquire as to whether he would consider selling the land around Ayia Varvara and about the price. In
the letter I explain that I plan to build a luxury hotel in Kyrenia,
which is such a beautiful place where many people would love to
come for holidays. Instead of a response, I receive an invitation to
tea!

Houstoun's home is lovely, built entirely of cut stone, to west
of Kyrenia, in the middle of the land that he insists on not cultivating. I go with my fiancée; he receives us in his garden and serves
tea. Eleni and I sip our tea as politely as possible, whereas he fills
a huge bowl, dips big chunks of cake into the tea, eats and feeds
the dog which is waiting next to him and looking curiously at me.
After some time, he speaks frankly:

"Regarding your letter and request to buy some of my land…
Unfortunately, I can't sell you anything."

"Why is that?"

"I have made some enquiries and Mr. Eftymiades, the judge,
has advised me not to sell it to you."

"Why not?"

"Mr. Efthymiades says that you're not capable of building a
chicken coop, let alone a hotel. He has also told me that those
who return from America are crazy, that they have overactive
imaginations!"

Sharp and to the point, his words leave me speechless! Fortu-

---

7 The nickname "Lordos" (Greek: Λόρδος) is derived from the English
word "Lord."

nately Eleni does not speak English, so she has no idea what was said; otherwise I would not have been able to swallow the insult. Embittered, I take Eleni and leave but, on the way back, she wants to know what happened. I tell her that they think I am incapable of building a chicken coop!

"At least he told you what they said, Costas. Maybe we can find another place for the hotel," she says calmly.

But where? The only land that we own in Kyrenia is her house, which is rented to Dr. Ieropoulos. The house itself is a mess and the surrounding area is dirty, I respond.

"One step at a time, Costas. God will make a way!" she says and her voice has certitude.

I feel encouraged!

"Are you suggesting that we start the hotel at your house? Would you agree to that?"

"If that's what you want to do, Costas."

I am touched – not simply because she agrees to turn her house into a hotel but because she is so supportive and loving toward me. Other than my father, she is the first person who is truly there for me.

Eleni's House

Eleni's house is a mess. Built at the edge of the mouth of the Koronos torrent, it is square two-storey building with large windows and a balcony that overlooks the sea. The area in front of the house is awash with seaweed and all kinds of other filth, which is carried downhill by the torrent two or three days a year. It's no coincidence that the river is nicknamed "Kotsirkas."[8] Near the house, at the top of the river's delta, a wooden bridge connects the two riverbanks. Its planks are rotten and the rail tracks, which the British used to transport boulders for the repair of the port in the

---

8 Kotsirkas (Greek: Κοτσίρκας) means "river of excrement."

previous century, are still there. Discarded metal from the same work lies about: mainly railcar wheels, rusted like the tracks that continue past the tithe storehouses and end beyond Proti Tsiak-kileri, at the huge quarry caves. A dirt road, or rather a footpath, passes in front of the house and ends west of the government's tithe storehouses. At harvest time, whether they like it or not, growers are required to deliver one tenth of their wheat as tax, in the amounts specified by Koltzis,[9] who travels around placing seals on crops. A terrible ruckus is created in this area because the animals loathe crossing Xylogiofyro.[10] The farmers try to get them to move using foul language, from the most ancient to the most vulgar Turkish profanities, including the most common "Ate oush! Tininisihtimini!" the meaning of which I have never learned. I am astounded by how much the animals resist crossing this bridge until I notice that, when they step on one decrepit plank, the opposite side rises up and spooks them. But the farmers or animal drivers do not restrict themselves to swearing; they also add flogging to the mix until the animals overcome their fear and move forward.

A makeshift stall for the doctor's mule is at the back of the house. Next to that, on a small rocky hill, stands the house of Bonnouis. Below are the caves, where the baker Poeros raises pigs, which smell horribly and attract flies, making a bad situation even worse. Not far from the tithe storehouses is the office-room of the attendant. Tirnavos held that position in 1913 but now, eight or nine years later, someone else is at that post. At a small distance stands the house of Elisseos Pittas from Karavas, directly across from the Kyrenia Municipality. Further up, on another small rocky hill, is Chamberlain's church – an attractive, stone-built structure yet disused because it's Catholic. Kyrenia has no Catholics what-

---

9 Koltzis (Κολτζιής): The employee who calculated the amount of crop and determined the tithe tax.

10 Xylogiofyro (Greek: Ξυλογιόφυρο) means "wooden bridge."

soever. The few resident Britons, who are all Anglicans, go to their
church, the one that Houstoun built near the Castle.

I explore the area further. Behind the tithe storehouses are the
slaughterhouses and the caves where the town's fuel is stored:
benzene in four-gallon containers and petroleum in large drums.
Further up, on the riverbank, stands my sister-in-law Styliani's
house, which is rented out because she lives in Bellapais with her
husband. Beyond that are the makeshift shop on Costis's property and my father-in-law's fields, where he cultivates vegetables,
lemon and other trees that provide the basics, mostly for his family. Further up still, near the Lapithos-Karavas road, are the buildings that house Paronakis's flour and olive mills. The entire area is
considered remote, the outskirts of Kyrenia, but I have decided to
make a start with my fiancée's house. The first order of business
is a major renovation! We will need a proper house to live in, regardless of my plans for the hotel. Later on, using the money that
I have collecting interest with Fieros, I can build something better,
something to my liking. Repairs it is then!

But repairs how...? The house is occupied. I return to Christis's
law office to draft a polite letter to Dr. Ieropoulos. One afternoon, just as I am coming back from my fields in Karakoumi, my
father-in-law informs me that the doctor wants to see me. We go
to his house together. A fine doctor from Hydra, Ieropoulos is
the type of man who will not allow anyone to challenge him; no
Kyrenian of those he has treated has ever dared to contradict him!
The only one who defies him is his wife. Mrs. Ieropoulos, who
hails from Larnaca, is always mouthing off because she is jealous
of the young matron at the hospital. We can hear their daily fights
all the way across the river at my in-laws' house, when I go there
for supper. We pretend not to notice and her suspicions are un-
founded in any case; it's simply a case of jealousy. Everyone knows
that Britons do not associate with locals easily; on the contrary,
they see themselves as a superior race.

The doctor is looking at me with incredulity. He takes the letter out of his pocket and shakes it threateningly at me.

"What is the meaning of this? You want me to leave the house?"

"Yes, Dr. Ieropoulos."

"What do you need a house for? Kyrenia has so many caves, why don't you go live in one?"

I am affronted but do my best to remain gracious.

"I want to open a hotel, Dr. Ieropoulos."

He laughs, obviously refusing to take my response seriously, so I became angry. I become very angry!

"Dr. Ieropoulos, if you do not leave of your own accord, I will take you to court."

"Do as you like! But I'm not leaving."

I go to see Mayor Charilis, who is also an attorney. He looks at me as though he does not understand what I am saying.

"What do you mean?"

"I want to take Ieropoulos to court because he refuses to leave my fiancée's house."

"You mean the doctor?"

"Yes, Mr. Charilis!"

He says nothing for a few moments, then cracks a smile and looks at me again.

"What can I say? I will not take the case. I'm the mayor..."

Not having understood why he has refused the case, I go next door to the office of Miltiades Shiakallis, who is said to be the best attorney in Kyrenia. He is anything but polite, however; he glares at me with ferocity.

"What? You think you can come here from hell's half acre expecting to get the man out of his home... Have you no shame?"

Seeing no reason to be ashamed, I continue:

"My father-in-law has given me that house as part of my fiancée's dowry..."

"Yes, but the doctor might as well have bought the house with the rentals that he's been paying all the years!"

"The rent is only £1.50 per month, Mr. Shiakallis, and it is my fiancée's house after all. We're getting married and we need it. Will you take the case?"

He refuses! In the end I find a lawyer: Dorotheos Carolides from Lapithos, who is married to Eleni Kel Panais, my fiancée's cousin. Carolides is a large man who sports a moustache. He owns a great deal of property in Lapithos, but he is not a big name lawyer in Kyrenia and does not have many clients. I explain the situation to him and he answers my questions. Then he looks at me with a smile as he twists his moustache.

"You ask 'why'...? The doctor, the mayor, Shiakallis, the lawyers, the moneylenders the landowners belong to the status class. Do you think they would ever let an immigrant spoil things for them? They would crush him in the blink of an eye!" he tells me.

Then he expounds on the status class, the esteemed persons that everyone must show reverence and bow their heads to... He even talks about how the wealthy endlessly profit from the blood and sweat of the workers, who barely make a living. He speaks about social justice, interesting things, but my mind is elsewhere: What will happen with my life? How will I make a living in Kyrenia?

"So will you sue the doctor to get out him of my fiancée's house?" I ask.

"Yes, but I will attempt to get him out of his own accord first, Catsellis!"

"Why don't you just bring his to court?"

"Because he's a doctor! And as you know, with doctors and priests, in spite how much money we give them, we're always indebted to them."

Kyrenians turn against me when they hear that I am trying to get the doctor out of my fiancée's house. At the coffee shop Savvis Severis mocks me, failing to acknowledge that he is almost bankrupt because of the unfinished ship at Proti Tsiakileri, behind the tithe storehouses! Antonis Vrahas curses me but in a friendly way.

"What can I tell you when... when..."

He does not understand why I would leave behind a large salary in America to come to Kyrenia to sue the doctor and stir up trouble. Every day 'well-wishers' come to tell me what this or that person has said. I am upset by the situation but say nothing until I hear that Yiannis Vrahas, my best friend, was bragging at the coffee shop:

"Leave the boy to me; I'll send him back to where he came from..."

Truth be told, I can stomach everything but this! During a walk that we take together in Karavas I can't hold back.

"I heard that you said this... Is it true?" I ask.

"Of course not! Would I ever say such a thing about you?" he says and his eyes start to water.

I believe him. A huge weight is off my chest – I have not lost my best friend. Nevertheless, I do not think he places as much faith in my plans as Eleni does. I am determined to carry on.

I ask Pavlos Hadjicostis for the £50 that I lent him at High Life Confectionary and for the money that he collected from Efstathios on my behalf in 1913. He asks for compensation:

"I've done so much for you, Catsellis!" he tells me but I'm no longer buying anything the man says.

"Yes, but I'm asking only for what I've lent you and what you collected on my behalf, Mr. Pavlos! Have you tallied up how much interest the money that you've managed for me since 1913 has accrued?" I ask.

If I were to demand it, the interest that he has been collecting on my money for nine years would exceed the original amount. Eventually he gives me the money, but now he is really angry with me; he was already vexed when the deal for the hotel in Nicosia sunk.

Eventually, Carolides convinces the doctor to move out without a trial. He moves into the house that my father-in-law gave his

eldest Yiannis on the Karavas-Lapithos road. Yiannis and his wife
Mirou live at the rear, where I am also staying. Carolides has accomplished the task without upsetting the status class, even if it
has taken until the end of 1921 to settle out of court. But I have no
complaints because I feel calm all this time; I have no urgent work
other than the fields in Karakoumi and, in winter, there isn't much
I can do there anyway. For the first time in my life I am enjoying
myself as I get to know Eleni. Little by little we become comfortable with each other.

The First Sea View Hotel,
1922

At the beginning of 1922, Dr. Ieropoulos vacates the house, which
is cube-shaped with two storeys, high ceilings, and a roof constructed with thick beams, wicker, seaweed and mud. The front
door, which faces the sea, leads opens to a hall with two rooms
on each side. The upstairs has the identical floor plan, except that
its front door exits to the balcony, which also overlooks the sea. I
throw myself into the renovations. On the ground floor, I convert
the two front rooms into sitting rooms. One of the rooms at the
back becomes a casual dining room-kitchen for the family, and the
other a large kitchen that will service the hotel. Since I cannot
find the same facilities in Cyprus as I had in America, I improvise.
A tin receptacle with grills inside, and with space around and below for lit coals, becomes an oven for roasts. When I test it, I am
pleased to discover that it makes a wonderful roast beef. On the
hearth I place some nice, handmade metal grills.

  Upstairs, one room will serve as our bedroom while the other
three are furnished with two iron beds each, with new cotton du-
vets and mattresses. The spacious hall will serve as the dining area
for guests. I install a European toilet upstairs but its tank must be
refilled every time it is used. So I also buy two tin tubs. There is no
running water in the house, but we have a well with a water wheel

at the back, albeit with brackish water. Since I have no animal, I do
the job myself. I turn the wheel and draw out water! My father-
in-law also gives me half his ration of water from the Municipality. There is already a clay oven in the backyard and I install two
sinks for laundry under the shed. Affixed to the balcony's central
beam is a rectangular sign that says in English "Sea View Hotel" – I
have always loved gazing at the sea! The renovations cost a total of
£128 and, regardless of what the sign says, this is not the hotel I
had envisioned.

So many people have tried to stand in my way. In an attempt
to foil my plans, some have even tried to convince my brother-in-
law Yiannis to demand Eleni's house in exchange for his own on
the Lapithos-Karavas road. They have not succeeded. My father-
in-law's word is firm, not that Yiannis would ever agree to such a
thing.

On May 21, on the Feast of Saints Costantinos and Eleni, Eleni
and I celebrate our name day at the newly renovated hotel; even
the Metropolitan of Kyrenia comes to perform a blessing. In the
afternoon friends and acquaintances cross the bridge of Xylogiofyro to pay us a visit. They wish us well and we treat them to food
and drinks: my friend Yiannis Vrahas and his brothers, the entire
Hadjiyiangos family from my mother-in-law's side from the opposite side of the river, my father-in-law's family, the Hadjiparaskevas family from Riatiko, my schoolmate Dr. Spyros, Neocles
Loizou, Mattheos Kariolos, Christodoulis Anayiotos. Even Pavlos,
the owner of Akteo, turns up. He is all smiles, obviously unconcerned that a second hotel has opened in Kyrenia next to the sea...

"Who's ever going to know about his hotel where he's opened
it, on the other side of Xylogiofyro?" he says.

And he is absolutely right! Three months pass from May 21
before I receive my first booking – an English couple with their
young daughter arrive from Egypt in August, but I am not given
the opportunity to enjoy their stay. Miss Trey and Miss Atthill, the
two English nurses, convince my guests to move into their room-

ing house in Pano Kerynia. I am livid! So I have it out with them: I tell them that they do not care about the locals, that they are preventing us from earning a living, and that they should give up their holier-than-thou act. Yet, these women are the last two people that deserve to hear such things; the two nurses have worked tirelessly and with dedication at the hospital for decades. If you had to fault them for something, it would have to be for attempting to proselytize the locals to their sect; they are Evangelicals. Sooner or later a few Kyrenians do join them, not because of their persuasion skills, but because two commissioners of Archangelos Church quarrel with the new Metropolitan Makarios Myriantheas. They convert out of spite. In all likelihood the nurses never meant to cause me any harm, yet I am still the loser in this situation. As I tell them off, they are wide-eyed with shock; without doubt, this is the first time they have looked at things from my perspective, so I do not regret speaking my mind. At least now they will know that they are doing harm when they solicit my guests. At the end of the day, they are nurses at the hospital; everyone should stick to what they know and let others be.

On two afternoons, Rauf Bey comes to the hotel with Pentayia's Dr. Smitter, who used to be the Tzar's physician before the October Uprising. They ask me to set a table for them next to the sea and order souvlaki. I look after them as best I can and they leave one golden lira for me. My first regular guest is the director of Kyrenia's post office, Munir Bey; he prefers my hotel to Akteo. He stays only on weekdays because on weekends he travels to Nicosia to see his family. My daily rate is six shillings for the room, and three shillings for breakfast and two meals. Since Munir Bey is a regular, I give him such a deep discount that I am left with no profit.

I do not remain idle; I start cultivating my fields in Karakoumi. Thank heavens this gives me something to do, otherwise I would go crazy without work; moreover, in time, the land starts to yield some crops. But I cannot make a living from any of these things or from the interest that I am earning from Fieros. To make matters worse, I am disconcerted by the animosity fired at me from every direction. This is what hurts most! When I go to the market with my two baskets, one in each hand, to do the shopping for the hotel, I hear ironic remarks everywhere – either whispers behind me or comments flung at me, mostly under the guise of friendliness when, in actuality, they are jabs and innuendoes. I realize that Akteo is the source of this negative feeling toward me because it lost one of its few regulars. Add to this the four or five suitors who did not succeed in marrying Eleni; they harbour resentment toward me, although I have done nothing wrong. What about everyone else?

Everyone – I included – is distraught about the developments in the East that are bad, very bad indeed! Refugees keep arriving in Kyrenia, not only natives of Asia Minor, but also Kerynians who settled there long ago and have left profitable business behind, forever lost. There is zero trade; ships are stuck at the port; Kyrenia's captains have fallen silent; everyone supports the refugees as best they can, with Metropolitan Makarios providing most of the assistance. And then there's the shocking news about the slaughter, about the destruction! What is more, chaos rules Greek politics; I try to make sense of things, to figure out what went wrong! I have always been an ardent supporter of King Constantine but he has been exiled to Italy. Nevertheless life goes on, one year rolls by, and the time we have set for our engagement has ended. We delay the wedding a little.

The Wedding

October 1922: I am getting married using the income from the hotel, a total of £15. On my wedding day I wake up in a sour mood. Without a steady income and under the weight of the tragedy of the Asia Minor Catastrophe, the responsibility of starting a family overwhelms me. Early in the morning, I am standing on the balcony of the hotel, while Kotsios Fieros prepares food for the wedding banquet. I have hired him as cook for the day since I am the groom. In America I had no problem: As a chef with a high salary, I could have treated Eleni like a queen. But the promise I have made to my father-in-law weighs heavily upon me. He does not want his daughter to be a queen in a faraway land; he wants her near him. And so I am obligated to stay in this wasteland, in this dead town – what town? – where almost everyone is hostile toward me. Standing on the balcony I can see all that is wrong around the hotel. In the three caves to the west, Poeros's pigs stink as terribly as the filth from Kotsirkas. And there is also the familiar unsightliness – dilapidated flat-bottom boats, disintegrating wagons and rail tracks. From the other side of the river, just above the sea, I hear the fiddle and the lute, a jubilant commotion; they are dressing the bride! I want to feel joyful but the responsibility of starting a family feels even heavier than before. I am agitated. I go downstairs and see Kotsios Fieros firing up the clay oven for the roasts, next to the small house at the rear. Realizing that he will need water for the dishes, I strap myself to the wheel and start walking around in circles to hoist up the small clay containers, which pour water into the sink. When the sink is full, I also fill up some tin containers. Then I return to the wheel. My groomsmen, Neocles Loizou and Paraskevas Agathangelou, who is Eleni's first cousin, arrive dressed to the nines in their black costumes.

"Costas, what on earth are you doing?"

"Is it time?"

They nod: Yes, it's time! They take me upstairs to dress me. I hear the bell of Archangelos in the distance, so I muster my courage and swallow my concerns. I am getting married and today this is all that matters; everything else can wait for another day. This is not the time to worry about the hotel, about the refugees, about King Constantine and Venizelos, about the East and the West!

The fiddle and the lute players in front, leading the way... In the church my father-in-law holds Eleni's hand and I am with my groomsmen. Eleni's bridesmaids are her sister Styliani and my sister Polyxeni's daughter Athena, who is twenty-two years old. All our family and friends are there. In the evening, we host a wedding dinner for close relatives and friends, approximately thirty people. But I have also invited the Turkish director of the post office. When someone remarks that inviting him was not appropriate, I respond that he is my only regular guest at the hotel and that I want him at my wedding; he is a good man and we should know the difference between what happens elsewhere and how we should act as human beings. Eleni and I do the money dance to the music of the fiddle and the lute, according to custom. Everything is done properly but modestly. A guest arrives at the hotel quite late; it's the crown attorney. I receive him still dressed as a groom. I give him a room and serve him dinner in the upstairs dining area. By the time I return to the wedding celebration, things are rather quiet. Apart from my siblings, nieces and nephews, and the siblings and relatives of my in-laws, Kel Panais, Agathangelos, Pavlis, Theodora Livertena with her husband are attending. Everyone has a good time but they do not stay late. Ours is a quiet wedding.

Shortly after the wedding, one of my sisters broaches the subject of transferring ownership of half the house to my name. Surprised by her demand, I ask why.

My sister does not want to say but I insist! Eventually she tells me that, if we do not have children, only Eleni's side would inherit.

"And why wouldn't we have children?" I ask.

She says that she has heard that those who return from America carry illnesses, venereal diseases and the like, and can't have children. I take this very badly indeed! Although I never wanted to be repaid, I ask for the money that I had sent her from America. I also sack her son who is working for me; he is rather slow at work in any case. Eleni means more to me now than my siblings. She supports me in her own quiet way. I can see that she loves me, although she is not one to say much. She is devoted to me and this is the first time in my life that I do not feel alone. Eleni is my wife and more important to me than anyone else in the world, siblings, relatives or friends!

First child – Lack of Work, 1923

The winter of 1922-1923 is heavy – snow atop Karamania across the sea and atop Kyrenia's mountains. One year has passed since the hotel opened and my income from it has been only £30. Kyrenia is full of refugees and the port is dead. The Phytos brothers, who were building Savvis Severis's ship, have moved away, leaving the ship unfinished. Even so, in the summer months, a few ships slowly start trading with the East again. In the fall crop is good; this is a very good year for oil. The oil mills can barely keep up with the workload. At least there is something positive! My income, however, is less than in the previous year. In the summer, Artemis and Lysandrides, two businessmen from Nicosia, come to stay at the hotel with their wives, who are sisters. But this does not improve my financial situation. My anxiety grows.

My anxiety grows because Eleni is pregnant with our first child! I am nervous; I feel strange; I am joyful but this is a different kind of joy. My schoolmate Spyros, who is a good doctor, looks after Eleni. Her time arrives at the end of November. It's a difficult delivery. Eleni is upstairs in the bedroom with her mother and sister Styliani, who are assisting Spyros and Theodora Hadjistephani, an experienced midwife and the doctor's aunt from his grandfather Hadjicharalambis second wife. I wait downstairs with my father-in-law and I am fit to be tied! I fret; I am filled with anxiety and fear… On November 23 our first child comes into the world, a daughter. Our first groomsman, the lawyer Paraskevas Agathangelou, is her godfather. We name her after my mother-in-law Despinou, according to custom. Despina has her mother's dark eyes and fair skin. I become so fixated on the baby that I become irrational. If a fly sits on her, I see red! But what can we expect when Poeros's pigs are a stone's throw away? No matter how clean we are, no matter how much order Eleni keeps in the house... It upsets Eleni when I get angry and that makes me feel worse.

I complain to Mayor Charilis about the pigs and demand that they be moved. He informs me that there is no law preventing Kyrenians from raising pigs in caves, when the owner of the property has given his permission. Nikolis Economou, the tailor, owns the caves. I make an offer for the parcel of land with the caves – half a rocky hill all in all – but he is not interested in selling, even if he has no use for it. What is more, now he has to make the effort to grow a few things on the land above the caves because of the familiar law, which states that all uncultivated land will be seized by the government. I believe his unwillingness to sell is due to Bonnouina, who has built her house on the remaining half parcel, to the west. Yet Nikolis Economou's sister sells me the parcel in between which is adjacent to our property. And it's not all rock; on the contrary its soil is quite fertile! I pay £30 for the land and plant cucumbers in early 1924. I strap myself to the wheel to water the plants; sometimes I am given water from a cistern further up. The virgin soil makes for strong plants that produce more harvest than I know what to do with – every day I fill up two baskets with cucumbers, which I sell to the greengrocers at the market. I earn £8 from cucumber sales, nearly one third of what I paid for the land! But the hotel is still struggling. Even so, I hire Phanou, the sister of Stavris Vottis, who is married to a lame greengrocer. Since one of his legs has a problem, they call him "Koutsosophocles" and his wife Phanou "Koutsosophoclena." Eleni's aunt helps with the housework now that we have the baby.

The Commissioner's Visit, 1924

In the middle of all this, I receive a message that the governor is coming to stay at my hotel. I am both excited and frazzled, for this

is the governor himself! I lose my cool. We carry out a thorough
cleaning and I even hire someone to plaster the walls. Since the
governor and his entourage need all four rooms, we arrange for
Eleni and the baby to stay in Bellapais with her sister Styliani, so
we can make our bedroom available to them as well. The governor is expected to arrive at noon. Everything is ready except for
the large water tank, which still needs to be filled. At last I have
bought a large tank, so I am no longer forced to keep lugging
water upstairs in buckets, two by two, to refill the European toilet. Our daughter is with my sister—in-law Styliani at her grandmother's house across the river; they are waiting there for Eleni.
In the yard the donkeys are saddled for the ride up to the village,
should the need arise. Eleni shuts the door to our private kitchen
and fills the tin tub with hot water so I can take a bath. Despite
her unruffled exterior, I realize that my tension is affecting her. I
quickly undress and just as I am about to step in…

"Don't! I haven't mixed the water yet! It's boiling hot, Costas,"
she shouts at the last moment.

I freeze! I was seconds away from a third degree burn… And
the governor…? Eleni pours in the two containers of cold water
that she has already prepared, and I bathe horrified at the thought
that I could have scalded myself and not been able to tend to the
governor. Once more I am gripped by that same childhood fear,
by that unbearable feeling of inferiority and insecurity. This is the
first time that I have felt it so intensely since my return to Kyrenia.
I share my feelings with Eleni.

"That's all in the past, Costas! All is well. Don't worry, I'll be
thinking about you in Bellapais."

Her tranquillity eases my anxiety. I regain my composure and
get ready. My father-in-law, who is a great help to me, arrives; he
is the only one with a dignified composure.

"If the governor doesn't like it here, he can find some other
place to sleep!" he says. And he means it!

Precisely at noon the governor arrives. His black car stops just
before Xylogiofyro because, in the shape that the bridge is in, it

cannot get across. Dressed in a slick uniform Kavazis, his Turkish aide, opens the door for him. Karanikkis, his driver, also steps out of the car. One or two other staffers begin to unload his things. He has brought his cook, so I am exiled from my own kitchen.

"Stand back! Stand back!" Karanikkis says to me and I take offense.

But there is nothing I can do. On the third day of their stay, I offer to prepare breakfast.

"Stand back, you don't know how they want their grapefruit sliced!" he says abruptly.

Incensed now, I pick up a grapefruit and cut it flawlessly

"You mean like this?" I ask.

Like that indeed! The driver eats his words and never tells me to step back again. On the last day, the tenth, I offer to cook the roast.

"You know how?" Karanikkis asks in disbelief.

I nod.

"Be careful because the governor has the meat brought in from Egypt!"

I say nothing more; I simply fire up my improvised oven and cook the roast. Just as the governor is about to depart, he turns to me:

"I truly enjoyed the beef!"

"I worked as a roaster in America," I explain.

"If I send you the meat, would you cook it for me?"

"Of course, it would be my pleasure!"

We shake hands and he departs.

I am pleased but I am also in a rush. I go across the river to my father-in-law's house to see Eleni, who has returned from Bellapais.

"So, how did it go?" she asks.

"Good, but if I had a better location it would have been…"

"Alright, alright… One step at a time, Costas!" she says.

I received £1 per day from the governor because he ended up bringing more things and staff than necessary. I also have the thirty golden liras from Pentayia's doctor, who has become a regular; he pays one golden lira every time he visits. The members of the Criminal Court also stay at my hotel now. No, I still cannot make a living on £30-40 a year but, since the governor's stay, I am convinced that there is no way I would fail, if I built a large hotel with all the necessary amenities. And this is something that Cyprus does not have: a hotel with attractive rooms, each with a full ensuite bathroom, and with a large kitchen where I can cook whatever I want. I have the money that is collecting interest with Fieros. Why am I keeping it there? I am not one to collect interest; I do not *want* to collect interest. Moreover, the interest that Fieros pays me is low, since he keeps most of it for himself. I go over everything again: Yes, my business is losing money but, as time passes, it loses less and less, even with three lousy rooms with six beds, two tin baths and one European toilet, whose tank breaks my back every time I fill it up with water, two buckets at a time, up a flight of stairs. As far as the kitchen is concerned, it is not easy but I always manage to present good food. This is certain because every week the governor sends me the beef that he brings in from Egypt so I can cook a roast for him. Since I have no fridge, in the summer I lower drinks in a basket into a borehole in the backyard to cool them. Around this time I also hire a full-time assistant, Yiorkos Adamou from Bellapais, who is a relative of my sister-in-law Styliani. He is a very nice young man who speaks English, since he is a graduate of Newham's in Nicosia. Above all he is smart and fast. He quickly learns everything: I teach him how to serve, how to fix drinks, how to prepare the rooms. He respects Eleni and me, and he is incredibly honest; if he drinks an orange juice at the hotel, he insists on paying for it. I start him off with a salary of £1 per month. So now I have someone in charge at the hotel while I run errands and it's obvious that, with Yiorgos, I can build bigger things without worrying about staff. And there is certainly no shortage of folks looking for work: Young people are constantly leaving the country because they can't find work where they live.

If I had a hotel, surely they would prefer to stay in their homeland than endure the hardship of going overseas. I go over my plans again and again, but I realize that I need experts to realize them. Where do I find these experts?

Plans for the Second Sea View Hotel – Second Child, 1925

In the middle of 1925 a young man by the name of Photiades returns from Athens; he is a graduate of the School of Architecture. I pay him a visit. I discuss my plans with him and describe exactly what I want to build and how – I give him details about the kitchens and the rooms. I instruct him to draw up plans as quickly as possible. He agrees to work on the project. By the time I return to the hotel from the market – one basket in each hand – the young architect is there, waiting for me. I take the baskets into the kitchen and return to the hall where he shows me the plans. The design for the new hotel is exactly how I had envisioned it. It has two floors: The drawing rooms, the kitchens and six rooms are on the ground floor, while on the first floor there are twelve rooms with private bathrooms, equipped with ensuite toilets and baths. The site where I intend to build the new hotel is the land that I bought from the sister of Nikolis the tailor, next to the existing hotel. Yiorkos Adamou is there now, drawing water from the well and watering the cucumbers. I call him and he comes to serve a drink to the architect. As I look over the plans again, I begin to consider the difficulties; I am especially concerned about materials. There is plenty of gravel at the mouth of Kotsirkas, more than enough in fact, but what about stone? The architect assures me that the stone at the back of my property is not only suitable, but also in sufficient quantities. This means that my plan can be realized!

The architect leaves and I, not wasting a second, start organizing everything. I have heard about an expert builder who has come to Kyrenia from Constantinople, Master Kyriakos. I go to see him.

"I am going to build a large hotel. Would you supervise the construction?" I propose. Master Kyriakos accepts.

My schoolmate Demetros, the son of Mihalatzis, is a painter; he does repair jobs for Houstoun and knows construction. I propose that he take on the responsibility of paying the labourers; he agrees. I return to the hotel and look at my employee rather intensely.

"Yiorkos, it looks like we're starting to build... What do you say? Are you ready to roll up your sleeves?" I ask.

"God willing, Boss! Of course..." he replies.

By that afternoon everything is set. I sit down and look at the sea for a while. Since I have been back in Cyprus, this is the first time that I feel that I am truly accomplishing something, truly living. I think about Eleni, but Eleni does not require that I ask her permission. She agrees with me and, more importantly, she trusts me!

Pregnant for the second time, Eleni is afraid of the labour; she really suffered with her first. So we dedicate our second child to Apostle Andreas in advance. And he helps! On September 17, she delivers a boy. Since our son has been dedicated, we baptise him at Apostolos Andreas Monastery. My sister-in-law Styliani is the godmother, and the boy is named Andreas. With two very young children now, Eleni has a lot on her plate; fortunately Koutsopho-clena helps with the cleaning and the laundry, both for the family and for the hotel.

Ancient Tombs

Most of my time is spent at the hotel but, at every spare moment, I am at the construction site working with the labourers. My employee Yiorkos does the same. While we are digging the foundations, we come across an ancient tomb! The law, which the British have established regarding antiquities, is strict: Anyone who finds something and fails to report it to the authorities receives a fine of

£100 and a prison term. So the moment we come across the entrance to the tomb, I notify the police. The police send a telegram to the Museum in Nicosia, and they respond that someone will visit the site the following day. My workers are sent home and a Turkish police officer arrives to guard the tomb. At night I bring him food. He is shivering since winter is well on its way. Although I do not feel the cold in bed, I can't catch a wink. I have heard so much about antiquities over the years, starting with my father's unlucky discovery. He found the objects, hid it in our house from where they were stolen, and the theft became the cause for my mother's death, the reason why we were orphaned. Then there were the artefacts that Karaviotes were clandestinely bringing to Malikkis's house at night... Malikkis would buy the objects for fez-fulls of money and sell them abroad, receiving payments in golden liras. The law instituted by the British may be strict but our age-old unwritten law says "finders keepers." At the present time, even the law states that one third of any antiquity discovery goes to the owner of the property. While Eleni is asleep and without her knowing, I get up, take two candles and matches, and go downstairs. I keep lookout for a while to make sure that the policeman is asleep; he is sitting at the corner, where he is sheltered from the wind. I listen to his snoring for a few moments then proceed with caution. I enter the tomb. Upon lighting the first candle I see a large cavity, which has been dug out of the rock. There are bones on the ground but these bones are not normal; they are much larger, huge in fact, like the remains of giants, not ordinary people. Or is it that they look this way to me? I do not know. Among the bones there are many vessels, pieces of pottery, small and large. I take a closer look. Nothing else, nothing of value... As I move deeper inside the tomb I discover, at the point where the roof slopes down, a smaller opening slightly above ground. I pass through it and find myself in another tomb. This one is smaller and its roof is shaped like a dome. I notice a hole on the ground. When I try it, I pass through without any difficulty. I descend into a third tomb, which is also full of bones and pottery but nothing more. Having finished my exploration, I decide to leave but cannot fit through the opening into the third tomb; it is as though it has shrunk. My arms seem to be in the way; I don't know how to position them and my shoulders do not fit as I attempt to climb out – they seem to be too broad for the opening. After the first unsuccessful attempts I am overcome with anxiety and fear. Suddenly it dawns on me that I am inside a grave. My mind becomes flooded with dreadful thoughts! Could it be that I have angered the giants who have left their remains here? Could they be trying to prevent me from leaving? I redouble my efforts. After a fair amount of exertion I manage to pass through the opening, exhausted and drenched in sweat, without a treasure but thankfully safe and sound. Still snoring away, the cop does not take notice as I creep back upstairs to bed. I am safe! And I've spared the ridicule. Phew!

The next day Markis, the representative of the Museum, arrives with two others.

"So are the workers going to help remove the vessels from the tomb and sieve the soil so we can see if there's anything of value?" he asks.

I look at him and the first thing I notice is a nervous tic, which causes him to repeatedly open and close his mouth. I am not at all pleased that, instead of building the hotel, my workers will be removing pottery and sieving soil from the tombs, but I say nothing. To make matters worse, Markis insists that the soil be sieved finely and with a great deal of care. When the workers finish the work, Markis goes through the pottery and makes his selections. He casts a few vessels aside, having determined that they are of no value, and places the rest in baskets as he prepares to return to Nicosia. I catch up to him as he is about to depart.

"Mr. Markis…Who is going to pay the labourers for their work today?" I ask and immediately see that he is startled by my question.

"What? The Museum has no money whatsoever, Mr. Catsellis!" he replies, opening and closing his mouth as always.

Anger builds up inside me but I say nothing; I realize that I am not going to accomplish anything by insisting. I pay the workers myself, and we continue working on the foundations. All I want is to move forward with construction.

In a few days we come across a second tomb! This time I have no expectations of finding treasures; on the contrary, I am dismayed because this means more delays and paying workers to sieve soil for no reason! When I look inside the tomb, I see a few pieces of pottery embedded in the rock; it would be very difficult to loosen them. At the entrance, high up, a calligraphic inscription of the name "Polynikes" is carved into the stone. I want to avoid dealing with the Museum and Markis again, if at all possible. McDonald, the governor of Kyrenia, is a regular at the hotel; I also know that he is a curator at the Museum. I decide to ask him to have a look at the tomb. If he determines that it contains nothing special, he may give me permission to proceed with construction. McDonald comes to have a look and, being a tall man, bumps his head on the inscription "Polynikes." Nevertheless, he examines everything and gives me permission to proceed. The next day Pavlakis, the police officer, notices the new tomb. He lives nearby, behind Bonnouis's house, and passes by the construction site every day on his way to work. He reports me to Police Chief Markos, who is a bit of a poser because he pursued the Chasamboulia. Markos sends a message that I should cease construction immediately.

"I will not stop building!" I tell them.

His people return to the police station and come back with an order that I am to report to the chief immediately.

"I have ordered you to stop building," Markos says abruptly as soon as he lays eyes on me.

His tone vexes me; I dig in my heels.

"And I've sent you a message that I'm not going to stop!" I respond in the same tone.

"Why not?"

I explain the situation – that my workers are losing wages and that I am forced to pay for work that should be paid for by the Museum, not to mention the delay and that the tombs are empty.

"I don't care! I'm going to send an officer there now to order them to stop working!"

I become extremely angry. I lean out of the window and call out to a boy on the street. I take three grosia out of my pocket and throw it to him.

"Hey boy, take this for your trouble. Go tell Master Kyriakos not to stop construction," I instruct the youngster.

Thrilled, the boy takes the money and rushes off, but Markos is livid.

"Come on, let's go see the governor!" he tells me.

Infuriated as I am, I do not inform Markos that the governor and I have already settled the matter. I follow him to the Administration Building, which is nearby. Markos asks to see the governor privately but, when McDonald sees me through the half-open door, he asks me to step inside. Markos gets a rude awakening and I exact my revenge for the way he has spoken to me, when the governor assures him that he is aware of the situation and that, as a curator for the Museum, he has already given me permission to proceed. The matter is settled but now Markos has it out for me; he cannot stand me, just as I cannot stand him.

And there seems to be no end to the tombs... Another appears at the location where the bar is going to be built. We discover six skeletons in a row and some pottery with nice decorations but nothing more. This time I notify no one; with the help of Hadjishiakallis, one of my employees, we hide the pottery at the root of the cypress tree, west of Eleni's house, under a mound of wood-shavings. We seal the tomb and continue building. I proceed in the same way when I come across more tombs.

One day, someone who is staying at the George Hotel in Nicosia, the capital's only good hotel, notices the pottery that Markis had discarded. He offers to buy it.

"You can have it," I tell him.

"How much?"

"Nothing!"

"No, that wouldn't be right. You have to let me give you something," the man insists.

A Turkish stonecutter is listening and, despite that he does not speak English, works out what the conversation is about.

"Take the money and we'll split it, Effendi!" he calls out to me.

"Okay, give me sixteen shillings," I say to the man in English.

The Turk and I divide the money between us. So eight shillings are my total proceeds from the ancient tombs, even if Kyrenia is abuzz with rumours that I have uncovered priceless treasures! But I have no treasures and my heart no longer skips a beat at the thought of ancient tombs. At some point I even dig up the pottery, which I buried under the wood-shavings, place it in three baskets, and deliver it to the police. I close the book on the subject of antiquities for good! The only thing that matters to me is completing the hotel as quickly as possible to the standards that I envision. But how do I accomplish this when I have run into money problems?

The Unexpected Lender-Saviour

The work is at an advanced stage; the ground floor is complete. Its roof is made of béton armé, poured reinforced concrete. This is the first construction of its kind in Kyrenia – no beams, no wicker, no mud. The roof of the upper floor is ready to be poured but I have little money left. It is not enough, so what do I do? I start considering returning to America despite having given my word to my father-in-law that I would never leave. The plan is that I would go there on my own, work as a chef for a short period of time, and return with enough savings to finish the hotel! How long would this take? One year, maximum two... My father-in-law is a sensible man; surely he would understand, surely he would not object. I would go there on my own while Eleni, his daughter, would stay in Kyrenia. Without speaking to anyone about this,

I secretly make enquiries and learn that immigration laws have changed in America. Now permits and other formalities are required that take a year or more to process. I am under pressure, so my blood starts to boil. Around the time that I am feeling this way, an American ambassador, who is travelling around, comes to the hotel. He chats me up and I tell him that I spent a number of years working as a chef in his homeland.

"What do you think of the United States?" he asks.

"It's the worse country in the world," I respond.

He is taken aback.

"Why is that?"

"Because when they wanted me to be filler in the war they made me an American citizen in 25 minutes. The only thing I had to do was raise my hand along with five or six thousand other men. The oath stated that I renounce all allegiance to any other country. I took the oath and now they won't let me return to the United States. What country do I go to now that I've renounced all others?"

The ambassador falls silent for a few moments then asks me to write all this down.

"Unfortunately, I don't know how to write in English. I've only learned how to speak the language."

"Can you give me your name then?"

I give him my name and my information from the United States Army. He departs and I am left with my construction project, crushed by worries over money.

The parliamentary representative for Kyrenia, who is a professional moneylender, had told me before he was elected that he would lend me money, should the need arise. Intending to take him up on his offer, I go to see him at his office – he is an elected official now. First he eats his words then tells me that it was not a smart move on my part to start building a hotel out there in no man's land. He asks whether I have taken into account that my expenses have exceeded my income since I opened the hotel.

Even if that were not the case, he says, the money would still not be available.

I think of approaching the harshest moneylender of all, Sovaros, who would skin you alive! When I ask for a loan, he demands that I hypothecate the construction in advance. He says that he will lend me the money after he sells the season's carob harvest! I shop regularly from Christodoulis Anayiotos, an old friend of mine from America. One day, when I happen to mention my predicament, he says that he has £600 collecting interest with Fieros. Since the interest that Fieros pays him is quite low, we agree that he would take his money back from Fieros and lend it to me at the higher interest of 7%. That way I would be able to finish the roof and build an additional twelve rooms, which would be partitioned with freshly painted, ready-made walls. I spend the money that I borrowed from Christodoulis very quickly but the hotel is still not finished! It's a building without windows, doors, equipment or furnishings. As things stand I certainly cannot begin operations and not only are all my saving gone, but I also owe £600 to Christodoulis. And Christodoulis's comments put more and more pressure on me every time I go to his shop. One time, while he is packing my purchases in the baskets, he tells me that Fieros assures him that "I'm gnawed on by foxes" all the way out there, in the middle of nowhere!

"Never mind that my wife keeps nagging me about the £600 that I lent you. I've told her 'don't worry; at the end of the day, if Catsellis doesn't pay us back, we can always take the hotel!'"

Is he saying this with intent, or is it simply a thoughtless off-the-cuff remark? No matter, his comments push me deeper into anxiety.

Amidst all this an unexpected letter arrives: I am asked to travel to Port Said in Egypt to obtain a visa for the United States, all expenses paid! The American ambassador has taken it upon himself to make this happen. I receive the letter in the afternoon but, since there is no carriage for Nicosia this late in the day, I set out on foot. I arrive in Nicosia at dawn. I jump on the carriage to Larnaca, where I see Mantovanis, the American consul in Cyprus, and make the necessary arrangements. I am back in Kyrenia on the same day. The only person I have spoken to about any of this is Pikriyiannis, since he is also preparing to return to America; he has not been able to make a go of it in Cyprus with his small hotel at the beginning of Victoria Street.

Now that everything is ready and the road to America is open, my inner conflict about leaving looms large! Standing on Xylogio-fyro, late in the afternoon, I reflect on the situation. It's autumn and, as I gaze at the sea, the sun is plunging into the water to the west, creating every imaginable colour. A few metres away I can see Eleni's house, the Sea View, our home and our hotel. Next to it stands the mass of the second Sea View, truly imposing! A nice sturdy building, freshly painted, with two béton armé slabs, which are the talk of the town, since this is the first time that something like this has been built in Kyrenia. It has poured concrete columns on its spacious balconies and well-constructed Corinthian-style columns at the front entrance. Inside, it has large drawing rooms and a dining room. I have worked so hard to bring it to this point; I have so many dreams but not that extra bit of money for the equipment and furnishings, which would enable me to begin operations. All I need is £200-300! I would save that amount very quickly in America but now that the road there is open, the road of the heart is closed. How do I say such a thing to Eleni, who is pregnant with our third child? She has been pampered by her parents all her life and now she is facing hardship with me without a word of complaint. She holds the baby with one hand and washes dishes with the other. She does any job she can do at the hotel; she is always at my side, always a great help to me. How do I tell her such a thing? How would my parents-in-law take the news, knowing that I have gone back on my word? And how would I ever respect myself again, knowing that I have broken my solemn promise to them? A man has nothing but his word! Never mind that I could not bear being away from my wife and children – I do not even dare think about that... Within the crimson hues of the setting sun I am wallowing in such darkness that I do not even hear the greeting.

"Good evening, Mr. Catsellis!"

I know that the man standing next to me on the wooden bridge is called Campbell – a sixty year-old English loner, who is renting a room at Pikriyiannis's hotel. Rumour has it that he is looking to buy a house. He has decided to settle permanently in Kyrenia. This is the first time that he and I have spoken, so I make an effort to smile at the man and return the greeting. I wait for him to continue on his walk so that I can be alone with my thoughts, but Campbell won't go.

"When will your hotel be finished?" he asks and points to the unfinished Sea View with his cane.

His words feel like a stab to my chest.

"It will never finish!" I announce with bitterness.

"Why not?"

"Because I don't have the money to finish it."

"How much do you need?"

"Give or take £300."

He takes something that resembles a notebook out of his pocket and a pen. He leans over and scribbles something.

"There you go... I am lending you the money so you can finish it, Mr. Catsellis!" he says.

It takes time to sink in... I don't understand what he is saying... I don't know what is in the hand which is extended toward me... A cheque... I take a closer look by twilight and see that it's a cheque for £300 made out to my name! I am so taken aback that I barely have enough clarity of mind to thank him, although Campbell does not seem to be expecting anything. He simply says "good evening" and continues on his walk.

I am standing as stiff as a board in the middle of the bridge. After a few moments, I look at the cheque again and the thought crosses my mind that the Englishman might be playing a cruel joke on me. But what if it's not a joke? What if this cheque for £300 is real? I have another look.

"If it is real, then this is a sign from God... It's a sign that God does not want me going back to America, that He does not want me breaking the promise that I made to my father-in-law, that He does not want me acting like a louse and causing heartache to Eleni!" I say to myself aloud.

I go home but do not divulge my plans; I say nothing about the arrangements that I have made for my return to America. I keep quiet but cannot catch a wink all night. I simply cannot believe that a complete stranger, someone I have never spoken to before, would offer this much help. It is not possible! I simply cannot believe it!

Early next morning I take the first carriage to Nicosia. The bank is located at Serai Square. Kyrenia's parliament representative happens to be there at the same time. He sees me come in; he also sees the cheque in my hand and cracks a smile.

"Ah, Catsellis, what poor fool did you talk into giving you money now?" he asks.

I say nothing. I am anxious to know the truth: Do I have the money or not? I sign the back of the cheque and hand it to the teller. My heart is about to leap out of my chest while he examines it. The prying parliament representative steps behind the counter, as if he owned the place, and leans over the teller's shoulder. The teller is Armenian – I know him because he came to my hotel as someone's guest for tea. When he notices the representative, he artfully turns over the cheque to conceal its information. Then he looks up for a moment, pointing to me with his eyes.

"Do you see this man, Mr. Representative? This man here will change Kyrenia on you!" he says and leans forward to count £300.

The Englishman was not playing a practical joke! The miracle is real. This is truly a sign from God: I am spared from having to leave Eleni and my children; I am spared from having to go back on my word. I can stay in my homeland and finish the hotel! As I collect the cash, tears well up in my eyes. Thick teardrops stream down my face... My dream is alive and about to become a reality. Campbell's dream is also alive and about to become a reality; he has found a location that he likes, high up on the mountain toward the road to Ais Larkos. He will build a house there and settle down.

Second Sea View Hotel – Third Child

However, with the money that he has given me, I still cannot finish the hotel because I decide to furnish the ground floor to my liking, without cutting corners. To begin with I buy a fairly good wood-burning kitchen, so I can showcase my cooking skills. I furnish the dining room, the large drawing room, and the six rooms on the ground floor. Large iron beds, Cypriot-style chairs, oil lamps and candles – every room has its own wood-burning fireplace and, most importantly, a toilet and a bath with hot running water. I buy boilers from Hadjikyriakos, who is the largest importer of such equipment in Cyprus, so I can heat up the water using wood.

February 1927: I move my operations to the ground floor of the new Sea View Hotel but also keep the three rooms in Eleni's house. Eleni gives birth to our third child on March 21, a daughter. My groomsman Neocles Loizou baptises the child that we name Athena, after my mother, although everyone calls her "Athenoulla."

Thanks to the attractive drawing room, the well-organized dining room and, above all, the proper kitchen, I begin to shine. I also have an oven at the back of Eleni's house where I cook roasts and bake cakes. One of my first guests, Artemis, who continues to come to the hotel with his brother-in-law, is a representative of Nile Storage, a company that imports packaged butter from Egypt: one shilling for a half-pound packet. I buy butter from him for my cakes, which turn out delicious as a result, especially the scones for my afternoon tea service. With these sweets, nice savoury treats, and Eleni's delicious homemade marmalades, my afternoon teas start to become well known. The Kyrenia-Nicosia road is neither bad nor long, and now many people have cars. Prosperous Nicosia residents with cars arrive after lunch to take afternoon tea, which is served with an assortment of sweets and savouries. When they return to Nicosia at night, they are so full that they do not eat supper. So I have a hotel full of guests in the afternoon, as well as a thriving lunch and dinner business. Now that I have enough clientele, I gain so much confidence that when Costantos, my old boss, and his wife complain that my pork chops are expensive, I don't lose my nerve; I am confident about the quality of my food. I suggest to him, quite simply, that he should eat where the food is not so expensive! I am charging 1½ shillings per portion. Despite having settled in at the new hotel, there is no end to the difficulties. I am always struggling to light my dining room with a faulty lux, which needs to be pumped again and again. I am still lowering drinks into the borehole at the back of Eleni's house to cool them, since no one in Cyprus knows anything about refrigeration. And now that I have more staff, I also have theft. Almost every time I pull up the basket from the borehole, it contains fewer drinks than I had lowered. There are times when the basket comes up completely empty and then I have a big problem. And there is also the daily torment of shopping with the two enormous baskets that I must lug back from the market, one in each hand.

Nevertheless, I have started to build up a good and regular clientele, such as the Constantinides family from Trikomo. Most of my guests are easy to please and some not at all. The Spinneys arrive; they are newlyweds. Mr. Spinney[11] is a good but difficult guest. He expects me to heat up the boiler in the middle of the night so he can take a bath. He comes to the dining room late and, one night, even demands that I find mandarins for him.

---

11 Arthur Rawdon Spinney CBE

"I can't go out at this hour to steal mandarins for you, Mr. Spinney," I tell him.

We have a bit of a confrontation but I like him all the same; he is a nice man with a good sense of humour, even though he often puts me in a rather awkward position. Newly married as he is, he makes a habit of kissing his wife in public. Since this causes me to blush, I often scurry away.

The business that I built up at the beginning of 1927 has made me impatient: I am anxious to finish the upstairs twelve rooms, but there is not enough money, despite that I have had good earnings during the winter. I repay Campbell, my saviour, who does not even charge me any interest. I buy the railway wheels and tracks from the Administration so I can remove them and clean up the area a little. Stavrakkos Constantinides buys the winch. I sell the wagon wheels for ten shillings each and keep two for myself; I use them to weigh down two empty barrels, which I connect with wooden planks. I build a swim raft for my guests. However, the hotel is essentially vacant in the summer months; everyone heads up to the mountains where it's cool. The idleness makes me even more anxious to finish the upstairs. The six rooms of the new hotel and the three at Eleni's house are not enough to accommodate everyone who wants to stay at the hotel in the winter. Moreover, now Eleni's house is overrun by our children, which need more space as they grow, whereas guests need peace and quiet, without youngsters making noise.

That summer Savvas Poeros returns from the United States; he has been there since 1916. He is one of the many Cypriots that I helped when they first arrived in America. I ask him for a loan but his brother Petros shows up the next day.

"You asked to borrow money from my brother?"

"Yes, I have."

"You should have asked me first!" he tells me in a harsh tone.

"Thank you, but I don't need it," I respond rather vexed.

I do need it but… I am caught between a rock and a hard place until Eleni agrees to take loan against her house. When we go to the Land Registry Office to complete the transaction, Petros Poeros says to Eleni.

"There goes your house, huh!"

Eleni gives no response. She is the only person who never loses faith in me. To this day I owe her a debt of gratitude for putting up her house as collateral.

With the money that I borrow, I throw myself into finishing the upstairs. I get no rest; I work day and night. I want everything to be the best it can be. I ask Photiades to install a closed circuit hot water system. Not only does he not know how to do this, he has never heard of such a thing. I explain to him how the system works and he agrees to do it, but I run into a problem with Hadjikyriakos. Hadjikyriakos insists that it is impossible for such a system to work and proposes to sell me more boilers. But I know that the system does work. I know what I am doing and what I am asking for because, for a long time, not only did I fire up the boilers at the school in Chappaqua, but the technicians there also taught me how to troubleshoot various problems. Hadjikyriakos is approximately sixty years old so I approach his son, who is twenty-five, but he is even more sceptical than his father. After a great deal of back and forth, I convince them to sell me a large boiler for the installation. I do not buy any more of the previous boilers. I speak to Photiades and he allows me to build a large water tank on the roof that I intend to fill, using a motor, with brackish water from the well at Eleni's house. When everything is installed, the system works perfectly! With the closed circuit system, the moment you turn on a tap, you get hot water in every room!

Yet I still worry that I may not have enough money to finish the upstairs. I struggle; I save as much as I can. At dawn I go to the market and return with two or three baskets in each hand. Then I work at the hotel, cooking with all the difficulties that not having refrigeration entails. As a result I end up serving chicken most of the time. The faulty lux in the dining room is killing me because I have to keep pumping it at the exact time when I need to be in the kitchen preparing well-executed dishes, just the way I like them.

I manage at long last! In the winter of 1927-1928, all twelve rooms on the upper floor of the Sea View Hotel are not only operational, but also first class. They are booked solid in the winter. I no longer put guests in Eleni's house. Eleni is pregnant again with our fourth child and things are not easy for her. She no longer comes to the hotel to help out; other than making her wonderful marmalades, she still takes care of the hotel linen. She buys fabric, sews everything herself, and supervises the washing and the ironing. Fortunately she has help from her sister Styliani, who travels from Bellapais with her husband, Costas Adamou, whom I employ. I put him to work as a server in the hotel dining room. Thank goodness, I have Yiorkos Adamou, whom I can count on for anything. In 1927 the Municipality decides to build an electricity generating station south of Koulas, on the footpath that leads to the Metropolis. They install two horizontal Ruston generators, 25 HP each. Two strong young men, Christos Kikkiros and the nineteen year-old Yiorkos – Eugenia's son and Eleni's nephew, from the Hadjiyiangos side of the family – are hired to erect the poles. In one year, when the electricity poles are up, the two young men are left without work. I hire them as chamber men. The first one is good but the second is absent-minded. When he forgets to put a towel in a guest's room, I sack him, even if he is my wife's relative. After all, the guest is not just anybody: He has advanced me £300 to collect and send every cocoon in the Kyrenia district to his silk weaving operation in Geroskipou, in Paphos. The arrangement helps him because he is spared the trouble of collecting the cocoons and me because the £300, which I receive in advance, enables me to upgrade the equipment in my hotel. Now that money is flowing, I put even more passion into my business; I want everything to be perfect! I manage to convince Nikolis, the tailor, to sell me his property – the rocky patch of land with the three caves. I get rid of the pigs, clean the caves, and one more stench disappears.

Now that the Municipality is generating electricity, I also improve the hotel's installations. As luck would have it, I come across an Englishman, a man by the name of McKenzie, who is a specialist electrician. He agrees to install a bell in each room. Another Englishman becomes so enthused with my cooking that he brings me a gift of groceries worth approximately £25. I do not know how to thank him, but I do know that it is time to do something else... I dare extend a dinner invitation to Houstoun and his wife, first because I respect the man, and second because I want to show him how unfairly I was demeaned in his eyes. I want him to see what I have built since – according to what he was told back then – I am supposedly incapable of building a chicken coop! Houstoun accepts the invitation. I receive him and his wife for dinner at the hotel, and look after them as best I can.

Seeing how well business is going, I submit a claim for the parcel of land where the old wheat storehouses are located. Tithing was abolished in 1925 and, since the land where the storerooms were built had been seized by expropriation from my mother-in-law Despinou for £7, I can claim it now that the reason for the expropriation no longer exists. My application is accepted but the government offers to sell me the land for £300 because they incurred the expense of building the storehouses and Tirnavos's office on it. The price seems inflated because the land is barely one skala and that's all I am interested in anyway. But since the parcel is so close to the hotel, even if Bonnouis's house stands in between, I take the offer. I also make an offer to purchase Kombonisi, a rock island across from the storehouses for 10 shillings. Early in the morning I go to court to make the payment, which includes £10 for land transfer fees, and the property is transferred to my name. The deal has cost me a total of £310. When I return to the hotel, I find Houstoun there, waiting for me. He looks at me from behind his monocle, does not return my greeting but motions that I should follow him.

"Come along!" he commands.

First we cross Xylogiofyro then Esso Geitonia. We pass the police station and St. Andrew's Church, which he built. We pass the Turkish cemetery and head east to the area behind the Castle. This stretch of land is expansive and beautiful; known as Tteppes, it has a massive boulder that moves toward the sea to the east, directly across from the Castle. This is where we stop. He raises his walking cane and points to the surrounding land.

"Shall I sell it all to you?" he asks.

"How much do you want for it?" I utter, when I am finally able to speak; I am astounded by his unexpected offer because Houstoun almost never sells land to anyone.

"I want £400!"

"No, I'll give you £300," I counteroffer.

"Alright then. Come along..."

I follow him south along the footpath and after approximately three hundred metres we arrive at the Administration. The sheds that once housed it burned down in 1926 and now it is being rebuilt with cut stone and lovely arches. We go straight to the Land Transfer Office and then I crash-land into reality... It dawns on me that earlier that morning I paid £310 for the wheat storehouses. I have no money!

"But Mr. Houstoun, I don't have the money to pay you now," I tell him.

"It doesn't matter. I will transfer the land to you now and you will have three years to pay me. I won't even charge you interest for the delay," he assures me.

And so Houstoun not only transfers ownership of Tteppes and the surrounding area to me, but also gives me permission to quarry stone from his property in Ayia Varvara, whenever I need it for construction.

CHAPTER 11

PASSION FOR CONSTRUCTION

Kyrenia, 1928-1974

Since building has become my second great love after cooking, I do not waste a moment; I commence work on the storehouse land right away. When I demolish the structures, I realize how much building material they contain. I have lime and cement, metal doors and hoes. I sell the tin roof to Paronakis for two grosia and twenty paras per oka. He sends Satrakian, one of his people, and together we weigh the tin with a balancer. I collect £99 from the roof alone! I also sell some other things and, when I add every-thing up, I see that the net cost of the land was only £40! And I still have unsold materials that I am keeping for future building projects. I plan to continue building because in 1927-1928 the hotel's eighteen rooms are always occupied. This is not taking into account the afternoon teas and additional sales in the dining room and at the bar. I cannot keep up with the work, not even with the help of Yiorkos Adamou or Costas Adamou, my brother-in-law, who has become a good server. I hire Sophocles Sophocleous, my companion in America. He is a good employee although his bulg-ing eyes are a source of trouble for me – some guests are afraid of him, especially Atremena – but what can I do? I am strict with all my employees; I expect them to execute every task to perfection, exactly the way I have shown them! But I am good to them; I pay them regularly and their meals at the hotel are good and filling. And that's not taking into consideration the gratuities they receive from the guests.

The Clubhouse – Fourth and Fifth Child, 1928-1930

On May 18 Eleni gives birth to our fourth child; again, it is not an easy delivery. She has dedicated this child to Panayia.[1] Now her sister Styliani is always by her side; since she has no children, she loves ours as her own. Styliani baptises our baby daughter Maria, after Mother Mary, according to Eleni's dedication.

In the summer months the hotel empties out again; people prefer to vacation in the mountains, even though I have used two more wagon wheels in barrels to construct a second swim raft. The first one, the one I built in the previous year, was lost at sea in the winter during a fierce tramontane. Few people prefer the coolness of the sea to the mountains but I do not fret; now that the business is built up, I can count on income in the winter every year. Besides, I have also bought land... I do not want to become a moneylender, who piles up money and lends it to the poor for interest. I like building; I like development. And I keep thinking that a decent clubhouse, on the land where the wheat storehouses used to be, is precisely what Kyrenia needs. Around this time a sixty-something English architect named W. D. Caröe arrives in Kyrenia with his niece. He specializes in building cathedrals and has a great love for our Byzantine churches. I share my thoughts with him and make him an offer. He agrees to draw up plans for the clubhouse. He shows them to me and explains how everything works. I like them.

I begin construction immediately. Houstoun keeps his promise and allows me to quarry, free of charge, as much stone as I need from his property in Ayia Varvara. An obstacle shows up, however,

---

1   Panayia or Panagia (Greek: Παναγία), which means All-Holy, is one of the titles of Mary, the mother of Jesus, used especially in Orthodox Christianity.

where I least expected: Karpis, the blacksmith, and his brother jointly own an adjacent property. They intentionally dig a deep trench through the middle of their land to prevent the carriages with the stone from passing. I discuss the matter with them and we come to an agreement: I pay £3 to the first brother and £12 to the second for the right to transport material through their land for three months. Since the work is not completed within the three months, I ask for an extension of another month, for which I pay £1 to the first brother and £3 to the second. I am hurt, not because of the money, but because of their attitude.

In the winter of 1928-1929 the hotel fills up again, while the clubhouse is under construction on the land where the old government tithe storehouses used to be. I put Christodoulis Anayiotos in charge of paying the workers and I supervise the construction at every spare moment.

In the summer of 1929, when the hotel empties out again, Theocharis Savvas, the taxi driver, is also without work. The son of the cook Savvis and Maria Arapou, Theocharis worked initially with Kotsios Karasavvas, who owned a Ford automobile. Karasavvas had a great deal of debt so he sold the vehicle to Theocharis in 1924. Theocharis has been the official taxi driver for my hotel since then. Being able to count on regular income from my guests, he has managed to buy one or two more cars. Taking advantage of the summer when we have no work, on the Feast of the Assumption, Christodoulis Anayiotos and I rent his cars. Theocharis drives our families, each with four children, to Kykkos Monastery. In Troodos we stay at Maklouf Camp Hotel, a tent hotel that operates only in the summer. Eleni's cousin Yiorkos, the son of Eugenia, whom I had sacked from the hotel some time ago, works there. I offer to hire him back for the winter months when the hotel in Troodos is closed, starting in the fall. This time I do not put him on rooms; I keep him close to me in the kitchen. He is a strong young man, who can whip sugar and butter with force

– in his hands egg whites are transformed into a dense meren-
gue and cakes turn out exceptionally light and fluffy. He enjoys
being in the kitchen so I gradually teach him the art of cooking,
although his specialty ends up being baking. He never manages
to cut meat portions as well as I do, but his cakes are better than
mine. He works exclusively in the kitchen and, when I eventually
promote him to first cook, he shines. The only thing is that he
avoids guests... When guests wish to thank or complement him,
he is nowhere to be found. Yiorkos the cook vanishes into thin air.
He has no desire to speak to anyone!

On November 5, 1929, Eleni gives birth to our fifth child.
Once more the godmother is Styliani, and our new daughter is
baptized her Aliki. By the end of the year, work on the clubhouse
is complete. It has a spacious main area and three smaller auxiliary
rooms: a storeroom, a washroom, and a billiard room. I furnish it
nicely and purchase Governor McDonald's billiard table for £60,
since he is leaving. I also ask him for a liquor license. I pay £22 for
the license, an astronomical amount of money for the time! But
the Clubhouse does not start out well – a number of well-heeled
Kyrenians come at night and gamble heavily until dawn. During
all those hours they order only a lemonade, or something compa-
rable, never paying for anything more. To make matters worse, I
am obligated to stay up all night. What choice do I have? And it's
not like I have nothing to do during the day...

Envy, Quarrels, and a Third Floor at the Sea View Hotel, 1930

In 1930 I get up at the crack of dawn to prepare everything at the
hotel. At first light I have to be across from the Clubhouse because
I am building a house where Tirnavos's old office used to be. An
Englishman named Mills, the buyer of all Cypriot tobacco, has
rented the location from me for a good sum of money. I am build-

ing a house for him, since this provides me with regular income. Then I return to the hotel for breakfast service and lunch preparations. I work, almost without a break, through the afternoon tea and dinner services. Then I go to the Clubhouse where I am forced to stay until dawn. And this part I find sickening! It's not just the lack of sleep – I have never needed a lot of sleep, a few hours have always been enough for me – nor that the revenue is ludicrous; the main thing is that I detest gambling, which is becoming more and more serious the way that my patrons are playing. I am stuck between a rock and a hard place: I have spent so much money on this building, how can I not operate it?

One afternoon, Yiorkos Karayiannis, who is a good teacher and a good man, is at the Clubhouse. He sees Vikentios, a government employee, walking by and calls out to him:

"Hello, Vikentios, come inside. Let me buy you a drink!"

"No, Mr. Yiorkos, I'll come when he lowers his drinks to twenty paras," he responds with resentment and refuses the invitation.

My drink prices at set at sixty paras, so this means that I would have to lower them to one third! Upon hearing this, I start to boil on the inside. *I will shut it down before I lower my prices!* I think to myself.

Later that night, when the gamblers leave, I close the Clubhouse. And I do not open it again; I spare myself both the nuisance and the remarks!

Many Kyrenians are antagonistic toward me, and not only with words. On winter nights, when the hotel is full, annoying barking and meowing is often heard. When I look into the matter, I discover that it is not feral cats and dogs creating the disturbance but people, who are doing it either for fun or with the intention of harming my business. I let things be, however; I say nothing because if I were to confront them, they would become even more antagonistic toward me. I reckon that they will eventually tire of this nonsense: How long can they keep coming around in the middle of the night to bark and meow? I am also hawk-eyed when it comes to theft but averting it is not always easy. Woodcutters make regular deliveries of firewood for the boilers; at some point, I realize that the amount of wood that is being delivered far exceeds my usage. How can this be? When I receive the next load of firewood, I sprinkle it with limestone powder; the following day I examine the new load and discover traces of limestone on the logs! The crooks are delivering a load in the morning then secretly loading it up at night, so they can charge for it again! When I catch them red-handed, they admit to their deception.

This year I also get into a dispute with an Armenian family over a small parcel of land that belongs to the brother-in-law of Lambiada, the daughter of Alexis Televantos. The property is at the cul-de-sac of Solonos Street, which starts at Sykamia on the main road of Karavas-Lapithos. It's not a large parcel but I have had my eye on it for some time; I really want it because, by turning the cul-de-sac into a road, I could create a fairly wide passageway from the Karavas-Lapithos road directly to the sea, west of the Sea View. This way my hotel would finally have a decent access route. Now guests arrive at the hotel by way of the market. They turn left on the narrow descending road just before Archangelos, come to the east side of Kotsirkas where they have no choice but cross Xylogiofyro, which is still in such awful shape that people are afraid go across. An Armenian manages to buy the piece of land that I want for £30. This upsets me tremendously but I say nothing. I wonder what he is planning to do with it because it is very small. Even so, he manages to obtain a permit from the British to build all the way to the property boundary, when the existing regulation states that there must be a minimum of ten feet from the building to the edge of the property line. I become angry and complain, taking my grievance as high up as the governor to no avail. The permit has been issued, a vacation home is in the process of being constructed, and the Armenian, who knows that I have taken action to have his building permit revoked, comes to see me in order to brag.

"Do you have any idea who we are? We, my friend, are made of money!"

He adds that he plans to come frequently to his vacation home because he really loves the sea.

"If you see the sea from that house, I'm going to see it from Ararat!" I respond stubbornly.

And I mean it! I have bought the land directly in front of his property from Nikolis the tailor, along with everything else in the area, except for Bonnuis's rundown house because he still insists on not selling. I am determined to build directly in front of the Armenian's house to completely obstruct his view of the sea.

On the Feast of Saints Constantinos and Eleni, Metropolitan Makarios pays us a visit. I tell him that it would be good to encourage more foreigners to come to Kyrenia because they spend money and put food on the table for many people. This way young people can stay in their homeland, not forced to migrate in search of work.

"You mean the British?" he asks.

"Mainly, the British, yes. They are good guests. They spend money," I respond.

"No, we do not want them here. They should leave!" he says sharply.

The Metropolitan and I are not understanding each other: I am speaking of British tourists and he is talking about the occupiers. I can't stand them either, especially the new governor of Kyrenia. His name is Dennis and I catch him shutting off the hotel's main power switch for no good reason. This happens more than once, many times in fact, especially when the British are playing the treasure hunt game. Although I catch him in the act, I can't imagine why he would do such a thing. Not that I could have ever imagined that the governor himself was responsible! I do not let him off the hook, however; I really let him have it in "French," as Eleni would say with a smile.

In the meantime, I have not left the Clubhouse vacant. When

British warships anchor in Kyrenia for six days, I open it last minute and operate it as a bar and restaurant exclusively for officers. I
do well because British officers like to drink; at long last I can say
that the £22 I paid for the liquor license was money well spent!
In addition, I open the Clubhouse regularly, once a month, when
tourists arrive in Kyrenia by ship for the day. Mantovanis sends
them to me from Larnaca. He sends me a message on the previous day with the number of guests, so I can set up the Clubhouse
and prepare food. The tourists arrive from the sea, by ship. They
come ashore, visit the Castle, travel up to Bellapais in Theocharis's
taxis, then come to the spacious Clubhouse to enjoy the lunch that
I have prepared. I charge 8-10 shillings per guest and there are
times when I serve meals to as many as 400 people.

Mantovanis's tourists get me thinking... If I had enough hotel
rooms, they would not have to leave Kyrenia on the same day. They
could extend their stay and enjoy the sights at a leisurely pace. Beyond the Castle and Bellapais, they could visit Ais Larkos, which is
also stunning, as are so many other things in the surrounding area!
And it would be more cost-effective for them this way, because I
charge 16 shillings per day per person including all meals, which
are skilfully prepared by Yiorkos and myself. But how can I possibly accommodate so many people with the eighteen rooms that
I have at the Sea View? I no longer place guests in Eleni's house,
which is full of children. We have five and she is pregnant again.
We are expecting our sixth at the end of 1930. Mills's house is
complete; the man has moved in and paid the agreed upon rent.
I make arrangements with W. D. Caröe to draw up plans for an
additional floor at the hotel. Yet Public Works will not give me
a building permit; they claim that the existing structure cannot
withstand the weight of another floor. I am certain that this is not
the case; I know how it was constructed. Photiades is a good architect and Master Kyriakos an experienced foreman, moreover, I
worked on site overseeing everything. The Building Permit Committee is composed of Governor Dennis, who doesn't like me,

and the feeling is mutual after I catch him turning off the hotel's main power switch, of Hall, the government's civil engineer who also rejects my application, and of Mayor Charilis. Since the first two are refusing to issue the permit, I approach the mayor to find out what his position is on the matter.

"We forbid you to build!" he says firmly.

"Well, I am going to build it regardless!" I say and dig in my heels.

"If you do, we will tear it down!"

"You do that!" I tell him and begin construction.

As a result of the emotional turmoil, an enormous boil appears on my back. I suffer greatly. Fortunately, a nurse is staying at the house that I am renting to Mills – she is the wife of a British government official. She has a look at the boil; using tongs, she removes something that looks like a string from inside it. She cleans it every day until it disappears, but it takes time. Boil or not, the Sea View Hotel has another floor! Not only does it not collapse, as they had predicted, but it is also "the only three-storey building in Cyprus, made of reinforced concrete," as elementary school teachers keep telling their pupils. The British do not tear down the addition and now I have twelve extra rooms. I add things up: Now that the Sea View has been expanded I have thirty rooms! My family has also expanded.

October Revolt –
The Annex with Twelve Rooms and a Dome –
Sixth and Seventh Child,
1931-1932

On August 12, 1931, Eleni gives birth to another son. We name him Stylianos and the godmother is my sister-in-law Styliani, who is very pleased that one of our children has been named after her. She has a special affection for this child; he is her favourite.

In October 1931 there is trouble: A movement starts up against the British. The Governorate in Nicosia is burned down and in Kyrenia people from all across the district gather outside the Administration Building. Some youngsters climb up, grab the British flag and rip it. Savvas Hadjilambis, the son of Lambous from Ais Grosis who is staying at the Metropolis, raises the Greek flag. Just as the British are preparing to shoot him, Metropolitan Makarios steps in the line of fire.

"If you're going to shoot, you should aim right here!" he tells them and points to his chest.

The British requisition the Clubhouse, they use it as lodgings for a company of thirty-one soldiers, including their sergeant and captain. From its roof they also monitor the Metropolis, which is located on the hill across. I am even obliged to provide food for them – twelve grosia per day per person for all three meals. I like neither that my building has been requisitioned, nor that I am forced to feed the British, but choice do I have? The movement fails. Our Metropolitan is arrested and exiled from Cyprus. Six teachers in Kyrenia are imprisoned. The priests of Ais Grosis and Diorios, as well as the deacons of the Metropolis, are arrested. My groomsman Neocles Loizou, my lawyer Dorotheos Carolides, Savvas Poeros, Kyriakos Poeros, and Savvas Karasavvas are sentenced to three months imprisonment. The same fate befalls many other younger men: first Savvas Hadjilambis and Demetris Galaktiou, as well as Chambis, the son of my brother Glioris. Fortunately most of them are found not guilty, so they are not detained at the Castle for too many days. They are released.

Thankfully, the British do not stay at the Clubhouse too long. Things calm down, the army leaves, and I instruct Caröe to draw up plans for ten rooms above the Clubhouse. He designs a dome at the centre, a faithful copy of the dome of the Church of Antiphonitis. Antiphonitis is an old Byzantine monastery, a lovely building with beautiful iconography, located between Ais Grosis and Kalogrea, east of Kyrenia. The entire design follows the Byzantine style and features arches. It is a square building with cov-

ered verandas and red roof tiles all around. It is very different to
the Sea View, because Photiades is partial to the Classical Hellenic
style that features columns, Corinthian capitals, and small white
poured concrete columns. On the ground floor of the Clubhouse
I build a stage toward the sea. I enjoy the theatre and Kyrenia does
not have a decent stage. When touring troupes arrive from Greece
they are forced to perform just anywhere and without proper installations. In fact, many do not come at all because the town does
not have the necessary facilities. I give the floor a slight incline so
the entire audience can see the stage, but not so much that I cannot use the area for dining as well. And so now next to the Sea
View stands The Annex. I decide to put in a tennis court; there is
plenty of room south west of the property, near the Pittas family home. When I start to level the ground for the tennis court, I
come upon an ancient tomb that stretches deep into the adjacent
property, which belongs to my classmate Dr. Spyros. Before I have
a chance to send a message to him, he hears of the discovery and
comes on site. We enter the tomb, which is quite large. I am not
holding my breath; I have come to realize that all these tombs
were stripped of anything of value centuries ago. At most, it may
have bones and some pottery, which no one appreciates. Only the
Museum cares enough to pick out the best pieces, discarding the
rest. I walk around inside the tomb but my mind is elsewhere – I
am thinking that the doctor's property is quite large...

"Doctor, how much do you want for this parcel of land?" I ask.

"Oh, I'm not interested in selling it," he replies and there is no
further discussion on the matter.

Meanwhile, even with thirty rooms at the Sea View and ten at
The Annex, I am still turning away guests not only in winter, but
also in summer because popular tastes have changed. Many people, foreigners and locals alike, now prefer the coolness of the sea
to the mountains. I order plans from W. D. Caröe for an extension
of the Sea View. In 1929 I bought a small parcel of land to the west
from tailor Nikolis, the one with the much-discussed caves; most

of it is solid rock. In 1932 the government needs stone for the construction of the waterfront across from Akteon. Akteon is now owned by Petros Vrahas, who has renamed it the Sea Side Hotel. I give permission to the government to quarry stone from my land free of charge – this serves them well since my property is very close to the area being repaired. In the process of quarrying stone another ancient tomb is discovered and this time it is intact! Porfyrios Dikeos arrives to inspect the site. I ask permission to enter the tomb – it's my land, after all – but he refuses. I insist; we get into a nasty argument, exchange heavy words, but he agrees in the end. The tomb has pottery with beautiful designs – the vessels are placed in baskets and transported to the Castle. When I see a golden ring on a skeleton, I ask for it! I am entitled to one third of all that is discovered on my property.

Dikeos refuses to give me the ring but I insist. I see Manifold to complain. She speaks to King, the first secretary to the governor. Eventually they give me the ring; it has a semiprecious stone and its gold is so soft that it bends very easily. This ring is the only gold I have from these tombs, even if everyone in Kyrenia believes that I have gained wealth and built all these things as a result of priceless artefacts and ancient treasures.

As a result of the government quarrying stone, the area opens up; in the meantime, Caröe's plans for the extension of the Sea View are ready. I am also ready to start construction. Early in the morning I run into Dr. Spyros outside the post office with his wife's cousin, Mayor Charilis. As soon as we exchange a "good morning" the doctor brings up the subject again:

"What do you say? Shall I sell you the land that I have near the sea?" he asks

"I do want it!"

"How much would you be willing to offer?"

"How does £300 sound?" I propose timidly.

"If they are golden, I accept!" the doctor replies.

"Listen, if you have any intention of selling the land to me, you're going to have to sell it for regular liras, the paper ones. I have thirty golden liras from the Pentayia doctor who was a guest at my hotel, because that's how he used to pay me. I'll give them to you, if you like. But that's all I have."

The doctor thinks about it for a moment and then, "Would you give me £350?"

"I'll give you £330," I counteroffer.

"Agreed!"

The agreement is made and the land is mine for £330. It stretches as far as Proti Tsiakkileri, to the bay where the Phytos brothers used to build large ships. The only thing there now is Savvis Severis's unfinished ship, a monument to past eras, to the seafaring life of Kyrenia and to the trade with the East. I seize the opportunity to buy the unfinished ship for £32, thinking that its wood would be good for burning in the big boilers of the Sea View and The Annex. Was I ever wrong! The wood is impregnated with so much tar that an enormous amount of smoke is produced; it does not burn. The purchase was a waste of money. Nevertheless Proti Tsiakkileri is now clean, even if one part of the doctor's land is requisitioned by the Municipality for use as a slaughterhouse, which is operating in some makeshift sheds. A narrow footpath or passage leads to the sheds, which are truly a terrible nuisance; not only is the setup primitive, but they are also the source of the foulest odour and filth. Although they throw the discarded en-trails into the sea, flies swarm in the millions to claim their share. Covered in blood, butchers and hamals carry slaughtered animals past the Sea View on their way to the butcher shops at the market – certainly not a pleasant sight for my guests!

Not only is all this exceedingly unpleasant, but there is also a hazard nearby – the large cave, where some old poles have been discarded, used to be an ancient tomb. Half of it is below ground; you have walk down twelve steps into the rock before you reach its floor. This is the Municipality's designated storage area for the

gas and benzene that barges deliver in containers from Famagusta. The representative merchants are Leptos and my groomsman
Neocles Loizou. Yet, excited as I am to acquire this parcel of land,
which I consider vital to my business, I do not give any of this
much thought. At this time I realize that The Annex – with its
imposing dome and its verandas with the red roof tiles, situated
where the waves fade on the spacious field to the west – is a better option for extension than the Sea View, which has a limited
amount of space next to it and where the ground is mostly rock.
I set aside my plans for the extension of the Sea View and instruct
Caröe to draw up plans for the extension of the Annex to the
west instead. The extension will include rooms, kitchens, and all
the essential facilities of a standalone hotel. The architect delivers the design, which is in the Byzantine style once more. The
extension features a second dome with rooms all around while,
on the ground floor, he has designed spacious drawing rooms with
Byzantine-style arches. Caröe situates the kitchens to the west,
directly across from Pittas's house, toward the mountain.

Not wasting any time, I start work on the expansion of The
Annex. The year is 1932 and my family is expanding again. On
October 8, Eleni gives birth to our fifth daughter; Styliani is the
godmother once more, and our daughter is named Vera.

Holiday in Athens – Two Good Purchases, 1933

In the following year all is set aside – hotel, construction, everything – for the first time since 1922 when I started, after eleven
years on non-stop work. Eleni is the reason – seven children,
seven difficult births – and, yes, she has a great deal of patience,
but now she has other problems. Something is wrong with her
stomach; every morning she cannot relax until she vomits bile.
Despite it all she continues to stand by my side, my right hand
person, without a word of complaint. Now that the hotel is run-

ning smoothly, she no longer works there, as she had done for years. Even so, she still takes care of the linen and makes sure that her homemade marmalades are always at hand. I use most of the marmalades in food services, but also give a few jars to choice clients as gifts. Even though her house has not been used as a hotel for many years, it is still overrun by cleaners, laundresses and ironers. She does not have a place of her own, somewhere private, and as a result most of her jewellery has been stolen – God only knows by whom, among all those who are always coming and going. Jewellery is too great a temptation for the poor. Eleni is upset, not so much about losing the jewellery or its value, but because I brought it for her from America as engagement gifts. Fortunately, my schoolmate Dr. Spyros, with the assistance of his aunt Theodora the midwife, has always been a great help to Eleni during all those difficult deliveries. Now Dr. Spyros suspects that there is something wrong with her gallbladder, so he sends her to Koureas, in Nicosia, to have x-rays taken. Eleni has a difficult time with the procedure because she must drink a ghastly liquid, which is required for the x-rays. Dr. Spyros examines the x-rays to make sure that the problem is indeed the gallbladder and suggests that I take her to see a good doctor overseas.

I will leave Yiorkos Adamou in charge as the hotel's general manager; he can also supervise construction. I can rest easy with him at the helm because he is honest, devoted and capable. My friend Christodoulis Anayiotos is only too glad to manage my payroll, because this means that approximately 200 workers have to stop by his grocery store to collect their pay. He opens credit lines for them; they buy their necessities from him and he never runs the risk of not getting paid, since he is the one handling their wages. Our seven children will be looked after by my sister-in-law Styliani, who loves them as her own. Eleni is having new clothing made; she is getting ready to travel!

We depart on the steamship Cyprus, not a large vessel. The first port of call is Attalia, where we stop for a day. When we go ashore, we discover that it looks a lot like Kyrenia. The owner of the restaurant, where we sit down for a meal, happens to be a Turk from Crete. He speaks Greek so we have a chat with him. In Attalia the ship loads livestock of 5,000 billy goats and 40 pigs. A bearded woman is among the new passengers that come on board; we all go around to have a look and satisfy our curiosity. When we reach open sea, the pigs in the ship's hold become ill and die; the sailors throw the bodies overboard.

In Athens we stay at a hotel close to Omonoia Square. I do not like it! It is not very nice and, of course, pales in comparison to what I have constructed in Kyrenia. But our primary concern is to have Eleni see the doctor, whose name is Loverdos. It would appear that Dr. Loverdos is quite renowned. We are told that he keeps monkeys in the basement of his house for medical experimentation. I gather information about him; I read in a newspaper that he has participated as an authority at an important medical conference. Dr. Loverdos examines Eleni and prescribes some medication, but we do not return to Cyprus right away. I insist that we prolong our stay so we can enjoy some vacation time for the first time in our lives! We keep company with Christofis Christoforides, a Kyrenian who is studying law at the University of Athens. We hire a carriage together and take a trip to Kifisia. Eleni truly enjoys the ride. I also take her shopping; she selects fabric, and we hire the best seamstress in Athens. Eleni keeps saying that she does not need new clothing since she had some made in Kyrenia before our departure, but I insist. Kyrenia is one thing and Athens quite another! I know that Eleni likes to dress well and according to fashion. We take photographs, go to the theatre, and see the sights. Twenty days pass, twenty days without any worries, wandering about Athens carefree. We have a lovely time because the medicine that Dr. Loverdos prescribed has helped Eleni; she no longer has problems with bile and the morning vomiting stops.

Back in Cyprus Eleni returns to the children, the housework, the hotel linen and the laundresses, while I return to the kitchen

of the Sea View and to the construction of the extension of The
Annex. While we were away, our eldest son fell from a low wall,
fortunately without any serious injury. I also learn that Paronakis
passed away and that his flour and olive oil mills will be sold at
auction, after having been idle for some time. For many years, this
dynamic Armenian operated the most well-known flour and olive
oil mills in the district of Kyrenia. At the time of the great oil production, in the 1920s, the mills could not keep up with the work.
Paronakis's mills are also among the most modern; unlike the old
wood mills, they are metal and in good condition. There are six
separate deeds for Paronakis's property, including land and buildings. Other than the mills, Paronakis also owns oil storehouses, a
bakery that Tziomounis from Karavas is operating, and a shop that
is also a souvlaki eatery. All this in a row on the west side of the
river, starting at the bridge, high up on the main road of Karavas-
Lapithos; the property boundaries come all the way down to my
father-in-law's fields, to the land that he has given to Costarakkos, his youngest son. If I manage to buy Paronakis's property, I
will be able to create a decent access route to my hotels, which is
something that I still do not have. Then I start thinking that, since
I am not on speaking terms with Paronakis's heirs – the people
who bought Televantos's property and built their vacation home,
thereby preventing me from opening a road to my hotels from
that side – they would not want me as a buyer. But I need this
property! I have a word with my friend Christodoulis Anayiotos
regarding the matter and he is interested.

"If the offer is low, not over £800, we'll take it!" he tells me.

I am quite certain that the price will not be that low; in fact, I
would be willing to pay much more for Paronakis's property. We
agree that Christodoulis will attend the auction but, on the eve
of the sale, my friend has to travel unexpectedly to his village of
Kalogrea; his mother has passed away and the funeral will be held
there. Now what...? I pay a visit to Zacharias, a tall, nice looking
young man and an excellent carpenter, who also trades in lumber.

Zacharias crafted the doors and windows for the extension of the Clubhouse. We come to an agreement, make the necessary arrangements, and Zacharias attends the auction. He tells them that he intends to buy the entire property so he can store lumber and roof tiles, providing that it is sold as one deed, not as six separate ones. Everyone believes his story and the bidding opens at £900 for the entire property. I do not set foot in the place; I stay at the Sea View but keep abreast of developments with the help of my brother-in-law Yiannis Vottis. He pretends to come down to the hotel from his house, which is located on the road above, in order to pick up cabbage leaves for his rabbits. And so Yiannis comes and goes, informing me about the latest bids.

"Now it's at £1,100, Costas."

"Tell Zacharias to go higher," I instruct Yiannis.

Yiannis returns to the auction and communicates my instructions to Zacharias in a way that he is not noticed. In the end, Yiannis returns to the hotel to tell me that the bidding has gone as high as £1,130. I hesitate – this is a considerable amount of money for the time.

"Tell Zacharias to offer one more," I decide.

"£1,131!" Zacharias shouts out.

Everyone waits for another bid, but no one makes a higher offer. Once Tilliros has closed the auction – "going once, going twice..." – Zacharias discloses that he has been acting on my behalf. Paronakis's heirs are displeased, but I pay them a visit and invite them to the hotel. I have them sit in the dining room, four or five people in total, and serve a lovely red mullet that I took delivery of that day. I take good care of them, we reconcile, and everyone is happy with the arrangement in the end.

But I am also thinking about the money... Zacharias has paid the £300 that I gave him and put in £300 of his own. To settle the balance I take a bank loan for £600 with a due date of six months. Before the end of six months I ask for an extension of another six, at which point the bank replies in writing that they are calling in the loan! I go to Nicosia, show them the letter, and demand an explanation. They are surprised to say the least! They insist that the bank has money and that they are in fact looking for borrowers so they can collect interest. But I am really upset; I refuse to take a loan from them. In fact, I avoid doing business with them for a long time because I suspect that the letter was sent after actions taken by certain people in Kyrenia who do not wish to see me succeed. With Houstoun having passed away in 1931, Kyrenia's Britons approach me with a request that I sell a piece of the land behind the Castle to retired Wing Commander Crawford Allan, so he can build a club for Britons. I borrow £500 from Kyrialides, who – they say – is a black-market hashish dealer, and settle the outstanding amount for the purchase of Paronakis's estate.

I continue operating the olive oil mill with Sophocles, my friend from America, in charge. Sophocles is a widower; his first wife passed away some time ago. He used to work at the hotel but when he messed around with one of the chambermaids, Katina, so much fuss was created that I had no choice but to let him go. Sophocles and Katina married eventually. Wanting to support him, now that I have the opportunity to do so, I hire him at the olive oil mill so he can earn a living.

The Dome Hotel: Two Domes and twenty-eight Rooms, 1934

But I am also in need of money! The year is 1934 and construction is at its peak. Caröe is insisting that the fence around the property be made of wood columns, which are provided by Chief Forester Annouis. They cost one shilling each. I propose something more reasonably priced but Caröe is adamant.

"If you feel they are too expensive, I'll pay for them myself!" he tells me. Of course, I would never agree to such a thing.

Caröe is also insisting that the roof tiles for the domes be authentic, made in Galata; I do not object. At the edge of the property, toward Proti Tsiakkileri, I am also constructing fourteen garages that will be used by hotel guests. While I am in this tight spot, Koukoush approaches me outside the hotel with an offer to lend me £1,200, on the condition that I repay him before the end of the year. I agree since I am earning money at the Sea View.

This year I work very hard because I have also taken on the supervision of the construction of Caröe's house. It is situated west of Kyrenia, next to a small bay, on rocky terrain. It's a lovely design, Byzantine-style columns facing the sea, built entirely of stone. To keep up with all my responsibilities, I have to get up between 2 and 3AM. I go to Caröe's house, pump water from Lordos's laundry rooms to fill the tanks before daybreak so that the workers are not standing around, wasting time. I supervise their work and pay them at the end of each week. Caröe has given me power of attorney and I withdraw money from his account for this purpose. It's a lot of work but I gladly take it on because I feel indebted to my architect. Then I return to the hotel for breakfast service and to supervise construction of the second hotel. I prepare lunch, afternoon tea, dinner... It is a brutal schedule but, before the end of 1934, the twenty-eight rooms of the new hotel are almost ready. I decide to name it "The Dome Hotel" after the two domes, which I really like, imposing as they are, like the dome of Antiphonitis. Moreover, it is an unusual name, which pays homage to the history of Cyprus. Literally overnight, with the help of Yiorkos the cook and Yiorkos Adamou, I move my kitchen operations from the Sea View to the Dome, making the latter the main hotel. That night we prepare and serve dinner at the Sea View and in the morning serve breakfast in the spacious dining hall of the Dome, out of the new kitchens. The kitchens are well-organized and highly efficient because they burn peat fuel. I have an entire barge shipped in, 100 tonnes – 800 okas to each tonne – that I store in one of the garages. This lasts me a long time because the kitchens burn only 100 okas per day. And so the peat lasts until I convert the kitchens to burn petrol. In the basement underneath the kitchens I install the first refrigeration unit in Cyprus. It is made by Walls, and I purchase it through Caröe. At the new hotel I have only choice staff; over the years I have held on to the best employees and gotten rid of anyone who was lazy or not good enough. I may be very demanding and strict but when I see that someone, among all those who come to me for employment, has a good head on his shoulders and the desire to work, I support them. I teach them the job and pay them well. At the hotel I have approximately twenty employees, all handpicked and enthusiastic. They earn a good living and love their jobs. They are poor kids from surrounding villages such as Bellapais, Karmi, Trimithi and Ais Yiorgis. I respect them and they respect me! Many young men also meet chambermaids at the hotel, get married, and start families. Sometimes I even help young men find nice girls to marry. During all this time my right-hand man is still Yiorkos Adamou, whom I can rely on for everything! In the kitchen Eugenia's son Yiorkos, whom everyone now refers to as "Yiorkos the cook," has also become a good and competent chef. I feel that the time has come to find a nice girl for him, too. And this happens eventually; a few years later he marries a relative of my wife, Eleni the daughter of Panais Koumas, and starts a family. All things considered, I can say that The Dome Hotel has nothing to envy of the good hotels in America and Europe. In addition to the large number of short-term guests, I also have a few guests that stay at the hotel all year round – first and foremost Mrs. May Pockington[2], or Mrs. Lila[3] as she is known in Kyrenia, because she is always dressed in lilac and her white hair is also coloured a lilac hue. She permanently rents an entire suite at my hotel.

---

2 Mother of Lady Chenevix Trench, known for her beautiful watercolour paintings, and grandmother of C.C. Trench, who has written a book for his capricious grandmother's trips and adventures, with the title *My mother told me*, William Blackwood and Sons, Edinburgh, 1958.

3 Lila (Greek: λιλά) means "lilac" or "violet."

Eighth Child – Accidents – Small Quarrels, 1935

In 1935 Eleni is pregnant again with our eighth child and gives birth at the end of the year. We have another son, whom we name Charalambos. Styliani is the godmother once more. This year I am almost blinded because of the refrigerator. Although it is a good fridge, once in a while it does not work properly because no one Cyprus knows how to service the motor. I go down to the basement to shut off the ammonia and do the opposite by mistake: I turn it on! Ammonia and oil spray my face, especially my eyes. Luckily, across from the hotel, the English nurse Mrs. Hall is still living in the house that I built for Mills some time ago. She rushes to my aid. She does not let me wash my eyes with water; she makes me wash them out with milk. I suffer terribly, especially in one eye, but mercifully there is no permanent damage to my vision. Even so, the accident causes much distress which is only compounded because Karalatzina, who is now very old, keeps walking past the hotel's kitchens shouting that I, her hired help, own buildings and land, whereas her son has squandered away most of his property. I keep telling myself to pay no mind to her but still find the situation rather unsettling.

Paronakis's mill is not doing well; it's all problems and no profit, even if Sophocles is doing his best. A suvar comes to make trouble one day; he complains that all his oil was lost in the mill. I shut down the operation! Sophocles opens a coffee shop in Kyrenia and earns a living for his family this way.

This year I complete construction of the Dome and Caröe's house, which took a total of eighteen months. He moves in and I pay him £410 for the architectural plans for the hotel, although he had said initially that he was not going to charge me. But since I am truly pleased with the design, with its formal Byzantine style, I do not argue the point. And then I receive an invoice for £72, a sum that represents his 6% commission for the bathware that he

ordered from England on my behalf... I know that the only work
Caröe put into that order was a letter to the bathware factory.
This upsets me terribly, so much that I lose my temper. Letter
and invoice in hand, I turn up at Caröe's house in less than three
minutes! When I arrive he is in the sitting room with a guest, but
this does not deter me.

"What is this you're asking for?" I ask.

"Commission," he replies.

"If you expect me to pay commission, I also expect to be paid
for supervising the construction of this house for one and a half
years!" I declare.

"You have no right to ask for such a thing."

"Why not? I don't owe you anything! Why should I work for
you for free all this time?"

"You are not a professional like I am!"

His remark makes me even angrier.

"Okay then, we'll settle this in court!"

The quarrel gets worse and worse until Caröe's guest intervenes by asking for details about what took place. The man listens
patiently to both sides and, in the end, finds that I am right. Caröe
not only stops demanding the £72, but also gives me a piece of
land on the Karavas-Lapithos road as a gift. It's a good parcel,
although rather remote. The important thing is that we remain
friends and maintain respect for one another!

I give the land that I received from Caröe to Bonnouis who,
at long last, has agreed to sell me his rundown house, west of the
Sea View Hotel. The property is not even worth £100 but I pay
£400 for it; beyond the land, I also give him the moulds for the
columns and agree to keep him on as the hotel's carpenter for
life. My friend Christodoulis Anayiotos brokered the deal with
Bonnuis; I have great respect for Christodoulis, who has been
in charge of payroll for my building projects for years. Yet feeling contented and comfortable with the agreement, Bonnouis
starts to slack off at work – I show patience for a while, until I

can no longer tolerate his laziness or his excuses. I let him have
it in "French" and dismiss him. Around the same time the debit
note for the £600, which my friend Christodoulis had lent me in
1926, matures. The interest rate has always been 7%, which is
considered quite high now that rates have dropped to 4%. But I
have the money so I pay 7% interest because Christodoulis lent
me the money at a difficult time, when I was in dire need; I owe
him a debt of gratitude. Even so, he seems displeased when I pay
him the interest and brings up Bonnouis in the conversation. I
explain that I reneged on the agreement to have Bonnuis work at
the hotel for life because he reneged first; instead of providing
the agreed-upon services, he was making a fool of me and not
doing the work. I add that it's no wonder that his nickname is
"Bonnuis," which is derived from the French "Bon nuit," which
means goodnight. Christodoulis is not satisfied with my explanation; he counters that he acted on my behalf in brokering the deal
and, since I have not kept my word, I am a... a heavy insult comes
out of his mouth. I become angry!

"Listen here: I have been working since I was twelve years old
and I'm not about to become beholden to anyone!" I tell him.

"Is that so? Then pay me the money that I have lent you!"

"Consider it done!" I reply.

And with that I find myself in a rather difficult position because
I have no cash at hand. It has not even been a year since the Dome
was completed – I have been pouring all my money into construction. What is more, I refuse to go to the bank; I am still angry with
them for calling in the loan. So I go to the Ottoman Bank instead!

"I understand that you're asking for a loan of £600? Why not
take £1,000 instead?" the bank manager proposes.

Christakis Loizides Aladkiastos, the owner of several large grocery stores, acts as my guarantor so that I can borrow £1,000 from
the Ottoman Bank. I calculate that I owe Christodoulis £630, including interest and repayment of the principal. But since I am
upset with my friend, I do not wish to deliver the money myself. I

decide to send my eldest son, Andrikkos, who is eleven years old. I give him the money and my instructions.

"Take this to Christodoulis Anayiotos and make sure to ask for the document," I tell my boy.

Andrikkos delivers the money but returns without the document. Since Christodoulis is also upset, he has had Costas Kazinieris calculate the interest to the day. Kazinieris discovered that I owe Christodoulis an additional one and a half liras because three days have passed since the date of maturity. I send Christodoulis the outstanding amount and only then does he give me the document, which shows that the debt has been paid in full. Although Christodoulis and I did not have a major argument, our long-standing collaboration comes to an end because of Bonnouis's laziness.

Five Daughters, Five Houses, One Road, Three Deaths, 1936-1938

As a result of all this I have cash at hand, the balance of the money I borrowed from the Ottoman Bank. The year is 1936. My eldest daughter is thirteen years old and beginning to look like a young woman. Now that she is in the first grade of gymnasium, I have stopped checking her homework because I only completed elementary school. But since all my other children are still in elementary school, every day I have them stand before me while I check their homework. My second daughter, Athenoulla, is bright but she exasperates me because, when I ask about her homework, she plays with her hair. I also have three younger daughters, five in total. Five daughters means dowries of at least five houses... So far I have I built only one, the house that Mills is renting. Now that I have money available, I start to think about Paronakis's olive oil mill, which has been closed for the past year. I have enough space to build a second house there, on the road of Lapithos-Karavas, with enough room to spare for a road towards the river. And I have space for two more houses further down. There is also the rundown house that belonged to Bonnouis — enough room for a house there as well. I begin demolition of Bonnouis house and order plans for three more houses from Photiades — all two-storey buildings with shops on the ground floor, situated along the Koronos River, with a wide road in front that will go all the way down to Xylogiofyro. Styliani's house stands in between but, since we are on excellent terms, she gives me permission to open the road in front of her house. I also make an agreement with my brother-in-law, Costarakkos; he gives me a piece of his property in exchange for helping him build his house. His parcel of land is quite large and he is engaged to Cleopatra, the daughter of Nicolas Savvides from Bellapais. The architectural drawings show twenty-one shops below the three residences. This way I will have the five houses that I need, one for each daughter. While working on the houses, I also begin earthworks on the west side of the river that will provide, at long last, a decent access route to the hotels, bypassing the downhill road that leads to Xylogiofyro!

At this time the government also decides to convert the wooden Xylogiofyro into a stone bridge. McLaughlin, the government's engineer in charge of the project, curiously watches how I am constructing the earthworks; he mocks me.

"The way you're building it, it will come tumbling down with the first rainfall," he says and laughs.

In my opinion it is his bridge that is not secure...

"Be careful that your bridge doesn't collapse with the first rain fall," I warn him.

Indeed, one night during a downpour, McLaughlin's bridge collapses, taking Faulkner, the manager of a marmalade factory outside of Kyrenia, and another person with it. Nothing happens to my earthworks, built as they are with concrete. They survive to this day!

My in-laws do not survive the year, however; first my father-in-law Stavris Vottis passes away and then, within twenty-two days, his wife Despinou also breathes her last. Everyone says that they loved each other so much that could not bear to be apart from each other, not even in death. We all grieve, especially Eleni, but Charon is not finished with us yet... Our youngest son has health problems. Many blame his poor health on "grief's milk" since he was breastfed by Eleni after the loss of her parents. Pale and frail, the child is always unwell; it pains me to see him this way. One day I give him a pear, one of those large ones that are imported from California, and I am elated when he finishes it. I take this as a sign that he has turned a corner, that he will survive; but it was not meant to be. Charon takes him from us in 1937 at one and half years of age! A few days later, celebrations for the coronation of King George are held in Kyrenia, and everywhere in the British colonies. Officials watch the parade from the balcony of the Sea View. Officer Tziambos gives the command and the police officers begin to march. They take over our house and from there hand out commemorative medals to the crowd, along with sweets in boxes with information about the coronation. Surrounded by so much fanfare and cheerfulness, while feeling shattered by the recent loss of our child, Eleni becomes hysterical. We rush her to Styliani's house, which is further up, so she does not have to see or hear the commotion. These are difficult times. Thankfully we have our seven other children; we try to console ourselves by having photographs taken of all our children standing in a row. We frame an enlargement that we have made.

Meanwhile, because I am building so much, rumours abound about a large amount of gold that I supposedly discovered in an ancient tomb. They say that we used Eleni's illness as an excuse to travel to Athens to sell the gold on the sly! People believe such stories because of the treasures which were discovered at Acheiropoietos Monastery in the past. At the same time, many are certain that I am on the verge of bankruptcy because they hear that I am borrowing money here and there for construction. It is true; I am building quite enthusiastically because I am providing homes for my daughters and because I have found a way to create an access route to my hotels. One day Dervis, the mayor of Nicosia, comes to the hotel.

"Is it true that you're in debt, Catsellis?" he asks.

"Yes!"

"How much?"

"Approximately £6,500, Mr. Dervis."

"Is that all?"

"Yes!"

"And you don't shit on those who are going around saying that you're bankrupt?" he responds in his characteristically foul language.

I am encouraged. Hadjilambros also arrives at this time; I recall how he used to mock me when I was a newcomer to America. Now he is here asking me for work. But I am not holding a grudge; in fact I feel for him, but my hands are tied. I do not need any more employees at present. Still, I think to myself how life and luck turn things around sometimes...

As life and luck would have it, I manage to get rid of a huge problem at last! Late one afternoon a barge arrives from Famagusta and offloads a cargo of 800 containers of petrol. Darkness falls before the hamals can complete the job, so they leave the petrol outside of the storage cave, right there on the field, out in the open! Some English nobles – dukes and duchesses, lords and ladies – happen to be staying at the hotel at this time. When they inquire about the containers, they become so nervous that a fire might break out that they can't sleep all night. I explain the situation to them – that I have repeatedly taken action to have the Municipality move the fuel elsewhere to no avail. The guests take it upon themselves to complain to the governor, who orders the Municipality to relocate the fuel storage area. The fuel is removed immediately but an extension of a few months is given for the relocation of the slaughterhouse, until a new facility can be built east of Kyrenia, in the Chrysokava area.

At this time the Municipality also decides to build a road to Proti Tsiakkileri which, until now, has been accessible only by a footpath demarcated by the old rail tracks. From the hotel's kitchen I see the men who have been sent to take measurements. I step outside with my apron.

"What's going on?" I ask.

"We're building a road," they respond.

"How wide?"

"Twenty-five feet."

Across from my kitchens, toward the mountain, there is a parcel of land that belongs to clock repairman, who had bought it for £7.

"Then you should take twelve feet from me and twelve from him," I say.

Although the clock repairman is present, he says nothing yet makes arrangements that none of his land is expropriated for the road, which is subsequently built along the rail tracks. Later on, Costas Fieros, who is now mayor, comes to see me. He demands that I knock down several columns and a corner of the hotel so they can widen the road. Fed up with the situation I really let him have it and, in the end, none of my property is demolished. Yet the road remains narrow because they never take any portion of the clock repairman's land.

After lunch service I like to sit down and look at the sea for a while. Across from the Dome, approximately fifty metres from the shore, some rocks jut out of the water, forming what is known as "Kombonisi." When I bought Kombonisi from the government a long time ago for 10 shillings, I became the laughing stock of Kyrenia for my presumed naiveté.

"What is he going to do with those damn rocks? What on earth would possess him to buy them?" they would ask mockingly.

But I am beginning to see how I could utilize them in my mind… In addition, the house that I am building on the land that I bought from Bonnuis is nearly finished. It looks good; Photiades has designed Corinthian-style columns and the like. I have rented it out to General Sprigs. With this house, I now have two but need three more for my daughters.

In the following year, in 1938, my earthworks project for the road on the west bank of the river is complete. Up on the main Lapithos-Karavas road, just after the bridge, another building has been completed. The house is upstairs and a number of shops are downstairs, on the ground floor. I rent one shop to my brother-in-law Costas Vottis, who turns it into a grocery store, and the one at the corner to Lanitis. The home is spacious, large enough to accommodate my entire family and the necessary house help. Its balconies face two roads and can be seen as far as Kamouza's downhill road. On its roof, at the corner, I have built a small arched wall on which I wrote the name "DOME," with an arrow underneath pointing toward the sea. Half of Kyrenia can see it! I transfer the property, both the residence and the shops, to my eldest daughter, Despina, since this is her dowry. Then our family moves in.

Due to the new living arrangements, I can only spend a certain amount of time with my family. I can no longer join them for lunch and dinner. As always, I wake up at the crack of dawn and go to Vourkaris General Store to do the shopping. My daily purchases are so large now that I can't carry everything myself, so Vourkaris provides me with delivery. Once I have made my selections, he brings the goods to the hotel himself. One day I happen to mention to Vourkaris that I am considering doing some additional shopping at the general store in Nicosia, because it offers a wider variety of products. Vourkaris laughs at me; I take offense and change grocers. I become a regular customer of Anastasis Paphites. Once in a while, I also travel to Nicosia in Theocharis's car; I become a regular customer of Christakis Loizides Aladkiastos, to whom I owe a debt of gratitude for being my guarantor for the loan of £1,000 from the Ottoman Bank. After I finish with the shopping, I oversee breakfast service and around 9AM I am back at home. My eldest daughters, Despina and Athenoula, keep watch on the balcony. When they see me approaching with the groceries for the house, they run to the kitchen and let their mother know that I am on my way. We always have breakfast together. Late in the afternoon, before dinner service, I go home to check the homework of the children who are still in elementary school. I am strict with them; I want them to be good students and to get ahead in life. I am especially strict with my sons. The eldest is studious but the younger one is a wanderer; he likes to roam around, going as far as Pano Kyrenia sometimes. I do not like this one bit! Every so often I am exceedingly strict with them but this upsets Eleni, who keeps any minor naughtiness from me. And when I try to spank one of them, she gets in the way to stop me.

When the original Sea View empties out, I demolish the house that was Eleni's dowry, thereby making the access route to the hotel a reality! It is a road that begins at the main Lapithos-Karavas road and continues along the west side of the river. Now the river is nice and tidy because of the sturdy earthworks that I have built. Next to my eldest daughter's house, I continue construction of a second house with shops. As soon as it is finished, I transfer ownership to my second daughter, Athenoula. Then I finish the house of my brother-in-law Costas Vottis, who is preparing to marry, as well as Styliani's house! And now I can begin work on my own land, where Eleni's house used to be. I build more shops on the ground floor and a third house upstairs that I transfer to my third daughter, Maroulla. The last shop, the one that faces the sea, turns out rather narrow because the road takes up a lot of space. So be it!

I manage to obtain a 99-year lease for the waterfront directly across from my property from the government; this way I can finally clean it up. I am constantly cleaning and doing earthworks, levelling the ground; I spare no expense. It turns out nice and wide, paved as it is with finely ground sandstone. Xylogiofyro and all the other junk are long forgotten; now cars can drive straight down to the hotels with ease! Kyrenians call the road that I am opening "Catsellis's road," but I think that they avoid using it

– rarely do you ever see a local walking along… Some even argue
that it adversely affects the old road, which passes in front of the
market, sharply past the rock of Archangelos, past Petros Vrahas's
hotel, before reaching the waterfront. I say nothing. My road is
nice; my guests arrive comfortably by car and park at the spacious
square next to the shore that I have levelled and cleaned up. And
my hotels are busy; they are always full! Truth be told, it does
bother me that the locals are not using my road. So I ask Christis
to write a letter to the commissioner, requesting that he inaugu-
rate the road and officially name it "Catsellis Road," as everyone
in Kyrenia already refers to it. All Kyrenians and many foreigners
attend the inauguration. After the ceremony I invite everyone to
tea, approximately 400 people.

The Death of W. D. Caröe
Extension to the Dome, 68 Rooms, Four Domes,
1938-1939

After the inauguration of the road I expect things to settle down
to a relaxed pace, but they do not! Why? The hotel is full – very
busy thank God – but I feel restless without building projects.
When Caröe passes away[4] unexpectedly I become upset! His funeral will be held at St. Andrew's Anglican Church. One of his
last wishes was that I serve as one of the pallbearers. I am deeply
touched by his request. I am keen to pay my respects in this way,
but the manager of the Country Club, retired Wing Commander
Crawford Allan, objects. He hates Greeks! Not only does he not
forgive or forget the uprising of October 1931, but also considers
us to be an inferior race, slaves essentially. With the exception of a
few lawyers and judges who are locals, Kyrenians are not allowed
entry to the Country Club. And God help any Kyrenian who dares
to swim in the sea behind the Castle! This stretch of beach is reserved exclusively for club members. How could he tolerate an

---

4 W. D. Caröe passed away in Kyrenia on February 25th, 1938.

ordinary Greek Cypriot among the other high and mighty pallbearers of Caröe's casket? Unable to observe my friend's final
wishes, I watch the funeral from the sidelines, filled with sadness
about his passing. Caröe died at the time when he was supposed
to be enjoying the house that he designed and built with so much
love; and a lovely home it is indeed! His son travels to Cyprus for
the funeral; he is also an architect, who works at his father's office
in the Westminster area with another partner. He stays in Cyprus
for a while to settle his father's estate, whatever he has inherited in Kyrenia. He sells the house for £2,500, an extremely low
price. The house is stone-built and the cost of construction alone
was £2,000, even with all the savings that I delivered by supervising the construction. And the land on which the house was built,
along with the fields around it, were bought for £300.

I ask Caröe's son to design an extension for the Dome. I do
not like operating both the Dome and the Sea View at the same
time, since I have to keep running back and forth from one to the
other. It's exhausting! The extension will be to the west, in the
area that the fourteen garages currently occupy. They are no longer in use since I now have the 99-year lease for the waterfront,
which stretches from the Sea View to the Dome. Now that this
area is neat, level, and covered with fine sandstone which pre-
vents it from becoming muddy in the winter, I have all the parking
I need for my guests. Caröe's son agrees to draw up plans and I
begin the extension immediately! I also manage to buy the old
slaughterhouse and the fuel storage cave for £62. The cave proves
to be very useful because we convert some of it into a septic sew-
er. In the following year, in 1939, the extension of the hotel is
complete. Now the Dome has four domes instead of two and 68
rooms in total.

World War II, 1939

In August 1939 World War II is declared! All my guests are gone, even the permanent ones, including Mrs. Pocklington, who relocates to a safer place, somewhere in Africa. The British round up all Italian and German citizens in Cyprus and place them under detention at the Castle; the majority of the detainees are Italians from old, wealthy families. I am given the responsibility of providing their meals, a task that I undertake in collaboration with my friend and schoolmate Yiannis Vrahas, who has returned – for the second time – from the United States; I employ him as stockroom manager for my hotels. The agreement is for 18 grosia per person per day, a very low amount, but what choice do I have? My hotel is vacant. In any case, I have access to inexpensive meat: I can buy a whole calf for £6 and a whole pig for £2 to £3. And my skill at breaking down meat helps us get the maximum number of servings, without any waste. From this service that we provide, Yiannis and I earn approximately £20 each at the end of the year! With his share Yiannis buys the rocky terrain directly across from the hotel, west of Proti Tsiakileri. This is a very good investment because it greatly helps his children later on, when the prices of seaside properties soar. The land sells for 1,000 to 2,000 times more than it was bought! The detainees are content because, beyond the satisfying meals that I provide, I also send extra wine when the Allies have a victory. I become so excited that I want them to celebrate such occasions, too!

Around this time the British Army rents the Sea View in its entirety. Soldiers move in and prepare their own meals because food is rationed. They do much of the cooking outside, in the back yard; they use large pots especially for boiling eggs. They ask me for some help such as preparing tea, for which I charge half a shilling. It's something, especially when there is nothing to be had anywhere! At the Dome only the bar is busy with British officers. According to regulations they must disarm before they have a drink, lest they get into trouble and kill someone when they are inebriated. As soon as darkness falls, the hotel's office fills up with revolvers and ammunition.

I zealously keep abreast of the news from the war but continue construction for the extension of the Dome. In May of 1940 Commander Krining pays me a visit.

"Would you be willing to accommodate Polish refugees for 4½ shillings per day?" he asks.

"If you make it five, yes," I propose.

The Polish refugees arrive while construction of the upstairs rooms and of the two new domes is at its peak. Since the new rooms are still missing some doors and windows, I accommodate the refugees in other rooms and turn the large drawing room into a dining area. Later on, the British slash what they were paying me for each person by half a shilling and give the money directly to the refugees so they can buy toothpaste and soap.

1940

October 1940: Greece enters the war and Kyrenia is aflame with patriotic sentiment! Greek flags re-emerge out of armoires and chests where they have been hidden since the uprising of October 1931. The blue and white flies everywhere! And I, amid the general enthusiasm over every Greek victory, send special treats to the detainees at the Castle. When Korytsa comes under the control of the Greek Army, I give £100 to the funding drive and pledge to double the amount if the student parade marched on my road! At the end of 1940 the Polish refugees depart, as do the British from the Sea View. Even though the war is raging, neither my hotels nor any of my other buildings are vacant; in fact, every available space in Kyrenia is being utilized, no matter how shabby. The Sea View is rented to the English School, which moves to Kyrenia for the safety of its students. Since it is also a boarding school, there is not enough space to accommodate everyone at the Sea View. I provide rooms where they can hold classes in many of the twenty-one shops on Catsellis Road. But since even that does not suffice, I also provide them with rooms at the Dome. Simms, the principal of the school, rents Styliani's house, while another teacher moves into the house that I built on the land that I bought from Bonnuis.

Even the Dome has a few guests; it is frequented by local merchants who are making a killing selling black market goods. And there's also the rich who, fearing bombing raids in Nicosia, move to Kyrenia for safety. The wives of Italians detained at the Castle also stay at the hotel since they want to be close to their husbands – the wives of Mantovani and Umberto, for example. Pentayia's doctor, Major Doctor Rose is also a permanent resident at the hotel at this time.

1941, 1942

Things get tougher in 1941 because now even Kyrenians fear bombing raids. Many move to nearby villages. The town is essentially evacuated! I send Eleni and the children to Ayios Epiktitos, where I have rented the house of Costis, Katelou's son. The village has an elementary school so the children do not fall behind in their lessons. After a short time, well before the end of the year, I bring them back to Kyrenia. I do not leave Kyrenia during the evacuation; there is work at the hotel, regardless of how little. And in 1942 half of the hotel is full! Officers of the British Military Hospital arrive, some from the forces in North Africa and some from New Zealand. They train; they make plans! Rumour has it that they are preparing to take the Dodecanese or something of the sort, in collaboration with two Greek majors; the name Colonel Tsigantes is being whispered. In the end, the plans of the Allies against the Germans are abandoned, and my guests begin to depart.

1943

At the turn of the year, at the beginning of 1943, the hotel is empty again. But not for long... The large drawing is nicely furnished with tapestry and curtains in blue hues – my guests call it the "Blue Room." I have a radio in the Blue Room; one day, while I am sitting there with my eldest son Andrikkos listening to the latest news from the war, one of my chamber men, Christophis, shows in an American colonel who has come to see me. I welcome the man and offer him a drink.

"How would you feel about your hotel being used as a leave centre for United States Army officers stationed in the Middle East?" he proposes.

I agree, and he asks about the cost. Although my prices are set between 14 and 16 shillings per person per day, this time I ask for 18 shillings including all meals, to give myself some bargaining room. But the Colonel does not bargain with me!

"Okay, then!" he says and we shake on it.

The first groups arrive from Egypt two weeks later. There are con men among them, specifically a man by the name of Winters who swindles me out of £100, but most of them are okay. Major Early, a nice man that I make friends with, gives my eldest son a recommendation letter for Princeton University. And to think that there I was, so many years ago, a young and abjectly poor immigrant wondering whether I would ever be able to send my son to Princeton! However, my son cannot go to Princeton for the time being; all regular transportation to and from the United States has been suspended because of the war.

The End of WWII
The Development of Kyrenia – Life Continues, 1944

In the meantime, we receive a marriage proposal for my first daughter. I give my consent and she becomes engaged to the son of Kyriakos Pattihis, the merchant and industrialist from Kato Drys. His son Nikos, who was educated in England, is a lawyer in Larnaca. Due to the war it is difficult to find many things on the market, yet Eleni manages to prepare a proper dowry for our eldest daughter. She gets married on December 29, 1943, and ten months later gives birth to a daughter of her own. The child is named Elena, after my wife Eleni. And so, in October 1944, we have our first grandchild.

In the following month the war ends, on paper at least. The killing slows down, thank God, although the atomic bombs become the cherry on the icing on the cake on August 1945. So be it! I keep reading about all this in books and historical magazines; I am astounded!

My hotel is full again. Many of my old guests return almost every year; they enjoy coming here. More Britons live permanently in Kyrenia now but frequent the Country Club; Allan has returned to Kyrenia after having fought in the war. Only Britons are allowed entry into the Country Club, where they have tea and play bridge or tennis apart from the locals. And they have exclusive access to the beach behind the Castle. Yes, they have their good and bad qualities, but they also come to my hotel. The military officers, who stayed at the hotel during the war, now return with their families.

The author of "Exodus"[5] begins his book at my hotel. Many locals are also regular patrons, especially the wealthy. Half of Nicosia comes for tea on a regular basis. And most newlyweds, even if they are not wealthy, spend their honeymoons at my hotel. A song in a musical theatre show declares that most Cypriots, especially firstborn children, are Kyrenians! All this is good for the town. And I am meticulously organized, with my core staff trained well, with Yiorgos as my chef, and with one or two younger men with a fondness and talent for cooking. Theocharis buys more cars, but other taxi services start operating as well. They are all busy be-

---

5 Leon Uris, *Exodus*, First Edition, 1956; a novel that was later made into a motion picture.

cause my guests want to go sightseeing to Ais Larkos, Bellapais and other villages; they want to visit our churches. They are also eager to purchase souvenirs. Zaris from Lefkara came to me when he was quite young with a suitcase of lefkaritika,[6] which I allowed him to display and sell at the hotel's entrance. Now he is married to Agni, the daughter of Yiorkis Hadjiyiangou, who is related to Eleni. He rents a shop from me on Catsellis Road where he sells needlework from Lefkara. My relative Nikos Stavrou, the son of my sister Milia, has opened a second shop with lefkaritika on Cat-sellis Road with his wife Elli, who is the daughter of Costas Em-manuel from Karavas. Styliani Hadjimina also sells her own nee-dlework. Ioulia Markidou, the daughter of Demetros Mihalatzis, has opened a shop with a variety of Cypriot products that she sells mostly to foreigners; she is also a real estate agent. Cypriot pottery is flying off the shelves. Potters no longer sell crockpots, dishes and bowls to the locals; now they are making decorative pottery, which they sell to foreigners. Yiannis Eliades, the "pot-ter" as he is referred to in Ais Yiorkis, is among the best; he is a refugee from Asia Minor-Pontus and highly skilled at the craft. Many young locals apprentice with him and go on to open their own businesses. And in our region the soil is among the best for the production of earthenware! The old Akteo/Sea Side Hotel has been renovated; it is now called the Coeur de Lion. Other Kyre-nians also renovate their homes and build hotels, each to his own ability. There is activity at the port again because foreigners want to go on boat rides, although some are looking for more... Tired of the suit and the desk job, the son of Mattheos Kariolos leaves the government, builds a large vessel, and takes foreigners all the way to Asia Minor. He also teaches them how to dive with oxygen tanks. Of the many English visitors who come to Kyrenia some decide to stay permanently – it is a lovely place with a pleasant climate. They buy land to build new houses or purchase old ones.

---

6 Lefkaritika (*Greek: λευκαρίτικα*) *is a form of handmade lace from the village of Lefkara in Cyprus.*

Lady Lock, who is passionate about Cypriot arts and crafts, buys the Dramia Chiflik below Ayios Epiktitos, renovates the old konak and moves in. Cypriot volunteers are back from the war and need jobs. They have no problem finding work in Kyrenia. Even students have no trouble getting jobs; if they can think on their feet, I hire them at fourteen or fifteen years old for seasonal work and pay them well! This gives me immense pleasure because, when I was young, I suffered greatly from not having any money. Only the gymnasium keeps moving here and there, from one rented location to another. A funding drive is organized and I make large donations so they can build a school. Loizides, my teacher, left his estate for this purpose, but the money he bequeathed ended up not being enough because first they delayed construction and then the war brought everything to a standstill. The Sea View has been empty since the English School vacated the premises. Christis, the president of the School Board, approaches me about renting it to them. They want it for next to nothing but I do not object; I let them have the building, which is converted into a gymnasium and a good boarding school for Kyrenia youth. Students from other places also use the boarding school, further contributing to the development of the town in this way. I am asked to become a member of the School Board. It's not my area of expertise but I accept: I do not want to appear as though I am disrespecting anyone by refusing.

I am fifty-six years old; I feel rooted in my homeland but still have much to accomplish. I have four more daughters to marry and two sons to educate and marry. I also have plans for more construction and development. The hotel still does not have its own water supply and Chrysanthis Strongilos from Lapithos has a spring in Thermia with an abundance of good, potable water. I am considering making an offer to buy his water for the hotel. Kyrenia does not have a decent cinema and my sister-in-law Styliani and her husband have given me their home on Catsellis Road; they are relatives so we have agreed on a price. Should the need arise,

I can always build another house for them further down; there is plenty of room next to the Sea View, at the spot where I cancelled the extension. I also have an open-air amphitheatre at the hotel; it is perfectly located and facing the sea, exactly like the ancients used to build them. And Kombonisi is directly across from the hotel. It's only a patch of rock but it's mine. I bought it from the government for 10 shillings many years ago. There are many ways in which I can make use of this rock isle. Kyrenians will surely make fun of me again but, if I put two empty barrels with holes on both sides into the sea and filled them with sweet-water concrete, I am certain that I would have impervious columns; that way I could build a bridge from the veranda of the hotel all the way to Kombonisi. Hotel guests would be able to go there for a swim! The water is deep but that is not a problem. I would dig up the center of the rock isle to make a pit, which I would then connect to the sea, creating a saltwater swimming pool at no cost. My guests would be able to go for a swim in the sea even in a fierce tramontane! I also keep thinking about the mountains. The Ais Larkos area is among the most rare; even Walt Disney sent his people to do drawings of the mountain for the motion picture "Snow White and the Seven Dwarfs" that he is producing. I could ask the government for a location near Ais Larkos, drill for water, and build a wing of the hotel on the mountain, surrounded by nature. The vistas alone would make it worthwhile! And I also have my property in Karakoumi; I never forget my land, like I never forget my father. I long to see a nice farm in Karakoumi with cattle, chickens and pigs. There are more than 100 residents living in my paternal village now, yet youngsters still travel to the elementary school in Kyrenia every day, some by bicycle, some by car; things are not as difficult nowadays but it's still not easy. I have vowed to build a school in my village. When will all this become a reality? That remains to be seen! Life is constantly moving forward with new and different things, just like the waves of the sea, never two alike.

CHAPTER 12

ADDENDUM

Inter-communal Trouble
and the Turkish Invasion of the Republic of Cyprus,
1963-1964 and 1974

Christmas 1963: Inter-communal violence breaks out in Cyprus between Greeks and Turks – pretexts, minor incidents and disputes that the Turkish-Cypriot leadership later admits to having incited (under the clear direction of Ankara) with the intention of fabricating an excuse. The Republic of Cyprus is just over three years old and Turkey is anxious to get her hands on it, after managing to have her say as a guarantor power through the Zurich-London Agreements. American foreign policy is equally impatient because, through Turkey, the United States would gain a direct military advantage in the Middle East. For the time being only the British have military bases, which they deem sovereign, in Cyprus, also on the basis of the above-mentioned agreements of 1959. The same old story repeating itself... The mighty of the earth and of the region want to seize the island for its strategic importance. But this Addendum will not analyze political facts; it will record their impact on the life of one man, a man who deeply loved his homeland and contributed to its development to the best of his abilities.

The Dome Hotel, 1964

Kyrenia, January 1964: I am twenty-six years old, married and displaced, because our house – among the last in town to the west, near the Turkish village Templos – has been turned into a guardpost! My nine-month old daughter Eleni and I are staying at the Dome Hotel with my husband Stelios, who is the youngest son of Costas Catsellis, the hotel's founder and owner. I am wearing black: Last January I lost my father at the age of fifty-nine to a heart attack and in July my first child, Costakis, to thalassemia at two and half years old. I do not like staying at the hotel, even if it is the most famous hotel in Cyprus. I miss having my own space; I miss the flower garden. But I have no choice in the matter, because even the farm that surrounds my paternal home has been given over to a squadron of volunteers; its large kitchen is serving as the general food preparation facility for those who keep watch, in case of attack, at critical lookout posts in Kyrenia. The woman who raised me along with my mother since childhood and who was living in my home – Eleni Panayi, the daughter of Glytzia from the village of Karmi – is at her house mourning the loss of her son. A prison guard, he was killed on Christmas Eve by Turks at the Central Prisons, in the first skirmishes in Nicosia; he was the first dead of the inter-communal conflict. And the hotel, with its 150 rooms, is all but vacant! Other than Costas Catsellis and his wife Eleni, only the families of his other two sons, who are now managing the hotel, are here. The army is using one wing of the hotel free of charge, while the hotel's office is functioning as the headquarters for the defense of Greek Cypriots of Kyrenia, in case of an attack. As for foreigners, only two elderly English women are still here.

Even so, almost everyone in Kyrenia comes and goes from the hotel with fear in their eyes. Thank God, we have not had any incidents here, even if the Turks have seized the mountain ridge to the south and are holding the strategic ridges of Ayios Ilarion, Prophitis Elias and Gomaristra above the large villages of Karavas and Lapithos. As a result, the road to Nicosia is blocked at Pogazi, which was called the passage of Ayia Ekaterini at one time. Greeks in Kyrenia are not afraid of their fellow Turkish townsfolk. The two communities have lived together, as friends and neighbours, in mixed neighbourhoods in Pano Kyrenia for years. The Turkish warships are the real threat – every night they shine their lights off our coast, threatening a landing operation. The events of 1922 and the gruesome slaughter of civilians in Smyrna are still fresh in everyone's memory. The region's Greek population was ruthlessly decimated. And the horrors of the 1915 Armenian Genocide are not that far in the past either – another extermination brutally planned and executed by the Turkish government. Many refugees-survivors of those events, both Greeks and Armenians, still live in Kyrenia. We have all heard first-person accounts of what it means to be caught in the path of a ruthless Turkish military advance – it means premeditated atrocities carried out against unarmed populations for ruthless expansionary goals.

    In all likelihood, three and half thousand years ago, a man named Kifeas arrived here from another Kyrenia in Achaea and established our small town, with its Greek population. Kyrenia is also home to 500-600 Turkish Cypriots, who have been here since the period of the Ottoman rule of Cyprus that ended in 1878. A community of approximately 400 Britons also flourishes here. They are permanent residents, elderly folk – almost all retired government employees from the British colonies – who have fallen in love with the mild climate and the beauty of the landscape. They are receiving instructions from their embassy; they are not afraid. In fact, most choose to believe that it is not Turkey that wishes to seize Cyprus, but Greek Cypriots that wish to exterminate Turkish Cypriots.

    Amidst all the fear and anxiety, I have some time to myself every day, early in the afternoon. While my daughter Eleni takes a nap, I come down from my room and sit on the north veranda, outside the bar. The only positive thing about this compulsory re- location to the hotel is that I am living right on the water. The threatening lights of the Turkish warships are not visible during the day. During the day the sea is the same sea that I adore, with her deep blue colour and fierce tramontanas that break as spec- tacular, towering waves against the rocks of Kombonisi, which is connected to the hotel by a bridge. Costas Catsellis – my father- in-law, now seventy-six years old – comes to sit here at the same time. For decades this had been the only break he would get in his eighteen-hour days; now he doesn't know how to occupy his time! He starts reading the newspapers and listening to the radio at dawn, trying to make sense of what is happening; he no longer prepares breakfast. Thankfully, around 9AM, the daily family ritu- al begins in his wife's small dining room, the only one in the south wing of the hotel. Every family member that happens to be at the hotel gathers here for breakfast. Eleni Catselli prepares tea, coffee and porridge. She serves seasonal fruit, halloumi, fresh anari,[1] yo- gurt, honey, rusks, warm country bread or koulouropoullo.[2] The latest developments are discussed and his sons try to calm him down, although they know how dangerous and volatile the situ- ation is! The only person who seems to have a calming affect on him is Eleni – sixty-two years old with her sweet and kind gaze, with her patience and tranquil philosophical stance toward all life events. They were married in 1922 and have been together for 42 years. In the last two decades, whenever Eleni is away for a few days visiting her married daughters – one lives in Limassol, one in Nicosia, and one in Famagusta – my father-in-law feels so much insecurity that he becomes accident prone. The man who has so much experience preparing meat portions cuts his hand while

1 Anari (Greek: αναρή) is a type of soft cheese.

2 Koulouropoulo (Greek: κουλουρόπουλλο) A type of simit; bread typically encrusted with sesame seeds.

cutting meat. Or he trips. His children chuckle about his minor accidents and, because Eleni knows how he feels, she never stays away too long. At breakfast, she prepares his porridge with calm and steady movements. She serves him and sighs lightly about the situation:

"We'll just have to wait and see," she says and Costas can eat his breakfast somewhat calmly.

In some ways, Eleni Catselli reminds me of my father; they are second cousins after all. Their grandmothers were sisters. After breakfast someone takes him by car to his paternal village, where he has set up a large farm with cattle, pigs and chickens. When the hotel is full, his clientele consumes most of the farm's produce, all of it fresh and carefully selected. There he "cheats time a little," as he likes to say. He is fond of the cattle and insists that the bull understands him, that he speaks to him just as a man would. By lunchtime he is back at the hotel's kitchen, where the amount of work is absurd. He has so little to prepare – meals for his family, for the military officers to whom he is providing accommodations, and for the two elderly English ladies. Not even forty plates in total! Of course, he never neglects to send food to Kyrenia's notable Turkish Cypriots whom, in an act of desperation and as a precautionary measure, Kyrenians have arrested and are holding as hostages, hoping to dissuade against attacks on Greek Cypriots in Kyrenia. He has also sent them thick wool blankets from the hotel.[3] His midday siesta lasts no more than 30 or 45 minutes. He lies down for a while and goes through every corner of the newspapers that he did not read in the morning. Be that as it may,

---

3 When things returned to normal, Greek Kyrenians released all Turkish Cypriots who were detained. One Turkish Cypriot complained to Costas Catsellis that the blankets they had been using during their captivity bore the emblem of his hotel. "What did you want me to do, Sapri?" Costas Catsellis asked the man, "Should I have left you there, cold and hungry in the middle of winter?"

he says that newspapers confuse matters. He prefers a strictly historical magazine because it presents evidence in support of any
historical event it discusses. He is keenly interested in gaining a
more spherical perspective on Greek history and the two World
Wars; these are events that he experienced, although he was not
in the position to know all sides of the story at the time. After his
siesta, he sits on the north veranda to gaze at the sea for a while.
In the past this was his only brief respite before afternoon tea
and dinner services, when he worked without a break until 10
or 11PM when the dining room closed. Idle now and not feeling
rushed, once in a while he moves from the veranda inside to the
bar, especially when it's cold. A little later in the afternoon, Eleni
joins him here for a short time. She usually drinks a weak tea or
plain water; she has diabetes so she is careful. At night he keeps
busy in the kitchen again and, depending on how his mood has
been affected by the ominous Turkish warships, returns to reading
the historical magazine. At times he listens to the radio. He listens
to the BBC but does not consider it to be objective. He says that
the British have interests in Cyprus and support the Americans
who want Turkey to intervene, never mind that they cannot stand
us because we ousted them, even if they have kept two sovereign
bases on the island and Troodos for themselves, where they have
installed spy radars. In light of all this, what could their official
radio possibly say? They may be objective about other things but
when it comes to the essentials, when it comes to their political
interests, all principles are out the window!
Nights are even more torturous, not only for Costas Catsellis, but
for all of us. On land everyone who can be conscripted has been,
although almost all are unarmed – mercifully there is no trouble
in Kyrenia – but what about the sea? How do you defend against
fully armed Turkish warships, equipped with the latest NATO
weapons systems? If there is an attack from the sea, the hotel will
be levelled first; it is no secret that it houses the headquarters for
the area's defense.

The First Recording of the Biography

Yet, early in the afternoon on the north veranda, neither he nor
I tire of looking the sea. The waves – he says – are always different, never two alike. Million, billions of waves over thousands
of years, each one unlike any other… He watches the waves and
sips his tea, a strong tea, which is imported specifically for the
hotel in enormous one-metre, tin, cube containers, lined with
thick aluminum that helps preserve the aroma and freshness of
their contents. He drinks one cup of tea, while I drink four or
five. This is why I always order tea for four persons. I notice him
looking at me with amazement, but he never says anything. We
are not very comfortable with each other. Although I have been
married to his son for four years, this is essentially the first opportunity I have had to spend time with him. The first few days he
spoke to me about my father; he says I look a lot like him but only
when it comes to my face, since Stavris Lordos was a big and tall
man. He had a shining bald head and a nicely shaped skull, which
emphasized his rosy complexion. His moustache was thick and
strong, seemingly avenging the absence of hair on his head and
making him appear mysterious, since it almost always concealed
his lips and his reactions. He dressed completely in white silk dim-
ity, adorned by a newly opened and carefully selected rosebud
with its pristine young leaf fastidiously fixed on his lapel. He was
quite handsome in his youth. He kept his hair long at the back and
sported wide brim cowboy hats. He brought the first motorcycle
to Kyrenia, played the mandolin, and sang cantadas, while women
secretly sighed. Women fancied him indeed, both the locals and
those who came from Nicosia for summer holidays. Later on he
married Elenitsa, the daughter of Yiannis Keperis, and had three
children. He set up a farm, which he cultivated with passion using seeds from abroad – unknown vegetables and flowers to our
soil, such as daffodils, jonquils and irises. His stables were full

of livestock: cattle, oxen and guineafowl, not only chickens, but
also ducks, geese, turkeys and pigeons. While Costas Catsellis was
pioneering in his field with the hotel, he was buying produce, yet
unknown in Cyprus, from my father since his guests were asking
for it: Brussels sprouts, curly parsley, unusual radish varieties...
My father enjoyed playing practical jokes, aiming to bewilder him.
Once during Carnival, he startled him when he wore a fez on his
huge bald head and had people claim that Farouk, the King of
Egypt, had just arrived at the hotel. Another time he went to the
kitchen to deliver produce from his farm and raised objections
when he saw him chastising a lazy chambermaid:

"Can I say something, Costas? Be nice! Treat the poor girls
kindly! And if they want some, give it to them!"

"Give them what?"

"Give them some lovin'..."

Shocked by Stavris's advice Costas looked into his eyes, which
were an unusual green colour with golden streaks, in the hope
that he was not actually saying what he thought he was saying.

"Do you mean...?" he attempted to ask but stopped when he
saw that my father was already nodding.

"Sure! If they want it, isn't it a shame not to...? What's wrong
with that?" he said with a smile that burst out from under his
moustache, leaving no room for doubt.

I am smiling, too. And my father... Someone described him
as the "great philosopher of life," kind, primal and progressive,
methodical and disorganized, impassioned about all that he loved,
unconcerned with social conventions, full of contradictions! He
cried when he read sentimental stories but, when he was angry,
his shouting could be heard from the farm all the way to Kato
Kyrenia. And Costas Catsellis, who has dared to recount the
chambermaid incident to me, is blushing even now, at the age of
seventy-six! In sharp contrast, my father considered the coming
together of humans and animals the most simple and natural thing
in life. And now I call "Father" the one who is sitting across from

me while my father, gone for over a year, has been assimilated at the cemetery's entrance (first grave to the left), in the company of his father Kyriakos Lordos. His bicycle, which tilled the streets and suburbs of Kyrenia for years delivering milk door to door, lies abandoned and rusting somewhere, while Karaolis, the white dog that always chased after him, breathed its last on his grave from sorrow.

This second father is different, so different than the first that he truly piques my interest. He knows that I am collecting material about Kyrenia and her people. Before the inter-communal conflict, I had asked him to tell me a few things about his life. I feel that now is a good time, so I propose that we begin.

"It's not like I've lived such a grand life..." he says, trying to dodge my questions.

"Well, with seven children and eighteen grandchildren, it certainly isn't small!" I counter.

He looks at me rather pensively and then...

"Eight children – one of my sons died, and if your Costakis had lived, I would have had nineteen grandchildren," he sets the record straight.

I will not take no for an answer:

"Exactly! Well...?"

"What you're asking for is so boastful!" he protests.

"You're not the one to judge that!" I counter again and wonder why he is refusing now, when he was willing to share all sorts of things about his life before.

Before the unrest I would see him every Sunday, when I came to the hotel for lunch. On the southeast section of the massive dining room with the Byzantine-style arches, there is a special table set up permanently for the family. Almost every Sunday, all his children, grandchildren, sons-in-law and daughters-in-law would gather around this table, having arrived from all over Cyprus. He always sat at the head of the table and, when he was not there, no one occupied his seat. It always remained empty. Now armed Turks have blocked the short road from Nicosia to Kyrenia that is barely 16 miles long. As a result of the conflict and the great distance one must travel to bypass the roadblock, most of his children do not come from other towns on weekends. When I remind him that he had agreed to talk to me about his life before, he reveals the real reason.

"Before…! Can't you see that everything is upside down? What will happen to us? What will happen to our country?"

I search for something to say that will give him courage; I am vaguely aware that he has weathered many storms in his life.

"Okay, but wasn't it worse during World War II?"

He says "no"! It was not like this during World War II, even if one tenth of Cypriots had enlisted as volunteers. Yes, there was war and anxiety then, too, but not this crushing, oppressive feeling. And there was also a tenacious collective resistance in the air from so many nations, which believed that their citizens were sacrificing themselves for freedom and high ideals. Now everything is upside down. Those same countries are not supporting us; they won't even speak up for our independence. What do they support? Everyone wants military bases in Cyprus and no one cares about her people. No one considers us; on the contrary, they want us out of the way – simply and callously, just like that! And we are small and powerless. I understand his fears and anxieties, the infernal turmoil in his soul – it's the same turmoil that is in all of us, especially in Kyrenia. Nevertheless, something compels me to persist with my questions.

"When were you born? Do you know?" I ask.

Eventually he begins to recount moments of his life; he starts at the beginning, timidly and with some difficulty. I discretely take notes in a notebook, which I try to keep out of sight, resting on my knees under the table. Each night I hasten to write everything down clearly and in great detail as it was recounted to me, while it is still fresh in my memory, even though within the dark window frame the lights of the Turkish warships are still visible, still

threatening a landing, still threatening war and slaughter. In the
end we both enjoy this exchange; it provides a temporary escape
from the anxiety about the fate that awaits our country and each
one of us. At night I prepare questions about what I have just recorded, and the next day we begin with clarifications. He answers
eagerly but his interest is especially piqued when I impart analo-
gous or related things from my folkloric research on Kyrenia. He
becomes excited when I happen to have written testimonials in
books or manuscripts. All this until the day the message arrives
that foreign journalists wish to interview him...

The Interview,
1964

Forming a slight wave that runs parallel to the shoreline, the hotel
extends east to west, with a wide central corridor that is identical on all three floors. With the exception of the ground floor,
on either side of these corridors on the two upper floors, there
are rooms: half with a view to the sea and half with a view to
the mountains. On the ground floor, after the entrance and the
reception area, the corridor leads to the management office and
to the drawing rooms on the side that faces the sea. A narrower
corridor begins a few steps past the office, dividing the hotel's
only south wing in two. The hotel's original kitchens used to be
here; on the east side of the corridor is the family's formal dining room with its gorgeous carved walnut furnishings. This room
opens only when Eleni has guests for afternoon tea or when her
children visit on formal occasions. Past the formal family dining
room are two small bedrooms, one for Costas and one for Eleni;
this way he does not disturb her when he gets up very early in the
morning. Another room is across the hall – a sewing room where
most of the hotel's linen is still sewn under the supervision of
Eleni and her sister Styliani Adamou, who has been more attached
to the family since her husband's passing in 1954. She lives alone

in her home, which is next to the Sea View, but spends almost all her time with her sister at the Dome. The casual family dining room is further down, on the same side; it is equipped with a small kitchen next door.

This is where we have all gathered — Eleni, his two sons, and I. We are waiting for him for breakfast. He is a little late and, when he arrives, he says that he did not catch a wink; he was up all night thinking about the journalists. He declares that he does not want to see them. They know about the trouble in Kyrenia and in Cyprus but are not willing to admit that all this has been orchestrated by Turkey in accordance with her expansionary agenda. Yet everyone can see that warships shine their lights every night, threatening a landing. This is what they should be writing in their papers! He has nothing more to say. He has done nothing that is worth recounting... Nothing, nothing at all!

Eleni is ready with the porridge, which she serves to him with a smile.

"Do you remember the time when we ran into Lipetris in that shop on Ermou Street in Nicosia, and he made up a poem about you right there on the spot? He said that you are the Bull and the Antibull..." she says.

"People don't tell reporters poems by Lipetris, Eleni," he counters in a dull voice while eating his porridge.

"But we have already said yes to the reporters. They are on their way..." his eldest son says, now truly concerned.

"You have so much to share, Father!" I confirm.

"Like what?"

"You've told me so many things!"

He shakes his head as if to shoo away an annoying insect.

"Old stories..." he says with contempt.

Then his two sons remind him of all that he has accomplished over the last two decades, things that they have experienced, things that he has not shared with me yet.

In 1946 he bought from the government two rocky patches of

land that were attached to the west side of the hotel, toward Proti Tsiakkileri, for £2. Everyone wondered to what end... When he poured concrete between them, a representative of Public Works came to see him to find out what he was doing.

"I am making Kyrenia bigger!" he replied.

He continued construction even though he was ordered to stop. He joined the rocks, laid down ground sandstone, and created a small square that has helped alleviate traffic on the narrow coastal road toward Proti Tsiakkileri. Even so he was asked to appear in court.

"I would be a fool to buy them, if I had no intention of utilizing them. And what I built, I did not build for myself, but for everyone!" he tells the court.

Now that the small square is finished – lovely, tidy and paved with sandstone as it is – no one would dream of demolishing it. Neoptolemos Pashalis drafted a law specifically for this case that was in effect for one day – as long as it took for the construction to be approved.

The year 1948 was of great significance because my father-in-law took a huge leap forward. He demolished the four domes and moved the hotel's entrance to the south and the kitchens to the east. There was no other way; another floor had to be added to the hotel to provide more rooms. The beautiful domes were sacrificed and now only the hotel's name attests to their existence. The hotel has 130 rooms and 240 beds, while the total number of first class rooms in the whole of Cyprus is only 325. In essence, more than one third of all first class hotel rooms on the island are at the Dome. But since the hotel was still in need of water, he bought a spring in Thermia from Chrysanthis Strongylos. He dug a deep, three kilometer-long trench, laid pipe, and brought fresh running water to hotel.

Amid this flurry of activity, at the end of the year, he ran into problems with his prostate. He had surgery in Nicosia but something went wrong; he almost died. When he recovered, having come face to face with death, he converted the company that he had built with so much hard work into shares, which were divided equally between Eleni, their seven children, and himself. On July 20, 1949, he received the incorporation certificate – "Catsellis Hotels Limited" – which he framed and hung in the hotel's office.

In January 1950, while he was walking up the steps of Archangelos to sign the Enosis Referendum – "We demand Union with Greece" – one Kynerian asked him:

"You came to sign, too, Mr. Catsellis?"

"Why wouldn't I sign? Am I not a Greek Cypriot?"

"I don't know. With so many English folk at your hotel…"

"Everyone in Kyrenia makes a living from my hotel guests. Tourism is one thing and nationalism quite another!" he responded and signed with a firm hand.

Eleni recalls how deeply it had wounded him that even one Kyrenian would question his patriotism.

In 1950 he completed the lovely movie theatre on Catsellis Road and the open-air theatre at the Dome, directly across from the sea. In the following year he began setting up a farm on his father's land in Karakoumi.

Next in line was Kombonisi, which he brought from the government in 1930 for 10 shillings. The first problem he had to tackle there was access. He filled empty barrels with concrete made with sweet water and secured them in the sea. Everyone expected the concrete to disintegrate in the salt water; instead it solidified! The concrete-filled barrels formed a series of immovable columns on which he constructed a sturdy bridge high above the water so fishing boats could pass below. That way, they would not be forced to go around Kombonisi to open waters on days when the sea was not calm. Then he connected the rocks around the small rock isle, dug out a deep pit at the centre, and bore a tunnel below connecting it to the sea. A natural saltwater pool was created where one can swim any time of the year, even during a fierce tramontane.

What is more, the water is always kept clean because the sea currents flow in through the opening.

They reminisce and reminisce until a staff member enters and interrupts the flow of memories.

"The foreign reporters are waiting for you at the bar, Boss!" he announces.

We all look at him without saying a word, but he is not budging. Then Eleni slowly gets up from the table and takes away the empty plate in front of him.

"It's time, Costas!" she urges gently

He avoids her gaze but realizes that he has no choice! He wipes his face with a napkin, gets up, and starts making his way down the corridor toward the bar. His two sons follow him; I do, too, albeit at a slight distance. Many reporters are there; they are already drinking their first beverages. Then an avalanche of questions about the disappearance of tourism, about the vacant hotel, about what will he do, about the enormous blow to the economy of the small town... And he with that indecipherable smile with which he has greeted each and every guest since 1922... With the exception of Eleni, no one knows what this smile conceals: Is it exhaustion, ferocious anger, a good mood, problems, or anxiety? At some point the questions stop. Silence! Yet that smile persists even when he opens his mouth again.

"Now that the hotel is vacant I have the opportunity to undertake major renovations. I have several changes in mind that I have been postponing because the hotel was always full. A luxury hotel, especially one with as much tradition as the Dome, should be renovated regularly," he declares simply, as if everything were perfectly normal.

After a moment of hesitation, the foreign journalists start to jot down what he said. He gets up before they have a chance to finish writing but remembers something, as he is about to take the first step:

"Please have another drink. And now, if you would excuse me, I have much to do. All these renovations require a great deal of planning."

I follow him; he is heading toward the kitchen. I wait and watch as he puts on his pristine white apron.

"Father, why didn't you say anything to them?" I ask.

"I knew they were expecting me to say something different... But I remembered my prostate surgery in Nicosia – a very close brush with death! It was night and I knew what was happening to me, but I said to myself: *No, I am not going to die!* I marshalled all my strength and I survived. It's the same thing now: They were expecting me to whine and whimper, to say that my hotel is finished, that Kyrenia is finished without any tourism. I would never give them that much pleasure! And tomorrow I will begin those renovations. I meant it when I said that this is the perfect opportunity, that the timing is right, now that I have no guests. The renovations will also help a lot of poor people, who have been left without work because of this situation."

He begins cutting a matured whole tenderloin into portions. Although he is given to the task, he notices me moving my head back and forth.

"What is it?" he asks.

I am stunned by his reaction, what can I say?

"I don't know, Father..."

He dips the steaks he has just cut into oil, making sure that all sides are coated. He sets a large one aside.

"You like it medium rare, right?"

I nod mechanically.

"That's the best way to eat it because that way you don't destroy the nutrition in the meat and it does the most good. And this one for Eleni," he says and sets a small one aside.

Yiorkos the cook – overweight and imposing with his eternally untied shoes – enters the kitchen at that moment, while the second cook, whom we call "Yiatros," flips crepes. He says "good morning" to Yiorkos, asks Yiatros whether the crepes are almost ready, but is obviously perplexed by my inquisitive gaze.

"Other than what I have told you, what do you know about me and the hotel?" he asks.

Until that moment it had never occurred to me that I would ever be asked such a question; I have no response. Even so the question begins to tug strings of memories within me.

What I knew

Indeed, what do I know about this man? Growing up on my father's farm, utterly self-centred like all small children that believe everything revolves around them, the Dome was part of my life, without ever having seen it. Every afternoon, at the time when day surrenders to night, when everything descends to twilight and the west tries to hold on to its violet hues, in that ambiguous light a peculiar otherworldly sound would begin to resonate... When I was a little older I learned that that sound was the gong of the large hotel with the domes calling its guests to dinner. I could hear it clearly because the farm was up on a hill, one kilometer from the sea, extending from the north to the south, perpendicular to the hotel. Perhaps this is why I always seek out sounds at dusk and, when none is there, I begin to sing *Phos Ilaron*.[4] I loved hearing the gong then; I waited for its metallic sound, which vibrated the air as though it were something natural. At the time it never occurred to me that there was a story behind it, nor did I ever think about what a hotel was, even if I could see its four domes.

I understood more about the use of the hotel when I went

---

4 Phos Ilaron (Φῶς Ἱλαρόν) is a Christian hymn in the Greek New Testament. Its Latin title is *Lumen Hilare*; it has been translated into English as *O Gladsome Light*.

there with my parents for tea at the invitation of an Indian military doctor. He was in the service of the British Army, most prob- ably at the British Military Hospital. He first came to the farm to buy flowers, got to know us a little better, saw a pretty cousin of mine, fell in love, and wanted to marry her. He was a guest at our house almost every day. Wanting to reciprocate our hospitality, he invited us all to tea at the hotel. I remember the beautiful drawing room only vaguely, since I was more impressed by the Indian man wearing khaki and a military turban. I admired him, so I held a grudge against my cousin because, in the end, she did not dare say "yes"; she did not accept his marriage proposal.

After the end of World War II, I watched a theatre production at the hotel: Sophia Vembo in "O Agapitikos tis Voskopoulas."[5] The performance was held in the large dining room but I, enchanted by the play, never gave any thought to why the room was there, or what it was used for when there were no theatrical performances.

I remember more clearly the first time I went to another draw- ing room, one with Corinthian–style columns. At the far end of the room, a young woman stood on a stage. She was saying some- thing, while her hands were tied to the front. I was barely four years old at the time; I remember trying to understand the plot. Again the space itself was of no concern to me; the only thing I knew was that the actors were senior students at the gymnasium. A friend of my mother's had brought me to the play. When we returned home and I was asked about what I saw, I said that there was a girl who loved her brother very much but was imprisoned and killed by an evil king. I became really fond of Antigone because for me, at the time, having a brother was an unfulfilled dream.

In the same hall and on the same stage a few years later, on January 30, on the Feast of the Three Holy Hierarchs, I recited a poem at an event organized jointly by all schools in the area. Since I was at ease with such things when I was young, I was often asked

5 Sometimes translated as "The Lover of the Shepard's Daughter."

to recite. Everything would have been perfect if, in the middle of my recitation, Sonia had not jumped up onto the stage to be close to me. She looked confidently at the audience and wagged her tail to signal our special bond. When I felt my beloved dog beside me, my voice quivered on a verse, but then I noticed that the Metropolitan was smiling in the first row. Realizing that this was not the end of the world, I continued reciting while Sonia, obeying my father's signals, jumped off the stage and went to him before I finished my recitation. At the time I knew simply that the large hall was a part of the Gymnasium of Kyrenia.

When I was eleven, there was much talk of an ancient tomb discovered at the site where Catsellis was building the movie theatre. For Kyrenians the discovery of ancient tombs was a routine occurrence, a commonplace event, yet my father – who always made sure that I was informed about all aspects of life – took me on site to have a look. I became so fascinated with what I saw that I refused to leave; I stayed with the labourers and the archaeologists, who gave me permission to enter the tomb. I was quite frightened climbing down the wooden ladder into the entombed cold and darkness, which could not even hope for a glimmer of light. But then I turned on the flashlight and saw, on the tomb's floor, a jumble of pottery and bones; a number of white eggs shone among them, while around them sarcophagi rested on ledges carved out of the rock. I leaned over one sarcophagus and saw a skull to which two golden laurel leaves were attached. The archaeologists said that the tomb had been stripped on the previous day by labourers, who opened it before the authorities arrived on site. Yet, behind the sarcophagi, several older skeletons were thrown about with their jewellery intact. The archaeologists taught me how to sift the soil and, during the three days that it took to thoroughly examine the tomb, I recovered many pieces of golden "macaroni" as I called it (i.e. tiny pipe necklace beads), as well as one golden earring that depicted Eros – a miniature Eros holding a quiver, with his curly head leaning backward while his cute belly protruded forward. The archaeologists made a record of the finding and placed it inside a matchbox. Then they sealed the tomb since it had nothing of special significance.

From the following year, when the movie theatre was completed, I never missed a school screening, sitting comfortably in its seats of dark red velvet; I have been a fan of the cinema since then. Even so I never identified the space with any particular person.

My education in the theatre continued at the hotel's open-air amphitheatre directly across Kombonisi, which acted as a sound barrier by muffling the roar of the crashing waves. I watched one of the best performances of "Iphigenia in Tauris" there. The landscape was such an appropriate backdrop to the story! I was in the sixth grade of elementary school at the time. I fell in love with the tragedy when I watched it, giving no thought to how the play got there or to the massive building behind the amphitheatre.

In the following year, when I first walked up the stairs of the Gymnasium of Kyrenia, the experience was, for me, the most natural thing in the world. The lovely three-storey building – with its tall columns and Corinthian-style capitals, with its balconies with the small concrete columns – was exactly as I had always known it to be. Although the sea stroked the spacious, tidy square at the front, the waves could not harm it because it was protected by a concrete wall, which also formed a ledge – a convenient place to sit. The girls were confined to the balconies at recess, while the boys roamed about in the comfortable square; although ours was a co-ed school, the rules stated the two sexes had to be separated at recess. Downstairs, at the front of the ground floor, spacious classrooms with large windows faced the sea. In the large hall on the first floor, in a meditative half-light, all the students would come together for the daily prayer, occupying the entire area around the Corinthian columns. The library was also there. On national days barricades were brought down to section off a large area for events on the northwest part of the ground floor. And the same stage, which had been used for the performance of "Antigone," would be set up here. Without any of the time-consuming, contemporary audio-visual means we, the students, sang; we learned to play musical instruments; we staged theatrical productions many times a year – two national days, Christmas, the Feast of the Three Holy Hierarchs, the end of the school year celebration, even an ancient tragedy at the beginning of summer. So many characters were brought to life on that stage – Athanasios Diakos, the ghost of the Dead Brother, the women of Souli who threw themselves into the Dance of Zalongo... Proud of their children and moved by good performances, everyone in Kyrenia watched the school plays. The kitchens were on the ground floor, at the back. We would go there to ask for a drink of water and to chat with the cleaning ladies, who also did the cooking, because the third floor was a boarding house for male students from out of town. And on the roof of the building, we, the female students, had our exercise classes. We wore short puffy underpants but had no fear of being noticed by the strict secretary of the Metropolis, Polykarpos, who always screeched about supposed immodesty and immorality. We never gave a second thought to the panoramic vistas from the rooftop, to the beauty of the nature around us, or to our youth; we simply took pleasure in this harmonious coming together of buildings, God and man, considering it the most natural and ordinary thing in the world.

The only disharmony I ever experienced intensely was in 1953, when the square was decorated for the coronation of Queen Elizabeth II. Those decorations were so different to what we would normally set up using myrtle, laurel, and blue and white fabric along the school's façade. Yet this is when I clarified within myself who we were and who were governing us; I was old enough to weigh such things and take a stance.

It never occurred to me, however, that the school building had been designed and built by someone, that it was rented to Kyrenia's School Board for a ridiculously low sum of money, nor did I ever imagine that it had been a hotel at one time. For me the hotel had always been the building across from our school, the Dome, which I passed every morning on my bicycle while delivering milk to our customers. My only stop in this area was a small house built on sea rock to the west – the home of a Scottish woman by the name of Ogilvy for whom I left a small bottle, half a pint of milk, every day. The photography studio, which belonged to an Armenian, was on the other side of the street, toward the mountain, between the taxi offices. I wanted to have my picture taken but not one of those formal eight-day portraits. So I offered to pay the shop girl to take a picture of me with her camera. The most informal place was the garden in front of the hotel. I posed there, even stepped into the small garden with the grass for a few shots. At the time, with all the insolence of adolescence, it seemed to me that the hotel was the only setting beautiful enough to serve as the backdrop for my regal mug.

But, in this, I was not alone; all Kyrenians took for granted that the guests of the Dome Hotel would sustain the shops, the taxi offices other than Theocharis's, the bars and the coffee shops that kept popping up everywhere – the first being Klitos's picturesque bar and coffee shop. Tourists of more limited means stayed at less expensive hotels, thereby helping to develop another sector of tourism.

I met Costas Catsellis for the first time when I was sent, as a member of a school delegation, to obtain his permission to stage a play at his movie theatre on March 25. When we arrived he was in the kitchen, with his pristinely clean apron as always, cutting meat portions. An older female student spoke to him and he simply replied, "yes, okay." The headmaster did not even bother asking us whether he had given his permission or not; it was as though he assumed that the school had the inexorable right to use his property whenever the need arose. Costas Catsellis himself did not make an impression in me but, then again, my mind was preoccupied with other things; I had been given a starring role in the one-act play. Even so, I enjoyed his theatre's attractive dressing rooms and lovely parquet stage. When I was in the fourth grade, we used this movie theatre often because the gymnasium had just moved into its own, albeit half-finished, building near the Metropolis. It was still not painted and lacked many facilities, including a hall where school events could be held. All events, other than the daily prayer, were housed at the Catsellis Movie-Theatre, to which we were always given access even if unthinking adolescents damaged the lovely seats, the walls, just about everything. On its stage I portrayed Antigone in "Oedipus at Colonus" and Triantafyllos in the play "Katsantonis" by Theotokas.

I entered the hotel as a secret courier for EOKA tasked with delivering letters to "Gigantas" – the code name for Costas Catsellis's eldest son. I would pass the reception area, turn left, hide in the office, and deliver the letter. I had neither the time nor the interest to dilly-dally and look around; the British meant business! In the summer of 1958 they carried out mass arrests all across Cyprus. Andreas Catsellis, a.k.a. Gigantas, was arrested. He was sent, along with most of his fellow Kyrenians that endured the same fate, to a detention camp near the Turkish village of Aourta. Costas Catsellis undertook the provision of food for the detainees while his youngest son, Stelios, came and went not only with food but also with messages for EOKA. I was also arrested at this time but my term at the Central Prisons in Nicosia was brief, only one month.

Back in Kyrenia and free, I spent a great deal of time at one of the houses on Catsellis Road, above a shop. Housed there, along with the PAEK Athletics Club, was the Association of Graduates of the Gymnasium of Kyrenia, which I served as secretary. The office of the general secretary was the laundry room, which still had its large hewn washbasin. The magazine "Politismos" was edited and printed here by hectograph. In another room I rehearsed for Molière's "The Bourgeois Gentleman," which was staged – where else? – at the Catsellis Movie Theatre! This is where I also met Costas Catsellis one afternoon, on the stairs; I was going down while he was coming up. I was wearing a dress made of local cotton because this was the era of passive resistance, when we boycotted English fabrics. I remember the dress being quite tight around my waist.

We stood there looking at each there for a few moments. It was the first time that we had sized each other up, and for good reason: If all went according to plan, he would become my father-in-law and I his daughter-in-law.

When he came to ask for me on behalf of his youngest son Stelios, it was August and quite late in the evening. He had just finished dinner service at the hotel and my father had been dealing with a difficult birth of a calf that ended tragically; the cow did not survive. Very little was exchanged between them before it was my turn to enter with the tray and serve the traditional sweet. This was the first time that I took notice of Costas Catsellis within the scope of my historical and folkloric interests.

But how would we ever find time for any of that – he with the hotel always full and I with motherhood and the tragic fate of my first child? I saw him only on Sundays at lunchtime, when I went to the hotel for the family meal, amid the din of the entire clan. The opportunity to get to know him only became available during the inter-communal conflict when I moved into the hotel, even though it was cut short by his meeting with the foreign journalists. Immediately after that meeting, he began renovating the hotel and had no free time while I, as the situation slowly returned to normal, went home where I continued the futile struggle to save my second and third children, who also suffered from incurable thalassemia.

I remember him on Palm Sunday, April 4, 1966, at the inauguration ceremony of the elementary school in Karakoumi. Not only had he donated four stremmas of land, which he had bought from old Mariannou, his brother Antonis's wife, but also built – using his own funds – the entire school building, which had been operating since 1960. Karakoumi had gone from a nearly nonexistent community of two or three dozen residents at the turn of the century to a population of over 200 at that time. It was a self-sufficient village and when, with the Independence, Tsiarkezos's house was rented to house the elementary school, Costas Catsellis began construction of a proper school building, which started operating right away. The inauguration ceremony was delayed due to the political situation but, on that spring day, Karakoumi wore its Sunday best, especially the school's large garden, which was in full bloom. The minister of education delivered a speech and then, when it was his turn to say the few words that he had written down in advance, he refused to put on his reading glasses. He thought that wearing glasses would be a certain sign that he was an old man and that everyone would consider him to be over the hill!

Costas Catsellis was anything but an old man or over the hill because, that year, he began construction for the addition of eight double rooms at the east wing of the hotel, above the kitchens. They were completed in the following year, raising the total number of rooms to 138. In parallel, the Sea View, which had been converted into apartments in 1953, was changed back to a hotel. When all the work was finished, it had 37 rooms and 69 beds. Even though the hotel was now a corporation, the 'old man' was the absolute ruler over two aspects of the business: the kitchen and construction. When it came to renovations he was especially irreplaceable because he was the only one who knew where the electrical cables and the pipes of the closed circuit water system were located, and how much iron each structural column contained.

Later that year, when six fellow Kyrenians and I founded the Folkloric Club of Kyrenia, we barely had to ask; we were welcomed into the hotel's west drawing room. This room had a beautiful stone-built fireplace with "1939," the year it was constructed, inscribed in Latin numerals above it. In the meantime, his donations to the Gymnasium of Kyrenia became more generous.

As fate would have it, two years later, I was given the opportu-

nity to not only bond but also live in close proximity with Costas
Catsellis again. His sister-in-law Styliani passed away on the eve
of her name day, on November 25, 1968. Eleni followed suit; she
breathed her last in just over three months, on March 2 of the following year. I remember him expressionless, without a tear or a
sigh; he only fainted in church during the funeral service... After
the death of our third child, my husband and I closed our home
once more and moved into the hotel for several months so we
could be near him. He made no changes to his private quarters
or to his work routine. He buried the pain deeply within him; it
revealed itself only at unexpected moments and in ways that only
those closest to him could perceive. Eleni's passing brought him
to terms with his own mortality, despite my reactions...

"No, you're not going to die!" I protested whenever he would
say something along those lines.

"Everything dies. People, animals, trees..." he would counter,
completely disarming me.

He honoured Eleni's memory by building a special wing at the
gymnasium to house a library, which would also serve as a lec-
ture hall. He named it "Elenios Library," after his wife. In parallel,
he added an additional 37 rooms to the third floor of the hotel,
bringing the total to 175 rooms and 305 beds.

The Pancyprian Association of Hoteliers, in collaboration with
the Cyprus Tourism Organization, decided to honour him "for his
tireless efforts in making Cyprus known as an excellent tourist
destination and as a pioneer in attracting European tourism to
Kyrenia, and to Cyprus in general." The ceremony was held on
Sunday, February 25, 1973, at the College of Tourism and Hotel
Management. The entire family gathered there early. When he entered the hall, I saw him take a seat at one of the back rows.

"Why are you sitting back here?" I asked.

"So many officials are coming, they'll sit at the front," he replied.

I realized that he was feeling awkward. I smiled, took him by
the arm, lifted him up, and led him to the first row.

"You're the one they're coming to honour. You want them to have to go around looking for you?" I said.

The representatives of the Pancyprian Association of Hoteliers and of the Cyprus Tourism Organization delivered their addresses. They presented him with a golden medal, which they hung around his neck. And when it was his turn to respond to their praises, once more, he refused to put on his reading glasses.

"I can see, I can see! I'm still holding on," he assured me.

The year 1973 came with another flurry of building activity; he began construction of a sweet-water swimming pool. Many people kept saying that he was continuing to build because he believed that if he stopped, he would die. To such comments he always responded with a smile, never saying a word. No, he was not consumed by a desperate need to hang on to life; he simply could not live without creating!

While this project was underway, the coup d'état took place on July 15, 1974. Again I moved into the hotel for safety with my fourth child, Despina-Maria, who was four years old at the time. A few days later, at dawn, the first Turkish fighter jet invaded Cyprus and sprayed the hotel's north veranda with bullets, precisely at the spot where he always took his afternoon tea. Other than the guests that were already there, many frightened Kyrenians came to the hotel to take cover in its basements. Yet the "old man," as everyone was calling him by now, did not take a single step down into that basement... He remained in the kitchen, preparing meals for his hotel guests and fellow Kyrenians, whom he considered and treated as hotel guests.

"My fellow townspeople have come into my home, why wouldn't I look after them?" he said to me.

But since Turkish objectives were as plain as day, I was determined to not surrender to fate. With a small child on my arm and another growing inside me – unarmed civilians as we were – I stressed that we should go somewhere until things settled down. No road was safe but I insisted that we take the risk. His grandson, Costas Zambarloukos, who worked at the hotel, decided to stay behind; he would manage the hotel in any eventuality. It was decided that my family, my mother, my younger brother, and the "old man" set out in the same car, God help us! Someone sent for him and he came from the kitchen to the entrance, where everyone had gathered for the departure, still wearing that clean white apron.

"Why should I leave? I'm an old man. I haven't harmed anyone. The worst thing they can do is kill me!" he said. He did not want to go.

I untied his apron and listed, nearly shouting, all the reasons why we had to go. I took him by the hand and led him to the car. We set out. The first two days we stayed in Nicosia at his daughter Athenoula's home. Most believed that we would return when the fighting stopped; the reality, however, would prove to be very different indeed. The invaders were not carrying out "a peaceful mission!" This is what they were touting solely for external consumption. Their objective was to seize a large part of the island at the very least, including the entire Kyrenia district, just as they had planned years ago. Those who remained in Kyrenia were detained at the Dome; only a handful of people were allowed to remain in their homes. And of course, no civilians of those who had sought temporary refuge elsewhere were ever allowed to return; on the contrary, the enclaved were systematically expelled either through blatant violence or under a number of pretexts.

The "old man," my family, and I went to Limassol, where his eldest daughter Despina lived. He stayed with her, while we rented a nearby house that had very little furniture. Yet one room was packed with enormous boxes of tea, one by one metres in size; it was a special order for the hotel that had not cleared customs in Limassol in time. We brought the shipment to the house, not knowing what else to do with it. We did not stay at that house very long because it was close to the city's central avenue and extremely noisy. We found other accommodations, just over two kilometers further up, in the Tsiros area. He could walk the dis-

tance to our house quite easily; every afternoon we had tea together. Since all my manuscripts had been left behind – one more
injurious loss among all the others caused by the violent displace-
ment – I asked him to recount his life story to me once more.
He enjoyed the process because he was breathing in the land of
his birth, albeit only in his mind. He visited us every day, even
after he finished recounting his life story. There was, of course,
his young granddaughter Despina-Maria, his twenty-third grandchild, and Stavrini-Christina, the daughter that I had given birth
to in the meantime. Even though he was 87 years old, he was
still in good health; his spirit was lively; he read the newspapers,
commented on developments, learned news of the enclaved at
the Dome, especially of his grandson. He had faith that we would
return. But things only got worse... In a few months they expelled the enclaved, both those who were detained at the hotel
and elsewhere; instead of being allowed to return to their homes,
they were forced to come to the free part of Cyprus. On January 3, 1976, his grandson, Costas Zambarloukos, was expelled.
They cleared out the hotel and started operating it themselves, as
though they were its rightful owners. The Sea View had been used
as barracks for Turkish troops since the first days of the invasion!
Costas Vottis, who was now blind and bedridden, and his wife
Cleopatra remained at their home, enclaved in Kyrenia.

One day he came to see me; he was quite distraught.

"Things are tough. It's not going to be easy for us to return!"
my father-in-law said in a trembling voice.

I tried to give him courage. He listened without saying a word,
without countering, as he would usually do. The next day he had
trouble walking the distance to our house. The doctor ordered
rest and that he confine himself at home for a few days. A few
days later, while he was moving around his daughter's house without difficulty, he suffered a heart attack. He died suddenly, like a
felled tree.

I recorded his death in my diary, from where I now copy the following passage:

Refugeedom, Friday, June 18, 1976

Last Saturday, on Soul Saturday, July 12, my father-in-law, Costas Catsellis, passed away. At the wake I read the "Book of Revelations" by John the Apostle. At the funeral I dispensed the funerary meal. What else could I do? I could not provide what he really wanted — to be laid to rest next to his wife in Kyrenia. I went to the cemetery early to bring the provisions for the funerary meal; there, my daughter Despina-Maria and I saw the open grave. A shallow grave, barely one and a half metres deep, dug out of a hard white soil, without a trace of moisture... So much has died inside me with his passing. I have spent years writing his biography, commemorating and recording the events of his life; I have spent so many years studying him. I lost something with his death, something that perhaps I know even better than I know myself...
　　The earth's different places are presences
　　with such strong personalities,
　　that certain people die
　　when they are forced to part with them.[6]

---

6 Marcel Proust from "Jean Santeuil."

PHOTOGRAPHIC APPENDIX

Father Yiannis Paphitis, whose church records book that lists births and marriages in Kyrenia between 1880 and 1905, is a valuable source of information.

The small house of Father Yiannis Paphitis (right), and the promenade, which was built with stone that Costas Catsellis provided to the Municipality free of charge. Archangelos Church can be seen at the rear.

The ridge of Ayios Ilarion, also referred to as "Ais Larkos," in Kyrenia mountain range.

Kimon Beach in 1911. In the distance is Chamberlain's Catholic church, to the right the tithe storehouse and, at the front, the improvised building which women would enter to go swimming.

Costas Catsellis (to
the left) as a volunteer
in the United States
Army in Maryland in
1918 with his friend
Yiannis Vrahas, when
the latter visited him
at the camp.

The bust of the Marquis de Lafayette formed by the soldiers of the
11th Division of the United States
Army that bore his name.

Costas Charalambous's registration as a volunteer in the US Army on November 5, 1918. The document, which bears his signature and contains mistakes and inaccuracies in the names and dates, was located in the relevant national archives in the US.

Costas Charalambous's discharge documents from the US Army in 1919. The documents were located in the relevant national archives in the US.

Phinitzia, the palm tree; the point of farewell and welcome of immigrants on the Nicosia-Kyrenia road. (The photo is taken from an album that belonged to George Ludovic Houstoun, 1892.)

Postcard of the port of Kyrenia during the 1920s, with its storehouses, homes and high balconies. Postcard of the port of Kyrenia during the 1920s, with its carob storehouses, homes and high balconies.

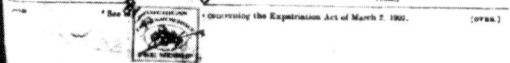

A page from Costas Catsellis's application for a US passport in 1923. A passport was issued but he never returned to the US. The document contains inaccuracies in the dates and in the spelling of names.

A page from Costas Catsellis's application for a US passport for his return to Cyprus, signed with his original surname 'Charalambous'. The application was approved on July 12, 1921, and he left the US in the same month. The document contains inaccuracies in the dates and in the spelling of names.

The siblings Costas and Eleni
Hadjiparaskeva (Vottis) in the
1910s.

The house – which was the dowry of Eleni Catselli – that served as the
first Sea View Hotel in Kyrenia in 1927 and next to it the second Sea
View Hotel The bridge of Xylogiofyro and some wagon wheels can be
seen in the foreground.

The Dome Hotel and, to its right, the two houses that Costas Catsellis gave as dowry to two of his five daughters.

The landfill project for the square, which was named Kimon Beach.

Several Kyrenians immediately after their release from prison for their action during the October uprising of 1931. Pictured in the back row from left to right: Neocles Loizou, Savvas Poeros, Kyriakos Poeros and Savvas Karasavvas. Pictured in the front row from the left to the right: Dorotheos Carolides and Captain Panais Michaelides.

Architectural drawing by the English architect W. T. Caroë for the Dome Hotel depicting the two domes (based on the dome of the Antiphonitis church). In the insert: The Sea View Hotel.

Eleni and Costas Catsellis most likely during their trip to Athens in 1933.

Seven of the eight children of Eleni and Costas Catsellis in 1937. Pictured from the left to the right are Vera, Stelios, Aliki, Maroulla, Athenoulla, Andrikkos and Despina.

Styliani Votti and her husband Costas Adamou in the 1940s.

Cleopatra and Costas Stavri Vottis during the 1940s. The couple remained enclaved in their home after the Turkish invasion of 1974. Costas passed away in 1980. Cleopatra remained enclaved in her home, despite an attempt on her life during which she was seriously wounded. It seems that the attempt was carried out by a Turk, who wanted to take her house. Cleopatra died in 2012.

Costas Catsellis in his kitchen with his chef, Master Yiorkos.

Costas Catsellis in his kitchen.

A bottle bearing the logo of Stavros Charalambides's farm.

Stavros Charalambides (Stavris, the son of Lordos) and his wife Eleni. Their farm in Kyrenia raised cattle and other products with which they supplied the Dome Hotel.

Sophocles Paphitis with his first
wife, the daughter of Kaniklides, a
barber from Nicosia.

Theocharis Savvas (left) with Kotsios Karasavvas, who was the owner of
Kyrenia's first taxi, No. 11, on May 1, 1923.

Costas Catsellis at the beginning of the 1940s.

Eleni Catselli at the beginning of the 1940s.

The three youngest children of Costas Catsellis and Eleni.

On the left, the first and second Sea View hotels just behind the Kyrenia Municipal Seawater Baths. On the right, the Dome Hotel with its first two Byzantine domes.

The Dome Hotel with Kato Kyrenia in the background. In the foreground, Proti Tsiakkileri with the unfinished ship purchased by Costas Catsellis.

Eleni Catselli with three of her
five daughters. From left to right:
Maroulla, Athenoula and Aliki.

The youngest four children of Costas and Eleni Catsellis. From left
to right: Aliki, Maroulla and Vera.
Stelios is seated in front.

The Dome Hotel with its four domes on the left, and a general view of
Kato Kyrenia in the 1940s.

The Kyrenia Castle and the surrounding area; an old post card.

One of the many postcards of the Dome Hotel with its second floor and demolished domes. At the sea, the bridge to Kombonisi with the natural seawater swimming pool.

The western side of Dome Hotel as it appeared after the addition of the second floor, which eliminated the four domes.

Dinnerware set and logo of the Sea View Hotel from the 1920s.

Dinnerware set and logo of the Dome Hotel from the 1940s.

The students of Nicosia's English School in 1940, when the school moved to Kyrenia, which was thought to be safer from possible German airstrikes. They rented the Sea View and operated it as a school and boarding school.

In front of the Gymnasium of Kyrenia (the Sea View Hotel) on March 25, 1951.

"Iphigenia in Tauris" staged by the students of the Gymnasium of Kyrenia at the open-air amphitheatre of the Dome Hotel in 1949.

The women of Souli portrayed in a theatrical performance, which was held in the large hall of the Gymnasium of Kyrenia (the Sea View Hotel) on March 25, 1949.

Portrait of Costas Cat-
sellis in the early 1950s.

Costas Catsellis with Dome employees in the early 1950s.

Aerial photo of Kyrenia as it was before 1960.

Aerial photo of Kyrenia as it
was after 1960.

Eleni and Costas Catsellis in
1960.

Costas Catsellis being honoured by the Cyprus Asso-
ciation of Hoteliers and the
Cyprus Tourism Organization
for his pioneering work in the
development of tourism on
February 25, 1973.

The last birthday of
Costas Catsellis in
1976, after the Turk-
ish invasion when he
was displaced and liv-
ing in Limassol, with
his grand daoughter
Despina-Maria.

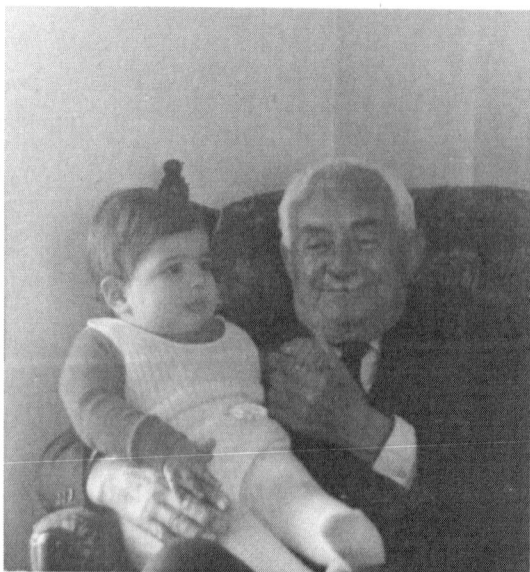

The last photograph
taken of Costas
Catsellis; in Limas-
sol with his young-
est granddaughter,
Stavrini-Christina.
Costas Catsellis had
23 grandchildren in
total, but only 20
survived.

Rina Katselli, the author of the biography of Costas Catsellis, with his grandson Costas Zambarloukos, one of the directors of the Dome Hotel, in 1974. Zambarloukos was the last to be expelled from the hotel by Turkish troops on October 19, 1975, after being enclaved there – along with many other Kyrenia residents – since the invasion of July 20, 1974. In the centre, the head of Costas Catsellis in bronze, as sculpted by a Scottish artist, a hotel guest.